The Bible Speaks Today

Series editors: Alec Motyer (OT)
John Stott (NT)
Derek Tidball (Bible Themes)

The Message of
Mission

The Bible Speaks Today: Bible Themes series

The Message of the Living God
His glory, his people, his world
Peter Lewis

The Message of the Resurrection
Christ is risen!
Paul Beasley-Murray

The Message of the Cross
Wisdom unsearchable, love indestructible
Derek Tidball

The Message of Salvation
By God's grace, for God's glory
Philip Graham Ryken

The Message of Creation
Encountering the Lord of the universe
David Wilkinson

The Message of Heaven and Hell
Grace and destiny
Bruce Milne

The Message of Mission
The glory of Christ in all time and space
Howard Peskett and Vinoth Ramachandra

The Message of Prayer
Approaching the throne of grace
Tim Chester

The Message of the Trinity
Life in God
Brian Edgar

The Message of Evil and Suffering
Light into darkness
Peter Hicks

The Message of Mission

The glory of Christ in all time and space

Howard Peskett

Vice Principal, Trinity College, Bristol

Vinoth Ramachandra

Secretary for Dialogue and Social Engagement (Asia),
International Fellowship of Evangelical Students

Inter-Varsity Press

Inter-Varsity Press
Norton Street, Nottingham NG7 3HR, England
Email: ivp@ivpbooks.com
Website: www.ivpbooks.com

Main text © Howard Peskett and Vinoth Ramachandra 2003
Study guide by David Stone © Inter-Varsity Press 2003

First published 2003
Reprinted 2004, 2007

British Library Cataloguing in Publication Data
A catalogue record for this book is available from the British Library.

ISBN 978-0-85111-326-5

Set in Stempel Garamond
Typeset in Great Britain by CRB Associates, Reepham, Norfolk
Printed and bound in Great Britain by Creative Print and Design (Wales), Ebbw Vale

*Inter-Varsity Press publishes Christian books that are true to the Bible and that
communicate the gospel, develop discipleship and strengthen the church for its mission in
the world.*

*Inter-Varsity Press is closely linked with the Universities and Colleges Christian
Fellowship, a student movement connecting Christian Unions in universities and
colleges throughout Great Britain, and a member movement of the International
Fellowship of Evangelical Students. Website: www.uccf.org.uk*

To my dear wife, Roz, in gratitude
(Howard Peskett)

To my beloved parents, in gratitude
(Vinoth Ramachandra)

Contents

BST | The Bible Speaks Today

GENERAL PREFACE

THE BIBLE SPEAKS TODAY describes three series of expositions, based on the books of the Old and New Testaments, and on Bible themes that run through the whole of Scripture. Each series is characterized by a threefold ideal:

- to expound the biblical text with accuracy
- to relate it to contemporary life, and
- to be readable.

These books are, therefore, not 'commentaries', for the commentary seeks rather to elucidate the text than to apply it, and tends to be a work rather of reference than of literature. Nor, on the other hand, do they contain the kinds of 'sermons' that attempt to be contemporary and readable without taking Scripture seriously enough. The contributors to *The Bible Speaks Today* series are all united in their convictions that God still speaks through what he has spoken, and that nothing is more necessary for the life, health and growth of Christians than that they should hear what the Spirit is saying to them through his ancient – yet ever modern – Word.

ALEC MOTYER
JOHN STOTT
DEREK TIDBALL
Series editors

Preface

All Christian mission finds its root and fountainhead in the God whom we worship, revealed in Scripture as Father, Son and Holy Spirit. Before all human sending (and the root of the word 'mission' means 'sending') we stand in wonder and gratitude before the God who sent his Son for us, and the Son who sent his Spirit to us. It was Yahweh, the Lord, the covenant God of Israel, who summoned all nations to himself with the words 'Turn to me and be saved all the ends of the earth: for I am God and there is no other!' (Is. 45:22). The church's privilege and responsibility is to testify by its life and witness to Jesus Christ, God's unique Son, crucified, risen and ascended, in fulfilment of the Old Testament scriptures. The church can fulfil its mission only as it is dynamically empowered by the Holy Spirit, God's empowering presence; and the church is most effective in its mission when its members are in continual life-giving contact with the Holy Spirit and when these encounters with the Holy Spirit are integrated into the life of the church. And the church is, in its very being, a missionary church, in so far as it shares the divine life of a sending God.

Underlying this book are the desire that Jesus Christ might be glorified more and more in the church and in the world, and the eager expectation that one day the whole creation will find its consummation in him, and God will be all in all.

Another underlying conviction is that the grand narrative of the Bible may be accurately summarized in the sentence 'God makes and chooses a people for himself, so that he may be glorified throughout the world.' Thus it is entirely appropriate that we should choose fifteen passages from the Bible, in accordance with the design of this series, all of whose messages converge in one way or another on this theme. We thus oppose those who deny the existence of any grand narratives, and who believe that the Word is a picnic to which the interpreter may bring any meaning he chooses. We do not deny that all readers bring to their reading certain

11

presuppositions which may be more or less appropriate. But we believe that readers may reliably assume that there is more in the text than the reflection of their own faces.

Structurally, the book is organized quite simply. Four chapters in part 1 set out the world horizons of our theme. Two Old Testament passages of paramount importance are embedded in two New Testament chapters which reflect upon the pre-eminence of Jesus Christ, who is the image of the invisible God, agent and goal of this creation, source and beginning of the new creation and the head of his body the church.

Part 2 considers four texts from the Old Testament which set out the international purposes of God, and the shape of the people whom he has called to be the instruments in the fulfilment of that purpose; the chapters also show the varying responses to the call of God in patterns which have been repeated up to the present. In these chapters critical theological issues are discussed; for example, concerning mission and cultural identity; the distinctive character of the people of God; poverty; nationalism; and the thorny issue of territory and the upsetting and unpredictable justice of God.

Part 3 explores five texts from the New Testament, reflecting on the freedom Jesus brings (according to the so-called 'Nazareth Manifesto'), the way he commands and the famous Great Commission he gave to his disciples after the resurrection; and considering also the meaning of Pentecost and the way in which mission was carried out in one case study from Acts.

Part 4 consists of two chapters that bring the book to a climax in wonder and worship, which is where all theology and science should end, reflecting on the consummation of creation's song and the coming down of the Holy City from God at the end of time. Then the mission of God and the mission of humanity will be complete in the new heavens and new earth in which righteousness dwells.

For over twenty years Vinoth has worked in his native Sri Lanka and in most countries of South and South-East Asia; and for twenty years Howard worked in Singapore with men and women from many countries of East Asia. It will not be difficult for the reader to detect differences of style in our chapters, and we have not felt it necessary to flatten every section out into the same style, because we believe that truth needs to be made clear to the understanding, but it also needs to be made glorious to the imagination! Occasionally we have used personal stories, with the pronoun 'I', and thus we think it may help readers to know that Vinoth wrote chapters 1, 2, 4, 6, 9, 11, 13, 15, and Howard, chapters 3, 5, 7, 8, 10, 12, 14. We invite the reader to see this book as an exercise in East–West partnership in missiological exploration. We have usually worked with the text of the New Revised Standard Version of the Bible in English; occasionally we have printed out the text in full, or made our own translation, when we wanted, for special reasons, to draw attention to the structure of a passage, or to bring out particular meanings. We hope that the reader will always read the Bible text before and alongside our expositions.

Mission is not an optional 'extra' for those few volunteers who 'like that sort of thing'. The church militant is God's people, Christ's body in this world, called to be God's agents and representatives, a community mandated to reproduce and grow so that Jesus Christ may be more and more glorified. We must also emphasize that Christian mission leads us again and again to the foot of the cross: all Christian mission must be shaped by the cross; the cross must never be behind us, but always in front of us. For this reason, we have drawn attention again and again to mission from the underside, to the connection between mission and suffering and even martyrdom, and to the importance of mission out of weakness, which has been the way mission has been conducted through most of the history of the church.

This book is a book of Bible expositions, not a mission-strategy document. Mission executives will not find here any detailed plans of action, although we interact with important age-old themes of effective mission; for example, the importance of cultural identity and sensitivity, great cities in need of God, the significance of *integral* mission, the connection of mission with ethics, the power of vernacular communication of the good news. Although we are not theological pluralists, we emphasize the need for detailed knowledge of, and sympathy with, those people who follow other faiths, and understanding of the faiths themselves.

We have also interpreted the term 'mission' widely, more widely than some mission and evangelistic agencies may find comfortable. We have been driven to this width of interpretation by loyal reflection on the Bible passages themselves. Thus we talk of human worth and human rights, of social equality and the value of human work, of earth-keeping and the integrity of creation, of the land of Israel, of colour and caste distinctions in the church, and of evangelical ecumenism.

Above all, we write in hope, a narrow path with dangers on both sides. On the one side is the danger of falling into presumption, the premature certainty that we are the masters of our future and that we can control the method and timing of its arrival. On the other side is the danger of despair, where, under the pressure of many sorts of stress, difficulty and disappointment, it is possible to

13

wonder if the longed-for future will *ever* arrive at all. Against these dangers we need, on the one hand, humility, for God is the Lord of our futures and all futures; and on the other hand, we need a larger view of God, as the God with stretched-out arms, and the God who will never disappoint us, for all his promises will come to pass.

Our hope is for the city of God, through which flows the river of the water of life, and in which grows the tree of life, producing fruit each month, whose leaves are for the healing of the nations. In the centre of this city is the throne of God and of the Lamb, and all God's servants will worship him there. 'And there will be no more night; they need no light of lamp or sun, for the Lord God will be their light, and they will reign for ever and ever' (Rev. 22:5). We thank God for all the foretastes we have had of this city and kingdom in our sharing with many communities in many countries of the world. And we invite our readers to join with us on the unfinished journey, for which the passages about which we write in this book are both chart and challenge.

HOWARD PESKETT
VINOTH RAMACHANDRA

Part 1
World horizons

Colossians 1:15–23
1. The glory of Christ

^{15}He is the image of the invisible God,
  the firstborn of all creation;
^{16}for in him all things in heaven and on earth were created,
  things visible and invisible,
  whether thrones or dominions
  or rulers or powers –
all things have been created
  through him and for him.

^{17}He himself is before all things,
  and in him all things hold together.
^{18}He is the head of the body, the church;
  he is the beginning,
  The firstborn from the dead,
so that he might come to have first place in everything.
^{19}For in him all the fullness of God
  was pleased to dwell,
^{20}and through him God was pleased
  to reconcile to himself all things,
  whether on earth or in heaven,
by making peace
  through the blood of his cross.

^{21}And you who were once estranged and hostile in mind, doing evil deeds, ^{22}he has now reconciled in his fleshly body through death, so as to present you holy and blameless and irreproachable before him – ^{23}provided that you continue securely established and steadfast in the faith, without shifting from the hope promised by the gospel that you heard, which has been proclaimed to every creature under heaven. I, Paul, became a servant of this gospel.

H. G. Wells, the visionary science-fiction writer, was a bitter opponent of Christianity. However, in 1937 at a party given for his seventy-first birthday, he announced to his guests, 'Gentlemen, I am 71 years old today and I have never found peace. The trouble with people like me is that the man from Galilee, Jesus of Nazareth, was too big for my small heart.'[1]

Who was Jesus of Nazareth? No weightier question can be asked. It is a question that springs at us from the pages of the New Testament. 'Jesus of Nazareth', observes one of the numerous scholars whose professional lives have been devoted to the issue, 'is one of those perennial question marks in history with which mankind is never quite done. With a ministry of two or three years he attracted and infuriated his contemporaries, mesmerized and alienated the ancient world, unleashed a movement that has done the same ever since, and thus changed the course of history forever.'[2]

Jesus of Nazareth, then, is a controversial figure. But the controversy that surrounds him is not like the controversy that surrounds other famous men and women. In the latter case, the controversy rages over the content and relevance of their teaching. So, today, Hindus in India argue over whether Mahatma Gandhi sanctioned the caste system, and political activists disagree among themselves as to how far the Gandhian principles of non-violent resistance are applicable under regimes more brutal and repressive than the British Raj. Marx and Freud have fallen into some disrepute in recent years, even as their theories have lost their persuasive hold on individuals and whole societies. Note that these are all debates that hinge on the assessment of a person's ideas or his 'message' for the world. They apply to anyone we care to mention, whether Confucius, Muhammad, Darwin or Nietzsche.

But not so with Jesus. The controversy over Jesus concerns *who he is*. For the historic Christian claim regarding Jesus of Nazareth is that no human category, whether that of 'charismatic prophet', 'religious genius', 'moral exemplar' or 'apocalyptic seer' can do adequate justice to the evidence of his words and actions. It is the claim that in the human person of Jesus, God himself has come among us in a decisive and unrepeatable way that constitutes an offence to a religiously plural society. It is this that provokes the scorn of the atheist, the puzzlement of the Hindu, and the indignation of the Muslim. The same range of responses were

---

[1] Cited in Stanley Jaki, *The Purpose of it All* (Regnery Gateway, 1990), p. 234.
[2] J. P. Meier, *The Mission of Christ and His Church: Studies in Christology and Ecclesiology* (Michael Glazier, 1990), p. 31.

encountered in the Graeco-Roman world that the earliest followers of Jesus inhabited.

An eminent historian sums up the extraordinary challenge that the followers of Jesus faced, and out of which a radically new conception of God as Tri-unity emerged:

> From the beginning Christianity carried within its bosom two convictions: that there is only one God, and that Jesus Christ is divine. It had for three hundred years refused to compromise on the question of monotheism; it had steadfastly refused to make any concessions to the tolerant polytheism of the culture of the late Roman empire in which it lived, and thousands of Christians had suffered and died because of this conviction. But just as deeply rooted in the heart of Christianity was the worship of Jesus Christ, not the cult of a deified man (which was common enough in the Roman empire), but the worship of the Son of God who had taken to himself human nature in the Incarnation. These two convictions had to be reconciled.[3]

Many New Testament scholars believe that underlying Colossians 1:15-20 is a fragment of an early Christian hymn. The rhythmic cadences give substance to this belief. The language of this hymn may have derived from Jewish Wisdom literature. For example, passages like Proverbs 8 and Job 28 in the Hebrew Bible were hymns praising wisdom as an attribute of God. Such literature was, at a very early stage of the church's life, applied to Jesus. So, it is likely that the apostle Paul is adapting a hymn, possibly well known to his Colossian readers in the middle years of the AD fifties, to bring out the theological significance of Jesus Christ for their life and mission.

The *He* with which verse 15 begins is the 'He' of whom Paul has been speaking in the immediately preceding verses; namely, 'the beloved Son' in whom is found 'redemption, the forgiveness of sins' (v. 14). He now elaborates on the glory of this figure, in relation to God, the world and the church.

1. Christ and creation

First, he is the image of the invisible God, making visible the invisible God. We know from the first book of the Bible that humankind was created as the image of God, dependent on God like

---

[3] R. P. C. Hanson, 'The Achievement of Orthodoxy in the Fourth Century AD', in R. Williams (ed.), *The Making of Orthodoxy* (CUP, 1989), p. 149.

the rest of creation but called into personal relationship with him. Moreover, a physical image of a king in the ancient world represented that king's sovereignty over the particular territory in which it was erected. The Creator's image on earth is humankind, male and female, who together represent and reflect his rule over the earth.

But our imaging of God's rule of justice and freedom has been corrupted, defaced by our rebellion. So we as human beings no longer reflect God to the rest of the creation. But in Christ we see the true Adam, humanity restored. In seeing him we see what human beings were called to be; and because we are created in the image of God, we see in Christ also what God is like. The concept of 'image' has this intrinsic ambiguity, enabling it to serve as a bridge between the divine and the human, the transcendent and the immanent.

Secondly, he is the *firstborn of all creation* (v. 15). What follows in the poem makes it clear that this is not to be understood so much in the sense of temporal priority (born first of all God's creatures) but of priority of rank (pre-eminent over all God's creatures). Israel in the Old Testament is sometimes referred to as the firstborn of God (Exod. 4:22; Jer. 31:9). And in Psalm 89:27, the Messiah, the Son of David is referred to as the 'firstborn' of God, the King over all the kings of the earth. Remember, too, that in the Old Testament, the firstborn in a Jewish family was the heir of everything that the family owned. So that in speaking of Christ as the firstborn of all creation the text is saying that the whole creation belongs to Christ. He is foremost in rank and therefore the rightful owner.

The thought expressed here is not that Jesus of Nazareth existed before creation in human form, but that the one whom we now know as Jesus of Nazareth had his origin even before creation and that it was utterly appropriate for him to become man. A British commentator points out the analogy of saying, 'The Queen was born in 1926' – this does not mean that she was queen then, but that the one we now know as the Queen began her life in 1926.[4]

Thirdly, he is the agent of creation: *for in him all things in heaven and on earth were created* (v. 16). And again our thoughts go back to the opening chapter of Genesis where we read of God uttering his Word into the void, and through his Word a *creation* springing into being. There is also a rich Jewish tradition that ascribes to Wisdom a role as the agency through which God created the universe (Prov. 3:19; Wisdom 8:5; Ps. 104:24). Like the concept of image, discussed above, the concept of wisdom serves to bridge the gulf between the

---

[4] N. T. Wright, *Colossians and Philemon: An Introduction and Commentary* (Eerdmans/IVP, 1986), p. 69.

Creator and the creature, the articulation in language of the self-revelation of God.

But, the next preposition (*eis*, 'for', 'unto', in the last line of v. 16) is never used in reference to Wisdom in Jewish literature. For, fourthly, Christ is also the goal of creation. In the context of the present hymn, the redemptive work accomplished 'in Christ' (v. 14) is presented as the key that discloses the mystery of the divine purpose in creation. He stands both at the beginning and at the end of the cosmic story. In Christ, creation and redemption are one. God has brought into being a creation that will find its ultimate significance in the glorification of Jesus Christ.

This creation, which belongs to Christ and has him as both its source and goal, includes *all things in heaven and on earth ... things invisible and visible, whether thrones or dominions or rulers or powers* (v. 16). It is not only human beings and the physical order that serve God's purposes in Christ, but also the invisible, non-human and supra-human, powers of the universe. Scholars disagree as to the referent of these abstract terms in the poem before us. Are these 'personal principalities of angels which influence the destiny of creatures, but are subject to God'?[5] Are they 'structures of earthly existence', a 'demythologizing' of pre-Christian Jewish apocalyptic which projected on to the cosmos the real determinants of human existence; that is, the physical, psychic and social forces at work within and among us?[6] Others have noted that some of the terms Paul uses here were almost technical terms in the complex, metaphysical systems of the pagan Hellenistic environment in which the church in Colosse found itself.[7]

Anything we say on this matter can only be tentative, as the scholarly jury is still out. But we are inclined to agree with those who make the following observations: (1) Although Paul clearly believes in the existence of 'angels, demons and personal spirits', as indeed do other New Testament writers, he shows a singular lack of interest in them. His preferred terminology when dealing with the 'spiritual realm' is more abstract and impersonal. (2) It is difficult to find authentic precursors to Pauline language about 'the powers' in pre-Christian Jewish apocalyptic. The latter regularly attribute names, ranks and duties to spirit beings in a way that Paul does not. (3) We must not import ideas from the Gospels and Acts in

---

[5] M. Barth and H. Blanke, *Colossians* (Doubleday, 1994), p. 202.

[6] See H. Berkhof, *Christ and the Powers*, 2nd ed. (Herald, 1977); W. Wink, *Naming the Powers* (Philadelphia: Fortress, 1986).

[7] See Chris Forbes, 'Paul's Principalities and Powers: Demythologizing Apocalyptic?' *Journal for the Study of the New Testament* 82 (2001), pp. 61–88.

interpreting Paul's language. Paul often personifies the abstract spiritual powers facing humanity, most notably the Law, Sin and Death. These are invisible, existential realities. (4) In Colossians, Paul is writing to a church attracted by the sophisticated propaganda of a mystical Judaism in which terms drawn from Greek philosophy ('Middle Platonism') may have played an important role. Paul is, then, using what all good communicators do; namely, appropriating the language of the audience to demonstrate the superiority of Christ. His concern is not to arrange these cosmic powers in some hierarchical pattern or to distinguish carefully between them, but to assert Christ's superiority over all such entities. All the 'powers that be' in the universe owe their origin to him, and are created to serve him.

Fifthly, he is the integrating centre of the whole creation: *He himself is before all things, and in him all things hold together* (v. 17). In other words, if it were not for Christ the whole universe would dissolve into chaos. Christ is the centre around which everything turns. The Polish poet Czeslaw Milosz came out of the horror of the Second World War to say, 'Nothing could stifle my inner certainty that a shining point exists where all lines intersect.' And this is why it is only Christian faith that can speak coherently of a *uni*verse, because behind all the diversity (and, indeed, chaos) of the world there is the same set of physical and moral laws which give order and value to the whole. The world has an intelligible, contingent order, held in being by the creative agency of Christ.

It is not only the universe but also our human selves that need an integrating centre. For without that centre our lives cease to have meaning. Friedrich Nietzsche (1844–1900), perhaps the most influential philosopher of the twentieth century, ended his life in a mental asylum. Writing to his sister, he declared, 'As I write this a madman is howling in the next room, and I am howling with him inside of me, howling for my lost integrity, sundered from God, Man and myself, shattered in body, mind and spirit, yearning for two clasped hands to usher in the great miracle – the unity of my being.'[8]

This is also why perhaps only Christians can speak coherently of a *uni*versity, for what is it that unites the different disciplines of biology and geology, astronomy and medicine, history and art? It is Christ. It is not by accident that in Western Europe the universities had their origin in the monasteries which were the centres of learning as well as prayer. Theology is the enterprise of relating all

[8] F. Nietzsche, *My Sister and I* (Bridgehead, 1951), p. 233.

human knowledge, as well as all our everyday activities, to God's self-disclosure in Christ. The triune God who is at work in the mundane world of economic life is the same God who sustains the arcane world explored by nuclear physicists. If education loses that vision, if Christ is no longer the integrating centre, then the sciences and the humanities fall apart. Communication across disciplines withers. As 'information' increases, specialists lose the sense of a bigger framework that gives meaning to the narrow subdivisions of knowledge that they carve out for themselves. Is it too radical to claim that the deterioration of universities around the world into tuition factories, churning out professionals unable to communicate with one another the fruits of their training, is due not only to the fragmenting forces of industrialization, but also to the loss of a shared vision of a creation sustained by, and responsible to, One beyond our self-contained systems?

But nature, as Pascal noted, hates a vacuum. And the place in the university that has been vacated by the biblical vision is taken over by some other discipline. Other gods rise up to take the place of the displaced God of creation. Despite the popular rhetoric of a postmodern 'suspicion of all metanarratives', recent years have witnessed a resurgence in attempts to explain all human behaviour and beliefs within an evolutionary, naturalist paradigm, or to assess human worth in terms of 'utility', or to reduce all moral discourse to a universal language of rights, or to evaluate education systems solely in terms of their impact on national economic competitiveness.

2. Christ and the new creation

The text we are considering moves on to speak of Christ in relation to God's *new* creation. And this is the turning point in the poem. The *he* of verse 18 is the same *he* of verse 15. The church – that worldwide company of men and women who have embraced the word of truth, the gospel (1:5, 6), and have thus experienced forgiveness of sin, freedom from the powers of evil and the beginnings of new life under the rule of Christ (1:13, 14) – is now organically related to Christ, depending on him for its life and direction. The head–body imagery expresses the truth that the church is the place where both the reconciling rule of Christ over the world and his solidarity with the world in its journey towards redemption is being realized.

This is brought out more forcefully in the next set of images: Christ is the 'source' or *the beginning (archē)* of a new creation, *the firstborn from the dead* (v. 18). The resurrection of Jesus on that first

23

Easter morning was the completion of creation, the vindication of the created order. It was an anticipation and inauguration of God's new world order in which the tyranny of sin and death has been broken. The risen body of Jesus is a glimpse of the kinds of 'spiritual bodies' (1 Cor. 15:44) we shall become on the day when Christ will *come to have first place in everything* (v. 18b). It is as if a little bit of the future has been cut off and planted in the present. Easter unveils God's purpose that the Christ who is *de jure* sovereign over the cosmos should become *de facto* sovereign by way of the cross; and also that all who put their trust in him will be raised to share his resurrection life. So Easter reveals not only the triumphant reign of God in Christ but also our own future as citizens of God's redeemed world order.

Moreover, it was not just as any individual person whom God happened to raise from the dead that Christ achieved pre-eminence, but because of what he has always been and what God has accomplished through his life and ministry. *For in him all the fullness of God was pleased to dwell* (v. 19). Here the full divinity of the man Jesus is stated without any implication of rivalry to God. That all that makes God *God* should take up permanent residence in Jesus (cf. 2:9) was something in which God took pleasure. And he also delights in reconciling to himself through Jesus *all things, whether on earth or in heaven* (v. 20). The grand events of incarnation and atonement are not forced upon the Creator by some external necessity, but are his free, loving and joyful movement towards his creation.

Observe how the poem echoes the same sequence *in him ... through him ... to himself* in verses 19 and 20 that we found in verses 16, 17. The *all things* of verse 20 are clearly the *all things* of verse 16; namely, all the power structures or spheres of authority in the universe. The 'powers that be' are created by God, in and for Christ, but they also stand in need of reconciliation to God. The act of reconciliation is described by the compounded verb *apokatallassō*, repeated in 1:22 and found also in Ephesians 2:16 but nowhere else in literary Greek. It presumes a state of alienation or hostility to exist in the world.

Theologically speaking, what is presupposed in moving from verse 16 to verse 20 in the poem is the reality of the 'fall'. Evil has spoilt God's creation. The powers have fallen away from God's good intention. So they are no longer God's servants for human flourishing. Power given by God to bring order and stability to the world is distorted and used to dominate and manipulate others. Although their origin is in Christ they exercise their power independently of, and therefore against, his purposes. The

24

consequence of their activities may be seen in empty belief-systems (Col. 2:8; 2 Cor. 10:4, 5), political oppression and persecution (Col. 2:15; 1 Cor. 2:6, 8; Acts. 13:27; Rev. 13), and in futile religious rites and practices (Col. 2:20ff.; Gal. 4:3, 8–11).

The universe, then, stands in need of peacemaking. And the means of peace, the way by which the universe is reconciled to God, is *the blood of his cross* (v. 20b). The blood speaks of sacrificial death and the renewal of the covenant between God and humankind. On the cross the rebellion of sin, and the disruption to the harmony of creation caused by sin is, once and for all, defeated. The powers that oppose God's purposes for all his creation are overcome. And now the effects of that victory through the cross are to spread like ripples into all corners of the world, until everything that remains hostile to God is pacified, all idols overthrown. Then the whole creation will share in the shalom of God's rule (Rom. 8:18–25).

The comprehensiveness of this text should not be used to assert that, at the end of time, every single human being will be reconciled to God, whatever his or her present relationship to God may be. This understanding seems to be ruled out by the context of the whole epistle, let alone most of the New Testament. The following verses (1:21 – 2:7) make clear that the reconciliation effected through the cross needs to be proclaimed and received in faith (1:23; 2:6); it is manifested in those who belong to Christ's body, the church (1:24), and continue steadfast in the faith (1:23) until they reach maturity in Christ (1:28). The emphasis in verse 20 is on the universal *scope* of God's salvation: it embraces nothing less than a total renewal and reordering of the creation. It is not limited to the human creation. Since reconciliation between personal agents requires the acknowledgment of wrong by the wrongdoer and the acceptance of forgiveness; it cannot be an automatic process that bypasses human decision.

Let us pause to consider the subject of this remarkable passage. Paul is speaking of a person who was put to death outside the walls of Jerusalem a couple of decades prior to this letter. In the Roman Empire crucifixion, though widespread, was viewed with universal horror and disgust. It was cruel and degrading; the victim was often flogged and tortured before being strung up on a cross on busy, crowded junctions as a deterrent to the masses. It was the most humiliating form of death in the ancient world: the penalty reserved for rebellious slaves and (what today would be called) 'terrorists' against the state. No Roman citizen could be crucified. Romans didn't even discuss the subject – they pretended it never existed. The great senator and orator Cicero declared that 'the very word "cross" should be far removed not only from the presence of a

Roman citizen but from his thoughts, his eyes and his ears'.[9] Crucifixion was a way of obliterating not only the victim but also the very memory of him. A crucified man had never existed. That's why not a single ancient historian thought it worthwhile to discuss the subject.

It is in a world such as this that we meet a group of men and women moving around the Roman Empire and announcing that among those forgotten, crucified 'nobodies', there had been one who was no less than the Son of God, the saviour of the world. Paul, in the passage we are considering, goes further. This crucified figure is the One through whom the universe came into being and also the One through whom the universe will be restored to its proper functioning.

The foolishness of such a message cannot be overstressed. If you wanted to convert the educated and pious people of the empire to your cause, whatever that cause may have been, the worst thing you could ever do would be to link that cause to a recently crucified man. To put it mildly, that would have been a public relations disaster. And to associate God, the source of all life, with this crucified criminal was to invite mockery and sheer incomprehension! This was indeed the experience of the first Christians.

This message, if true, subverted the world of religion. For it claimed that if you wanted to know what God is like, and to understand God's purposes for his world, you had to go not to the lofty speculations of the philosophers or to the countless religious temples and sacred groves that dotted the empire, but to a cross outside the walls of Jerusalem. For the Jews a crucified Messiah/Saviour was a contradiction in terms, for it expressed not God's power but God's inability to liberate Israel from Roman rule. For pagans, the idea that a god or son of god should die as a state criminal, and that human salvation should depend on that particular historical event, was not only offensive; it was sheer *madness*.

This message, if true, also subverted the world of politics. It claimed that Rome's own salvation would come from among those forgotten victims of state terror. Caesar himself would have to bow the knee to this crucified Jew. It implied that by crucifying the Lord of the universe, the much-vaunted civilization of Rome stood radically condemned. Little wonder that the Christians' 'good news' was labelled a 'dangerous superstition' by educated Romans of the day.

Now, it is the madness of this 'word of the cross' that compels us

[9] Cicero, *Pro Rabirio* 5.16; quoted in M. Hengel, *The Crucifixion of the Son of God* (SCM, 1986), p. 134.

to take it seriously. There is something so foolish, so absurd, so topsy-turvy about the Christian gospel that it gets under our skin: *it has the ring of truth about it.* No-one can say that this was some pious invention, for it ran counter to all notions of piety. And nothing was gained by it.

3. Missiological challenges

What are the implications for Christian thought and mission of the truths we have been exploring in this text?

First, Christian thinking is always *Christ-centred*. Many in our churches, let alone our world, have too puny a view of Jesus. When they speak of him – if they speak of him at all – it is usually as their personal saviour, or friend, or the 'founder of Christianity'. Jesus did not come to found any religion, but to bring God's purposes for both Israel and his entire creation to their fulfilment. And while he is indeed our personal saviour and intimate friend, he is far, far more. It is only in relationship to him that God, the world and humankind can be understood rightly. For he makes the invisible God visible; he is the agent of creation and redemption; he is the one truly human being and the archetype of the new creation; and he is the one through whose death and resurrection the cosmos will be reconciled and made whole.

The American preacher A. W. Tozer once said that what we think of God will determine what we think of everything else. And what we think of God will depend on what we think of Christ. If our thoughts about God are not centred in Christ, then we shall drift back into monotheism or paganism. The latter is seen, for instance, in the prolific writings of the theologian John Hick whose so-called 'Copernican revolution' in theology is an appeal to Christians to see Christ as simply one of many planetary witnesses orbiting around the universal experience of 'God'.[10] And for such theocentrism to be acceptable also to non-theistic faiths such as Buddhism or Taoism, he proposes further that the 'God' at the centre of this 'universe of faiths' be referred to as an unknowable 'Real' or 'Mystery'. The 'Real beyond God' is neither a person nor a process, neither good nor evil, neither one nor many. Of that Real we cannot think or speak. We can only speak, in a mythological way, of our culturally

[10] First proposed in *God and the Universe of Faiths* (Macmillan/St Martin's Press, 1973). Hick's fullest exposition of his pluralist thesis is *An Interpretation of Religion* (Macmillan/Yale University Press, 1989). A popular, recent account (including responses to criticisms) can be found in his *The Rainbow of Faiths* (SCM, 1995). For the present author's fullest critique of Hick, see Vinoth Ramachandra, *The Recovery of Mission* (Paternoster/Eerdmans, 1996), pp. 120–125.

and historically conditioned responses to the Real. These are the religious traditions of humankind. In Jesus Christ all we see is one such response among many to the Real, the latter mediated through the theistic myths of Jewish religious thought.

Observe that unlike Copernicus's original revolution, which was to dethrone the earth from the centre of the solar system, Hick's religious system puts the human back in the centre of things. For all its hospitable accommodation of the world's religions, it is ultimately biased against the theistic traditions. It simply rules out, a priori, the possibility that the Real is ultimately, and not simply in some of its evocations, personal. For to entertain this possibility one must then also be willing to acknowledge the further possibility that this God wills to reveal himself and to enter into personal relationship with his human creation. Hick has effectively excluded any meaningful concept of divine revelation from his metareligion of religions. He has silenced God. All we are left with are distorted human attempts to grasp reality. And writers such as Hick understand themselves to be occupying a superior vantage point from which they can recognize the distortions of others.

The church has, from the earliest times, had to combat religious philosophies reminiscent of this modern form of pluralism. Neoplatonism, for instance, separated the god of creation (the 'Demiurge') from the unknowable, impersonal One. Some commentators believe that, lurking in the pagan background to the letter to the Colossians, is a philosophical doctrine similar to this and to the second-century gnostic schools. The 'fullness' (*plērōma*) of the One was diffused throughout the cosmic chain of being, with physical matter at the lowest level of existence. To speak of the incarnate Christ as the one in whom 'the whole fullness of deity dwells bodily' (2:9) is to explode that ancient world-view. It is also to confront head-on the modern gnostic tendencies of religious pluralists such as Hick.

Christian mission stands or falls with the absoluteness of Christ, whose glory is unveiled in the good news of Christian proclamation (cf. v. 23). For no matter how wonderful a person he may have been, and however God may have been present through him, if Jesus was not more than human, the Christian church has lived a lie. Its creeds and practices have been based on falsehood. It has elevated a mere human being to the level of God and worshipped him. We are guilty of the most monstrous idolatry, and the Jewish and Muslim critics are right.

Secondly, Christian mission is *integral and universal*. The vision of the creation and final reconciliation of *all things, whether things on the earth or things in the heavens* through the cross of Jesus

Christ has been summed up by the great Dutch philosopher and statesman Abraham Kuyper: 'There is not a square inch in the whole domain of our human existence over which Christ, who is Sovereign over *all*, does not say: "Mine".'[11] God's concern embraces not only individual men, women and children, but also the physical and biological environment which sustain their lives, and the social, economic, political and intellectual structures that shape the forms of their existence.

Mission, then, is primarily God's activity. God is reaching out to his world through Christ and his Spirit. He is engaged in liberating the cosmos and humankind from its captivity to evil, and it is his purpose to gather the whole creation under the Lordship of Christ. God's love is centrifugal – radiating outwards to the whole creation – and 'sending' and 'being sent' is integral to his nature as a community of divine persons. Indeed, until the sixteenth century the term 'mission' was used exclusively to refer to the Trinity – the sending of the Son by the Father, and of the Holy Spirit by the Father and the Son. The Jesuits were the first to use 'mission' in describing the spread of the Christian faith among people (including Protestants) who were not members of the Catholic Church.[12] This use of the term unfortunately coincided with the colonial expansion of the European powers, with the result that the term has acquired distasteful overtones of cultural hegemony and aggressive conquest that linger to the present day.

The emphasis on the triune God as the subject of mission delivers the church from both an idolatrous self-centredness and also a narrowing of the scope of mission. The *missio Dei* points to God's reaching out in redeeming and reconciling love to all the creation. The *missio Dei* embraces both the church and the world, and the church is called to the privilege of participation in this divine mission.[13] Indeed, the correlation of 1:18a with 1:20 implies that the church is the focus and primary means towards this cosmic reconciliation. For it is the community in which this reconciliation

---

[11] From the inaugural address at the Free University of Amsterdam, 20 October 1880, in *Abraham Kuyper: A Centennial Reader*, ed. James Bratt (Eerdmans/ Paternoster, 1998), p. 461.

[12] See David J. Bosch, *Transforming Mission: Paradigm Shifts in Theology of Mission* (Orbis, 1991), p. 1.

[13] The use of the Latin term *missio Dei* has been increasingly popular since the Willingen conference of the International Missionary Council (1952), sometimes more as a slogan than as a well-articulated concept. See the discussion in J. Andrew Kirk, *What Is Mission? Theological Explorations* (Darton, Longman & Todd, 1999), pp. 25–26.

has already begun (1:21–22) and whose responsibility it is to practise it and to proclaim its secret (3:8–15; 4:2–6).

For Paul it is a matter of sheer privilege that he has become a herald of the good news of God's peacemaking activity (v. 23). The latter extends to the 'fallen' powers of the created order. We have seen, in our exegesis of the text, that we should neither 'demonize' the powers, locating them in some wholly malignant, other-worldly realm outside our responsibility, nor identify them completely with human powers. Even the hostile activity of non-human powers is this-worldly, operating through human structures and institutions, while the latter are not simply material or visible. Walter Wink refers to their 'inner spirituality or interiority', that 'inner, invisible spirit that provides [any power with] legitimacy, compliance, credibility, and clout'.[14]

We all know of powers created to serve human ends, but which seem to take on a life of their own that passes out of human control and which sets them up as substitutes for the true God. If the God-given Torah and temple could become idols, wielding a blinding power over the Jewish contemporaries of the Colossian Christians, then how much more the gifts of family, sexuality, culture, ethnicity or government. Many people experience sheer helplessness in the face of generations of dysfunctional family relationships, culturally entrenched practices of social or sexual oppression, religious systems that promote self-righteous legalism or a corrupting fatalism, long-standing ethnic hatreds often erupting in waves of collective brutality, or tyrannical political regimes that sow terror and distrust in their wake.

The gospel unmasks the idols of personal and public life, and subverts the fallen powers through the powerlessness of the cross (Col. 2:15). The gospel addresses individuals, but also all their activities, whether it be in family life, the arts, science and technology, business corporations or governments. Gospel preaching announces God's intention to fill the universe with the glory of Christ, and it is the task of all Christians to work out what that means in the areas in which they are involved: 'neither a secularized church (that is, a church which concerns itself only with this-worldly activities and interests) nor a separatist church (that is, a church which involves itself only in soul-saving and preparation of converts for the hereafter) can faithfully articulate the *missio Dei*'.[15]

Thirdly, Christian mission is also *eschatological*. Paul, languishing

---

[14] Walter Wink, *Unmasking the Powers: The Invisible Forces That Determine Human Existence* (Fortress, 1986), p. 4.

[15] Bosch, *Mission*, p. 11.

in prison, knows only too well that the world refuses to acknowledge that its reconciliation has been secured through the cross.
But the proof that God's future is already impinging on the present
is found in the little communities, like that in Colosse and other
parts of the Mediterranean world, where men and women have
been set free from their 'estrangement and hostility' (1:21). These
are communities of 'hope', a foretaste of the reconciliation to come.
It is through their gospel living (1:10) and gospel preaching (1:27)
that the cosmic goal of renewal and transformation will be
accomplished.

All our human activity (in the arts, sciences, in the worlds of
economics and politics) – and even the non-human creation – will
be brought to share in the liberating rule of God, and this grand
vision centres on the cross of Jesus Christ. It is there that a vision of
hope opens up for the world. And you will not find any hope for the
world in any of the religious systems or philosophies of humankind.
No faith holds out a promise of salvation for the world the way the
cross and resurrection of Jesus do.

Hope is one of the wonderful gifts of the gospel, enabling men
and women to live transformed lives in anticipation of God's final
victory over all the powers of evil and decay. Christian hope, in the
words of Walter Brueggemann, is the 'exultant conviction that God
will not quit unless God has had God's full way in the world'.[16]
Such hope is based not on the success of our church programmes
and our strategies of global evangelization. Furthermore, it rests in
the promise of God that all things will be reconciled to God through
the blood of Christ's cross. *This is the Gospel that you heard, and
that has been proclaimed to every creature under heaven* (v. 23;
cf. 1:6).

This ringing affirmation reminds us once again of God's eternal
intention, and draws our attention to the cosmic scope of the divine
mission:

God has in principle announced the gospel to every creature
under heaven. Although, however, the proclamation is made to
human beings, we would be quite wrong, in view of 1:16, 18
and 20, and the emphatic reiteration of 'everything' there and
elsewhere in Colossians, to limit its *effects* to them. From whales
to waterfalls, the whole created order has in principle been
reconciled to God. Like a sovereign making a proclamation
and sending off his heralds to bear it to the distant corners of

---

[16] Walter Brueggemann, *The Bible and Postmodern Imagination: Texts Under
Negotiation* (SCM, 1993), p. 40.

his empire, God has in Jesus Christ proclaimed once and for all that the world which he made has been reconciled to him. His heralds, scurrying off to the ends of the earth with the news, are simply agents, messengers, of this one antecedent authoritative proclamation.[17]

---

[17] Wright, *Colossians and Philemon*, p. 85.

Genesis 1:26–31; 2:15–20
2. Life and dominion

Václav Havel, the philosopher-president of the Czech Republic addressed both houses of the Canadian Parliament on 30 April 1999 at the height of the NATO bombing of Serbia. His speech was entitled 'Kosovo and the End of the Nation-State'. Havel expressed his conviction that the greatest political challenge of the twenty-first century would be to secure the recognition by all nation states of the limits to their sovereignty. All states must submit to the rule of international law, based on universal human rights. At the conclusion of his speech he observed:

> I have often asked myself why human beings have any rights at all. I always come to the conclusion that human rights, human freedoms, and human dignity have their deepest roots somewhere outside the perceptible world. These values ... make sense only in the perspective of the infinite and the eternal ... Allow me to conclude my remarks on the state and its probable role in the future with the assertion that, while the state is a human creation, human beings are the creation of God.[1]

1. A subversive counter-story

In simple yet profound language the opening chapter of the Bible introduces us to God and his creation. The narrative portrays God's creative work in pictures. The Spirit/Breath of God hovers over the world like a mother bird over its young, pointing to both the transcendence of God over his creation and also his intimate, caring

---

[1] Václav Havel, Address to the Canadian Senate and the House of Commons in Ottawa, 29 April 1999, 'Kosovo and the End of the Nation-State', *New York Review of Books*, 10 June 1999, p. 4.

involvement within it. Like a human craftsman, God 'speaks' and 'sees', 'works' and 'rests'. The Word of God, which is his self-communication, is uttered into the void and events spring into being. The universe God creates is ordered and intelligible, because it has its origin in this rational Word. To use later Christian language, the activity of creation depicted here is a trinitarian activity: God creates through the agency of Word and Spirit. In saying that the universe is created by God, the writer also indicates that the universe is open to God, not a closed system; it is open to new possibilities of transformation. God's relationship with his world is one of both loving intimacy and creative, commanding power.

The world is created rich in diversity. The Creator blesses living beings with semi-autonomy, the capacity to 'pro-create' (1:22). Creatureliness, individuality, diversity and change are all pro-nounced 'good' by the Creator. He takes delight in what he brings into being and builds into them potentialities for development. The earth must produce cattle, creeping things and wild animals. The waters must give rise to the swarming activity of sea creatures. In other words, the creation is equipped by the Creator to bring forth novelty in obedience to the Creator's call. Other biblical passages such as Psalm 104 (the subject of chapter 14) and Job 38 – 41 expand the thought of Genesis 1, showing in delightful picture language God frolicking with his creatures and calling forth their awesome powers.

The whole universe, then, is distinct from yet dependent on God for its existence and sustenance. All its wonderful capacities for renewal, adaptation and development are built into it by the Creator, but all these complex systems and patterns work in response to the divine Word. Moreover, the fact that God not only creates time, but creates *with* time and *in* time would have had profound implications for ancient Israel, as indeed it does for modern society. Israel would learn to value time as the fabric of history in which God is involved. Redemption, unlike in other religious world-views (including Hindu and Buddhist thought), will function *within* time and not as a deliverance *from* time. The Creator personally engages with his creatures in their striving towards the goal of a perfected creation.

That an evangelistic/polemical intent lies behind the Genesis creation narrative becomes clear when it is read against the back-drop of the popular beliefs and practices of Israel's neighbours. While employing literary forms found in the creation myths of other cultures, the content of the narrative is deeply antimythical in its thrust, as we shall see. It repudiates many popular religious ideas of the first and second millennia BC. A seventh-century Babylonian or a Canaanite in fourteenth-century Ugarit (both centres of great civilizations) would have been shocked by the teaching of Genesis. It is a powerful witness to the uniqueness of Yahweh, the Lord of creation.

For instance, we note the following striking contrasts:

i. Theism vs polytheism. There are no rival gods nor helpers in the work of creation, unlike in every other religious epic about origins. The latter narrate the birth of the gods, their loves and their battles. No-one is ultimately in control of the world. Its fortunes depend on which deity is currently in the ascendent. The gods (as in Hindu mythology) are personifications of various aspects of nature, and nature itself is deified as a living goddess who nurtures all living things and exacts a terrible vengeance on all who fail to worship appropriately.

Why does the writer put the creation of the sun and the moon on the fourth day, after the creation of light, when it would have been obvious to everyone that they were the sources of light for the earth? The reason becomes obvious when we recall that the worship of the sun and moon was very common in the writer's world (e.g. the great Chaldean city of Ur where Abraham came from was a famous centre of moon-worship). Also, then as now, many believed that human life was controlled by the motion of the moon and the planets. The sages of Babylon kept detailed records of heavenly motions for the construction of astrological charts. Political decisions depended on the accuracy of such charts. Even today it is common to find politicians, business leaders and even university teachers in many parts of the world for whom horoscopes and 'auspicious days' are more real than anything in modern culture. The Genesis narrative 'debunks' this superstition. The heavenly bodies are simply creations of God, lamps hung in the sky, with no divine power of their own. They are neither to be feared nor worshipped. Indeed, there is no word for 'nature' in Hebrew. Even the noun for creation is not very common; only the verb. What we call 'nature' is but a fellow-creature with human beings: both are dependent on and nourished by the Creator alone.

ii. God's Word vs cultic ritual. In many societies, the powers of chaos and evil were warded off by the magical incantations of special religious 'manthras' (e.g. the popular *pirith* ceremonies in Sri Lanka and other Buddhist countries today). These human words, accompanied sometimes by appropriate actions, were believed to sustain the stability and fecundity of the world. But what does Genesis teach? It is the Word of God, not human words, which ensures the stability and continuing fruitfulness of the world. This radically 'demythologizes' the reigning religious world-views.

35

iii. A good creation vs a capricious, even evil, world. Once again, contemporary world-views would have understood 'salvation' as an escape from the sensory, empirical world of human existence. There was no value or purpose attached to the physical realm of space–time events. Meaning was to be sought in detachment from the external world which, in any case, was less real than the 'spiritual' realm. This view is contradicted by the doctrine of creation, which sees the world as possessing an intrinsic worth and meaningfulness (though later corrupted and disfigured by evil – see Gen. 3) because it stems from the rational will of a good and loving Creator. Existence itself is declared blessed.

iv. Humans, the crown of creation, vs humans, an 'accident'. The teaching on humankind given in the opening chapter of Genesis is unique. Unlike the common religious creation myths which depicted man as an 'afterthought', an 'accidental' offspring of the gods, the entire narrative of Genesis 1 builds up to a climax in the account of human creation. That this is a turning point in the story is brought out by the author in three ways: (1) the language shifts from the repetitive 'Let there be ...' to the more self-deliberative *Let us make* ... (1:26); (2) the self-deliberation is then followed by the act of creation (1:27), showing perhaps the deeper involvement of God in this aspect of his creative work; (3) the fact of human creation, male and female, is repeated three times in the same sentence (1:27), presumably for emphasis. Similarly, in Genesis 2, although all living creatures carry the breath of life (1:30), it is only in the case of human beings that this breath is breathed into them directly by God (2:7).

Observe too that God commands human beings (v. 28) to be fruitful. This stands in marked contrast to the fertility cults of the surrounding nations, in which the worshippers sought to persuade the gods to be fruitful. Life is a gift from God. His blessing confers both gift and task.

v. Humans, the image of God. What this chapter teaches concerning humankind is startlingly revolutionary. The stone or metal image that an ancient king set up was the physical symbol of his sovereignty over a particular territory. It represented him to his subject peoples. But here it is humankind that constitutes *the image of God* (1:26, 27). It is men and women who represent God on the planet Earth. It follows that when human beings fashion images out of the created world and worship them, they worship something inferior to them and thus dehumanize themselves. It also follows that the way we treat our fellow human being is a reflection of our attitude to the Creator. To despise the former is to insult the latter (Prov. 14:31; Jas. 3:9). In ancient Egypt and Babylon the king was occasionally called the image of God. However, the Genesis narrative asserts that it is not only the kings and powerful lords of the earth who constitute the image of God, but all people everywhere. Observe too that it is *male and female* (1:27) together who are created as God's image, and so women are called to share in the dominion of the earth alongside men. This high view of the woman was unique among the cultures of the time, and has remained unique well into the modern age.

Babylonian society, like both other Mesopotamian and Egyptian civilizations, was hierarchically structured. At the top of the social pyramid was the king, who was believed to represent the power of the divine world. Just below him came the priests who shared his mediatorial function, but to a lesser degree. Below them were the bureaucracy, the merchants and the military, while the base of the pyramid was formed by the peasants and slaves. Thus the socio-political order was given religious legitimation by the creation mythologies of these societies. The lower classes of human beings were created as slaves for the gods, to relieve them of manual labour. And, since the king represented the gods on earth, to serve the king was to serve the gods. Consequently, the Genesis 'counter-myth' undermines this widespread royal ideology. It 'democratizes' the political order. All human beings are called to represent God's kingship through the whole range of human life on earth. And God's rule is not the rule of a despot, but the loving nurture of a caring parent.

vi. Universal vs chauvinistic nature of religious epics. The creation epics of the surrounding civilizations were designed largely to explain why the local god of that city/civilization was currently in the ascendant (as e.g. the triumph of Marduk, the god of Babylon). But there is no mention of Israel or the Hebrew people in the creation account of Genesis. Uniquely blessed though they may be in receiving this revelation from the Creator, they are not inherently different from other peoples. All are creatures made in the image of God. There are no distinctions of language, race, caste or class mentioned in the text. The only distinction within humankind is that of male and female, but it is a distinction that is anchored within an equality of worth.

2. Mission as counter-storytelling: on human worth

Thus men and women, according to the Genesis narrative, possess a unique nature. They are *creatures*, belonging to the rest of the animal kingdom: created on the sixth day, along with all the other creatures of the earth, and said to be formed 'from the dust of the earth' (2:7), pointing to our creatureliness and relatedness to the earth (as if to say, 'they didn't drop from heaven like some immortal gods'). Modern science helps us to understand our connections with the rest of creation: our bodies are made up of chemicals cooked in the interior of stars a very long time ago, we share most of our DNA with other living organisms, we live on the exhalation of plants, and our well-being depends on the maintenance of sensitive balances in the biosphere.

But, despite some sentimental accounts of dolphins and chimpanzees, there isn't a creature on the planet remotely like us in cognitive capacities. Physical continuities often leap into mental *discontinuities*. Humans alone are stamped with the image of the Creator, called into a *personal* relationship with him which defines human life as more than merely biological. Human beings alone are addressed by God. To the Creator, we exist not only as his objects but as subjects. Human uniqueness consists not simply in the fact that we converse with each other, but rather that God talks to us and invites us to respond. In other words, we are invited to become part of that conversation which is the divine life.

Moreover, human personhood is constituted by relationality. Just as God relates to us and at the same time remains other than us, so within the human community we are related in diversity. Personal freedom implies a space between each other that is to be respected, and yet we do not find our fulfilment as persons apart from God and one another. Thus the 'other', far from being a threat to my unique identity, is the one without whom I would have no identity. It is this fact of personhood, established by creation, that confers dignity and value to every human life.

God is mystery, and man and woman in God's image are mystery. When we stand before another person, however destitute, disabled, diseased or degraded, we stand before something which is the vehicle of the divine, something which, in Martin Buber's classic terminology, is a Thou and not an It. We can acknowledge the gradualness of development into personal encounter, while affirming the reality of personhood from the moment of human conception. We can and do, of course, treat people like 'its', as simply physical objects – for instance, in pornography, in reductionist scientific theories, through non-therapeutic medical experimentation, or by indiscriminate killing in warfare. We do so at loss to our own humanity. The death of God does not, as Nietzsche believed, lead to the glorification of man; but rather takes from men and women any claim they may have to be treated with reverence by their fellows. The Genesis story goes on to show how, when the man and the woman sought to become gods, rather than gratefully accepting their unique dignity as the image of the only God, they perceived the other as both a threat to each one's autonomy and as an object to be manipulated in a world of manipulable objects.

The revolutionary uniqueness of this view of human life is felt not least in our (post)modern societies, and it is an important aspect of Christian mission to narrate this vision of humanness in the teeth of all the other definitions of humanness that abound in the media, the academy and the business world. Human beings are to be treated as having an essential value that is neither given (e.g. by the state) nor can it be taken away by human beings; it can only be recognized. They are not useful commodities whose value depends on what they can or cannot command in the marketplace. The moral implications of this vision are finely expressed in the words of the French biologist Jean Rostan:

> For my part I believe that there is no life so degraded, debased or impoverished that it does not deserve respect and is not worth defending with zeal and conviction ... I have the weakness to believe that it is an honour for our society to desire the expensive luxury of sustaining life for its useless, incompetent and incurably ill members. I would almost measure society's degree of civilization by the amount of effort and vigilance it imposes on itself out of pure respect for life.[2]

What would such respect for human worth involve for us as Christians in God's world?

a. Caring for human suffering

Despite its blemished history, time after time the church has stood out in all cultures as the pioneer in initiatives to provide health care to the poor, bring aid to the imprisoned, the homeless and the dying, and to improve conditions of physical labour.

Christians in India, for instance, have long been in the forefront of movements for the emancipation of women, with missionary societies from Britain and the United States in the nineteenth century often giving the lead where the colonial government was hesitant to tread for fear of upsetting local sensibilities. Some of the finest medical hospitals and training schools in India owe their existence to Christian missions. Many Hindus would rather go to a Christian hospital than a government hospital, because they know

---

[2] Quoted in C. Everett Koop, *The Right to Live, the Right to Die* (Tyndale House/ Coverdale, 1976).

the quality of personal care in the former is so much better. In areas such as leprosy, tuberculosis, mental illness and eye diseases, Christian missionary doctors and nurses pioneered new methods of management and surgery. Moreover, the training of women doctors and nurses was first introduced into India by Christian missionaries. For many years the entire nursing profession was filled with Anglo-Indians and Indian Christians, as other communities regarded nursing as menial work fit only for uneducated girls and widows. It has been estimated that as late as the beginning of the Second World War 90% of all the nurses in India, male and female, were Christians, and that about 80% of these had been trained in mission hospitals.[3]

From a different social context – the refugee camps on the Thai border which were set up following the Khmer Rouge holocaust in Cambodia – Don Cormack, an OMF missionary, wrote poignantly:

It was the cheapness, the low value placed on individual human lives which was the scandal of 1979. I realized it when I went looking for a frail young mother sent from a jungle border camp to a nearby hospital because she was bleeding to death after a premature delivery in the forest. After some days of waiting, the husband asked me to try to locate her. When I presented her name at the hospital, the nurses roared with laughter: 'You don't think we bother with the names do you! If you don't see her here, then she is out there somewhere in that big hole.'[4]

Cormack continues, however:

In each camp a core of Christians stood out as a loving, caring people who eschewed evil. The church did of course have its own internal tensions and discipline problems. Most were only babes in Christ. It was interesting too that, invariably, Christians were found in positions of responsibility in the camps: hospital orderlies, interpreters, handling relief aid etc.[5]

b. Safeguarding human rights

Despite the rising number of democratic regimes around the world,

---

[3] See C. B. Firth, *An Introduction to Indian Church History*, rev. ed. (Christian Literature Society, 1976), p. 208.

[4] Don Cormack, *Killing Fields, Living Fields: An Unfinished Portrait of the Cambodian Church – the Church That Would Not Die* (MARC, 1997), pp. 284–285.

[5] Ibid., p. 318.

Amnesty International reports that more people than ever before are being subjected to rape, beatings, electric shock and other forms of torture by the state. The organization's researchers found incidents of 'widespread' torture by agents of the state in more than seventy countries between 1997 and 2000, some of them liberal democracies.[6]

What finally makes a society worth living in is not the amount of consumer goods available in shopping malls, nor the effectiveness of its social-welfare schemes, nor even the lack of discrimination in employment and education, but the sense all people should have of being valued and appreciated by their neighbours. The biblical understanding of the *imago Dei* restores the language of 'human rights' to its proper anchoring within a larger framework of our mutual responsibility for one another under God. Where rights are regarded as purely formal, legal entities – disembedded from practices that affirm the relational nature of our human personhood – the public sphere of civil society withers. We are reduced to a set of mutually antagonistic groups, each asserting its rights against the other.

Michael Perry, an American law professor, has argued cogently that 'there is, finally, no intelligible secular version of the idea of human rights, that the conviction that human beings are sacred is inescapably religious'.[7] This is not to deny that many who do take human rights very seriously are agnostics and atheists where religious convictions are concerned. But it does raise serious doubts whether a vision of human rights can be argued for coherently and sustained effectively in societies which lack an appropriate theological understanding of the human person.

> If we have no reason to believe that the world has a normative order that is transgressed by violations of human rights … and if we nonetheless coerce others, and perhaps even, at the limit, kill others, in the name of prosecuting human rights, then are we coercing and killing in the name of nothing but our sentiments, our preferences, our 'inclination of the heart'?[8]

Our argument goes further than Perry's. It is not enough to speak of a vaguely 'religious' view of persons in an abstract sense as if there were some universal genus called 'religion'; but, rather, a specific religious view; namely, a biblical understanding of human

---

[6] Reported in *Guardian Weekly*, 26 October – 1 November 2000, p. 7.
[7] Michael J. Perry, *The Idea of Human Rights: Four Inquiries* (OUP, 1998), p. 35.
[8] Ibid., p. 39.

personhood. The dominant schools of Hindu practice, for example, do not recognize the fundamental equality of human beings. Those outside the caste system, the Dalits, are not even human:

> According to the native Hindu theory, individuals belonging to a particular caste share identical particles. These particles are different from the particles that constitute other individuals in other castes. This is why it is necessary to maintain distance between castes, lest these particles commingle ... Unlike racial stratification where visible differences govern social interaction, the caste system has to rest eventually on the belief in natural differences.[9]

It is the biblical concept of *imago Dei* which, more than any other, has provided the ontological grounding of human rights which purely secular accounts lack. It is doubtful whether respect for all human beings can flourish in societies untouched by the biblical vision. Medical historians have pointed out, for instance, that the care of defective newborns simply was not a medical concern in classical antiquity. The morality of the killing of sickly or deformed newborns appears not to have been questioned until the birth of the Christian church. No pagan writer – whether Greek, Roman, Indian or Chinese – appears to have raised the question whether human beings have inherent value ontologically, irrespective of social value, legal status, age, sex and so forth. 'The first espousal of an idea of inherent human value in Western civilization depended on a belief that every human being was formed in the image of God.'[10]

That God, out of his special love for humanity, bestows on us certain inviolable *rights*, is a politically radical concept, not only in the Third World but also in Europe and North America. It is God's love for all human beings that authorizes the poor and oppressed to stand up and claim their rights to sustenance and freedom. Injustice is a violation of God's own being. Both the Bible and Christian tradition have taught that the poor and oppressed have legitimate claims on us, so that striving for economic, social and political arrangements that help them secure their rights is a matter of doing justice, not merely engaging in acts of compassion. Moreover, while we reject the secular notion of autonomy (understood as self-

---

[9] Dipankar Gupta (ed.), *Social Stratification* (OUP, 1991), p. 25.
[10] Darrel W. Amundsen, 'Medicine and the Birth of Defective Children: Approaches of the Ancient World', in Richard C. McMillan, H. Tristram Engelhardt, Jr, and Stuart F. Spicker (eds.), *Euthanasia and the Newborn* (D. Reidel, 1987), p. 15.

determination) as the basis of human rights, nevertheless we must recognize that God's love empowers his creatures to free themselves from narratives and practices that demean their humanity and to stake their claim in the world as the icons of God.

Thus the church, both in its public proclamation of a different understanding of humanness and in its demonstration of this in the church's own social practices, is called to bring before the public gaze the 'forgotten' people in our societies – the poor, the disabled, the elderly, the outcast. If ethics is the Achilles heel of late-modern secular culture, then the ethical becomes the site of gospel proclamation. To champion human rights in global and local contexts, and to argue that such respect for human dignity only makes sense within a biblical world-view is to bring political action and evangelical proclamation into a powerful harmony.

c. Promoting social equality

When an indigenous Christian leader from northern Argentina was once asked what the Gospel had done for his people, he replied that it had enabled them to look the white person fully in the eye.[11]

The vision of human beings created in the image of God does not entail that everyone should be equal in power, wealth, intelligence or physical health. No society, from a family to a nation, can function without socially differentiated roles. But what matters is how such differences are regarded, and in particular whether they serve to construct a social hierarchy in which some people are made to feel inferior to others. To regard people as divine image-bearers does entail promoting a society where there is not only equal treatment of all before the law but also equal respect shown to all. A society where there is equality of respect is one where no-one has to grovel or beg before another, where women enjoy equal pay and employment opportunities as men, where the views of employees are welcomed and listened to by their employers, where mistress and maid can eat at table together, where the disabled and the elderly have a voice in the affairs of the community, where the caretaker's name is remembered by the university professor ...

Wherever there is social equality, people feel that each member of the community enjoys an equal standing with all the rest that overrides their unequal rankings along particular dimensions.

[11] J. Andrew Kirk, *What Is Mission? Theological Explorations* (Darton, Longman & Todd, 1999), p. 71.

Christians do not have to choose between an idea of equality that is purely ideal and abstract, an equality before God without social implications, on the one hand, and a totalizing egalitarianism that is destructive of all forms of society, on the other. As Oliver O'Donovan argues, what is required is neither of these choices, but 'a coordination of our understanding of equality with our understanding of the humane forms of community'. He continues, 'To have any substance a claim for equality must reflect decisions about what differentiations are constructive and healthy for human existence and what are not. But those decisions in turn reflect a judgment about which differentiations help, and which hinder the meeting of person with person on a basis of equality, with neither of them slave or lord.'[12]

3. Mission as counter-storytelling: on human work

Be fruitful and multiply, and fill the earth and subdue it; and have dominion over the fish of the sea and over the birds of the air and over every living thing that moves upon the earth.

(Gen. 1:28)

Because human beings are created in God's image, they are called to rule the earth as God's vice-regents. This, of course, is no licence for the unbridled exploitation and subjugation of nature. (Is it conceivable that the Creator, having repeatedly declared his pleasure and delight over his creation, should now turn to the crown of his work and command them to destroy that same creation?) Humankind is here commissioned to act as God's representative over the earth and its creatures and therefore to treat them in the same way as the God who created them. And we have seen how God's rule over the universe has been depicted as one of ordering, life-generating, life-sustaining, empowerment and personal enjoyment. Humans are called to be 'subcreators' under the sovereign Creator in enabling the whole creation to flourish and reach its appointed fulfilment in time.

This is spelled out in the following chapter where 'subdue the earth' finds its 'semantic parallel'[13] in *till it and keep it* (2:15). The word translated 'till' is *'ābad*, the normal Hebrew word meaning 'to serve'. The word is commonly used in a religious sense of serving

---

[12] Oliver O'Donovan, *The Desire of the Nations: Rediscovering the Roots of Political Theology* (CUP, 1996), p. 263.
[13] Victor P. Hamilton, *The Book of Genesis, Chapters 1–17* (Eerdmans, 1990), p. 140.

God (e.g. Deut. 4:19) and in describing the priestly duties of the Levites in the tabernacle (e.g. Num. 4:23–24, 26). The second verb, 'keep' or 'tend', is the Hebrew šāmar, the root of which carries the meaning 'to exercise great care over', to the point, if necessary, of guarding. The same root is used in the next chapter to describe the cherubs who are on guard to prevent access to the tree of life in the garden (Gen. 3:24). 'The garden is something to be protected more than it is something to be possessed.'[14] Thus human beings have been entrusted with the priestly duty of caring for the earth and its creatures under God.

Unlike many religious myths of creation, physical work is not a menial chore relegated to men by the gods; nor, unlike much Greek or Indian philosophy, is the zenith of human activity found in inner contemplation. Creative work of some kind is indispensable to human flourishing. If God works in, with and for his creation, then men and women imitate God in their work of harnessing the powers of the created order, serving his creatures, and enabling the earth to bloom. 'When you find a man who is a Christian praising God by the excellence of his work,' wrote the novelist Dorothy Sayers, 'then do not distract him and take him away from his proper vocation to address religious meetings and open church bazaars. Let him serve God in the way to which God has called him.'[15]

Herein lies our mandate to be at the forefront of scientific and artistic activity. In relation to God, humanity and the universe form one *world*. Human beings do not impose an alien order through their work on a chaotic universe. Rather, in scientific and artistic activity under God the inherent intelligibility of the universe comes to expression and articulation:

Just as God made life to reproduce itself, so he has made the universe to express itself, to bring forth its own structure and order in ever richer forms, and in that way to find its fulfilment as the creation of God. This is what takes place through man, for man is that unique element in the creation through which the universe knows itself and unfolds its inner rationality.[16]

The biblical view of creation implies that we are neither owners (to do with the earth what we please) nor mere guests (to enjoy

---

[14] Hamilton, *Genesis*, p. 171.
[15] Dorothy L. Sayers, 'Why Work?' in idem, *Creed or Chaos* (Harcourt Brace, 1949), p. 59.
[16] T. F. Torrance, *Reality and Scientific Theology* (Scottish Academic Press, 1982), p. 68.

passively but not to intervene in 'natural processes'). Developing the earth's potential and conserving its fruitfulness are twin aspects of responsible planetary stewardship. It is what has come to be dubbed 'sustainable development' in recent times; namely, creating wealth in such a way that we leave for future generations a planet that has not been robbed of its life-giving and life-sustaining capacities.

Thus there is no absolute right to private property. Human beings have been entrusted as stewards with what belongs fundamentally to God.

> The earth is the LORD's and all that is in it,
> The world, and those who live in it.
>
> (Ps. 24:1; cf. Ps. 89:11)

Thus when Israel was given the land of promise to indwell (a paradigm of the human inheritance of the earth), they were told 'The land [the basic means of production] shall not be sold in perpetuity, for the land is mine; with me you are but aliens and tenants' (Lev. 25:23; also Exod. 19:5; Ezek. 46:18). The requirements of human survival take precedence over an individual's right to his property (e.g. Deut. 24:19–22). Neither governments nor multi-national corporations are the owners of the earth's resources. God holds them responsible for the development of those resources for the sake of all human beings who share the planet; and for the exercise of that development in such a manner that respects the integrity of his creation.

The Mosaic covenant spelled out how human dominion was to be exercised. For example, it forbade the exploitation of natural resources to extinction (Deut. 22:6–7) and, contrary to modern practice, not even warfare justified indiscriminate deforestation (Deut. 20:19–20). Animals and the land are included in the weekly and seventh-year Sabbath, 'that your ox and your donkey may have relief, and your home-born slave and the resident alien may be refreshed' (Exod. 23:10–12; Lev. 25:6–7; Deut. 5:12–15).

God's concern that all humankind should participate both in the development of the earth and in the fruits of that development stand as a massive indictment on a global economic system based on greed and waste – one oriented not around meeting the needs of all humankind (more than 40% of whom are too poor to be part of the global economy) but on stimulating the insatiable wants of the few, which puts the rising profits of company directors before the rights of men and women to meaningful work, and that views the earth not as a living creation to be respected but simply as another commodity to be consumed.

Returning to the Genesis story, the 'week' of creation finds its ultimate goal in the 'blessing' and 'hallowing' of the seventh day. The biblical scholar Gordon Wenham observes that these are 'striking terms to apply to a day'. He continues:

> Divine blessing on men and animals leads to fruitfulness and success, and it is paradoxical that the day on which God refrains from creative activity is pronounced blessed … Similarly it is unusual for a day to be 'hallowed', that is, made or declared holy … The seventh day is the very first thing to be hallowed in Scripture, to acquire that special status that properly belongs to God alone. In this way Genesis emphasizes the sacredness of the Sabbath.[17]

What the creation narrative does is to *relativize our work*. We find our true identity not in our work of ruling the earth, but in our relationship with God. Work is an important aspect of our worship to God, but it is not worship *per se*. Pausing to enjoy the fruits of our labour with our fellow human beings and to give thanks to God for the gifts of life – this is what restores the true perspective on our work. So rest and celebration are built into the created order. This was the basis of the Sabbath law in ancient Israel. Its primary intent was to set human labour within the only perspective which gives it meaning; namely, the worship of God. It is still a revolutionary concept to follow in an age devoted to the frenetic, soul-destroying idolatry of work.

The conditions of late modernity leave many people rootless and dissatisfied even with well-paid work. Sociologist Richard Sennet observes that

> One of the unintended consequences of modern capitalism is that it has strengthened the value of place, aroused a longing for community. All the emotional conditions we have explored in the workplace animate that desire: the uncertainties of flexibility; the absence of deeply rooted trust and commitment; the superficiality of teamwork; most of all, the specter of failing to make something of oneself in the world, to 'get a life' through one's work. All these conditions impel people to look for some other scene of attachment and depth.[18]

[17] Gordon J. Wenham, *Genesis 1–15*, Word Biblical Commentary (Word, 1987), p. 36.
[18] R. Sennet, *The Corrosion of Character: The Personal Consequences of Work in the New Capitalism* (W. W. Norton, 1998), p. 138.

THE MESSAGE OF MISSION

The church is called to witness to the truth that men and women are created for joy and wonder. It is worship that disciplines our greed, humbles our arrogance, restores true community and straightens our vision. In the words of David Wells:

> That the cathedral in an [sic] European city ... is not 'useful' for any purpose other than worship is powerfully symbolic. The architectural language proclaimed forcefully the centrality and freedom of grace – that it was not for sale and could not be bought. To worship is to be liberated from the merciless markets of life, to declare by God's grace that one is not for sale. It is to be for God, for his use and service, to be set free to marvel at his astonishing greatness and glory. This is the liberation, the marvel, towards which we must work as we encounter the naked, lonely men and women ... who have only themselves to converse with in the desolate spaces of their inner life.[19]

4. Mission as earth-keeping

Creation exists not to serve human interests but to reflect the glory of God.

> In his hand is the life of every living thing,
> and the breath of every human being.
> (Job 12:10)

> Praise the LORD from the earth,
> you sea monsters and all deeps,
> fire and hail, snow and frost,
> stormy wind fulfilling his command!

> Mountains and all hills,
> fruit trees and all cedars!
> Wild animals and all cattle,
> creeping things and flying birds ...

> Praise the LORD!
> (Ps. 148:7–10, 14)[20]

Animals, though subject to humankind, are viewed as our companions in 2:18–20. The act of naming the animals (2:19–20)

---

[19] D. Wells, *Turning to God* (Paternoster, 1989), p. 127.
[20] See also Pss. 96:11–13; 98; 148:1–4; Is. 55:12.

48

can be taken as a rudimentary form of scientific enquiry, the name in antiquity summing up the essence of a creature and so implying an intimate knowledge of it. 'The works of the LORD are great, sought out of all them that have pleasure therein' (Ps. 111:2 AV) is the text that stands at the entrance to the Cavendish Laboratory in Cambridge, England, one of the most famous centres for experimental physics in the world. So, the earth and its creatures are entrusted to human care, and we have a mandate from God for the study and enrichment of life on the planet.

The romantic view of premodern societies that has accompanied the disillusionment with science and the notion of progress in the post-Christian West has also led to some popular readings of the Genesis story that lay the blame for environmental destructiveness on the cultural influence of the Bible. It is the alleged 'anthropo-centrism' of the Genesis account that is said to be responsible for the ecological crisis. But this is a bizarre claim from the perspective of those of us living in non-Western cultures which have not been tainted by the allegedly 'anthropocentric' teaching of Genesis and yet who suffer environmental damage on a huge scale – the pollution of air and water supplies, the disappearance of rainforests, desertification and soil erosion – whether due to poverty, neglect, civil war, political corruption or blatant commercial greed (not all of which can be laid at the feet of Western corporations and govern-ments). The pollution and pillage of nature, whether as a result of ignorance, greed or selfishness has been characteristic of human cultures all over the globe and at all times in the past.

The microbiologist and environmental campaigner René Dubos once observed how 'the classic nature poets of China write as if they had achieved identification with the cosmos, but in reality most of them were retired bureaucrats living on estates in which nature was carefully trimmed and managed by gardeners'.[21] Dubos's verdict is that 'If men are more destructive now than they were in the past, it is because there are more of them and because they have at their command more powerful means of destruction, not because they have been influenced by the Bible. In fact, the Judaeo-Christian peoples were probably the first to develop on a large scale a pervasive concern for land management and an ethic of nature.'[22]

I am tempted here to quote John Calvin (1509–64), for it is often the Protestantism of Calvin that is the villain of the piece in the writings of those critics who blame the environmental crisis and the evils of capitalism on the 'Protestant work ethic'. Whatever some of

[21] R. Dubos, *A God Within* (Sphere, 1976), p. 114.
[22] Ibid., p. 115.

his followers may have said and done, let us listen to Calvin's own comments on Genesis 2:15:

> The earth was given to man, with this condition, that he should occupy himself in its cultivation ... The custody of the garden was given in charge to Adam, to show that we possess the things which God has committed to our hands, on the condition that, being content with the frugal and moderate use of them, we should take care of what shall remain. Let him who possesses a field, so partake of its yearly fruits, that he may not suffer the ground to be injured by his negligence, but let him endeavour to hand it down to posterity as he received it, or even better cultivated. Let him so feed on its fruits, that he neither dissipates it by luxury, not permits it to be marred or ruined by neglect. Moreover, that this economy, and this diligence, with respect to those good things which God has given us to enjoy, may flourish among us: let everyone regard himself as the steward of God in all things which he possesses. Then he will neither conduct himself dissolutely, nor corrupt by abuse those things which God requires to be preserved.[23]

Christians in many Asian societies have been in the forefront of efforts to protect animals from wanton killing and to prevent soil erosion by developing improved farming techniques. The much-maligned Puritans of sixteenth-century England campaigned tirelessly against cruel practices such as bear-baiting and cockfighting; and their legacy was continued in the Methodist movement and the evangelical awakenings of the eighteenth century. The British prime minister Horace Walpole is said to have remarked in 1760 that a certain man was known to be 'turning Methodist; for, in the middle of conversation, he arose, and opened the window to let out a moth'.[24]

Andrew Kirk's verdict is eminently sane:

> The Judaeo-Christian tradition has nothing to be ashamed of with regard to its teaching on humanity's relationship to the environment. It does not need to borrow from other traditions to supplement its own shortcomings, though it may listen carefully and respectfully to the views of others. It has all the resources

---

[23] J. Calvin, *Commentary on Genesis* (1554; repr. Banner of Truth, 1965).
[24] Keith V. Thomas, *Man and the Natural World: Changing Attitudes in England 1500–1800* (Allen Lane, 1983), p. 180; quoted in Philip J. Sampson, *Six Modern Myths about Christianity and Western Civilization* (IVP, 2000), p. 85.

necessary, in the words of Jan Jongeneel, 'to pursue a middle path between the Scylla of the divination of nature by traditional religions ... and the Charybdis of the modern desacralized exploitation of it'.[25]

However, it must be admitted that environmental concerns have not been a prominent feature of mission studies, whether in the West or the developing world, until very recently. At its Vancouver Assembly of 1983, the World Council of Churches (WCC) rightly drew attention to the way the quest for economic justice, social peace and the 'integrity of creation' went hand in hand.[26] In recent years nation states, or regions within states, have gone to war for control of petroleum supplies, diamonds and water. Excessive deforestation or overgrazing of cattle leads to soil erosion which, in turn, leads to the expansion of deserts which, in turn, leads to mass migrations which, in turn, leads to strain on the available resources of neighbouring countries to handle the influx of refugees, and this can, in turn, lead to war. The 'slash and burn' policies in the world's great forests (especially in Brazil and Indonesia) are due to pressures to grow cash crops and produce beef for export markets. In the long term these destructive practices lead to permanent impoverishment of the soil and a worsening of rural poverty.

While every country has to deal with local problems of air and water pollution, there has been a growing recognition in recent years among many scientists and environmental activists that the massive ecological challenges facing the world require a coordinated global response. Foremost among these challenges are (1) the escalation and proliferation of nuclear weapons technology; (2) the threatened extinction of rainforests, which would also involve a massive loss of biodiversity; (3) the threatened extinction of many animal species (tigers and some whale species being the most publicized); and (4) the climatic changes, particularly global warming, brought about by the loss of forest cover and the profligate use of fossil fuels by the most industrialized nations of the world.[27]

The Intergovernmental Panel on Climate Change (IPCC) has successfully brought together many hundreds of scientists from all

---

[25] Kirk, *What is Mission?* p. 175.

[26] *Gathered for Life* (World Council of Churches, 1983).

[27] America with 4% of the planet's population emits 25% of all the greenhouse gases, mostly from cars, air conditioners and power stations. Japan is the world's second industrial economy, but it emits fewer than 9 tons of carbon per head a year, less than half America's emissions, and close to the EU's average of 8.5 tons. See *Climate Change 2001: Impacts, Adaptation and Vulnerability*, <www.ipcc.ch/pub/wg2SPMfinal.pdf>.

over the world in the preparation of reports concerning global climate change. They assess the likely impact of such change and the technologies required to mitigate such change. Although there has been much debate about the details, a widespread consensus has emerged from their work that has provided an essential basis for the UN Framework Convention on Climate Change. Sir John Houghton, a Christian professor of meterological science, points out that scientists carry an 'awesome responsibility to present to policy-makers and the public accurate, relevant and balanced information regarding what is known with reasonable certainty and what the uncertainties are'. He commends the IPCC as a model of cooperation that 'could be followed in other areas of science (e.g. that of genetic modification) which impinge strongly on matters of international policy or regulation'.[28]

But the climatologists have no legal basis for imposing worldwide energy restrictions. Herein lies the rub. If global ecological problems such as global warming have any solutions, they can only come from a sense of human empathy and solidarity that might temper the short-sighted greed of purely commercial society.

Understanding the problem and recommending solutions is one thing. Getting individuals and nations to repent of their profligate lifestyles for the sake of the global good is another. A white child born in New York, Paris or London will consume, pollute and waste more in his or her lifetime than fifty children born in a developing country. But it is these poor children who are the most likely to die from air and water pollution. Christians, especially those in the rich nations and among the wealthier classes of poor nations, need to preach and demonstrate a gospel that has the power to liberate men and women from individual and collective idolatries, and to work with all who aspire for a more responsible use of the world's resources.

[28] Sir John Houghton, Guest Editorial, *Science and Christian Belief* 13.1 (April 2001), p. 2.

Isaiah 44:24 – 45:25
3. The incomparable God

1. From China with anger

In 1953 David Macdonald Paton, an Anglican priest who had spent ten years in China as a Christian teacher and administrator in Beijing, Chongqing and Fuzhou, published a book entitled *Christian Missions and the Judgement of God*.[1] This book was a blast of anger and frustration at (what the writer deliberately calls) the debacle of the missionary exodus from China after the Communist revolution there.

The main thesis of the book is as follows: God used the Communists as the instrument of his surgical will to bring about the ending of the missionary era in China: this was an act of his judgment and mercy. Most missionaries (wrote Paton) were naive – they did not understand imperialism; by their very existence in China they were a political fact and factor (even if they were as harmless as doves); they did not understand the power of Marxism as a vehicle of Chinese nationalism; they did not understand that there is no such thing as 'pure gospel': the gospel always incarnates itself in a particular culture. The missionaries planted in China a church that was in structure, ethos, architecture, hymnology and other ways foreign, alien and impotent. They had held on to power far too long and many of them had no deep respect for the Chinese and their culture. The result was that the Chinese church was not deeply rooted in Chinese culture; the missionaries had created an unhealthy dependency that needed to be rooted out.

---

[1] D. M. Paton, *Christian Missions and the Judgement of God*, 2nd ed. (Eerdmans, 1996).

The book caused a storm in 1953, partly because of its truculent tone in places, partly because Paton showed little understanding of those whom he called fundamentalists, sects and millenarians; and partly from (and on behalf of) hundreds of smarting missionaries who had been bundled out of China after long or short terms of service. Actually some of the things Paton said had been said over thirty years earlier by another high church British Anglican, Roland Allen, though in a more pacific way. This is not the place to discuss Paton's arguments or those of his critics in detail. But what neither Paton nor his critics foresaw was that through the trials and sufferings of the next fifty years the Chinese church would grow fifteenfold into a community of millions, sometimes through the very methods of hard labour and exile designed to stamp it out. History turns out to be a teacher of unexpected lessons. And so it was in the times of the writer of Isaiah 45.

2. An exclusive claim

The electrifying climax, towards which this particular section of Isaiah moves, are the words of 45:22, 23:

> *Turn to me and be saved,*
> *all the ends of the earth!*
> *For I am God, and there is no other.*
> *By myself I have sworn,*
> *from my mouth has gone forth in righteousness*
> *a word that shall not return:*
> *'To me every knee shall bow,*
> *every tongue shall swear.'*

There is an invitation in the words *Turn to me and be saved* ... There is also a declaration: *To me every knee shall bow* ... The validity of the declaration and the invitation are based on the central claim in the text, *I am God and there is no other*. This claim is emphasized by a solemn oath formula, *By myself have I sworn* ... and it is asserted that the claim is utterly reliable, *in righteousness*, and irrevocable, the word *shall not return*. Nowhere in the Old Testament, or indeed in the whole Bible, is there a clearer assertion of two fundamental biblical truths: there is only one true God; and because of this fact, the whole world is summoned to worship him.

The New Testament makes a further, deeper claim to uniqueness. These words in Isaiah are applied to Yahweh, the only God. In Philippians 2:10, 11, in his 'Hymn of Christ's Glory', Paul quotes these words of Isaiah as being applied by God to Jesus Christ. In Romans 14:11 also these words of Isaiah are put into the mouth of Christ, who has just been declared the 'Lord of both the dead and the living'. An Indian Christian was asked what had drawn him from his Hindu background to become a Christian. His reply was that it was the sheer *worshipability* of Jesus that had drawn him: there was no other who so desired and deserved his worship, his utter consecration.

In our multicultural, pluralistic times, and with our memories of religious hatred and bigotry, these exclusive assertions about the *incomparability* of God are almost bound to arouse reservations and even outright condemnation from some. But every missionary religion is bound to make such claims; without them how could it spread? In many parts of the world where worshippers fear many gods and spirits and their arbitrary and unpredictable demands, the news that there is only one true God who deserves to be worshipped; and therefore that there is only one God whom they *need* worship, is a joy-filled liberation. The God whom the Bible depicts is jealous for our exclusive loyalty: he will not share our allegiance, any more than a married reader of these words is willing to share the fidelity of his or her spouse.

3. The context of Isaiah 45

The context of Isaiah 45:22 is fascinating and instructive. These chapters of Isaiah presuppose that his Jewish listeners are coming to the end of a long exile in Babylon. A deliverance from Babylon is approaching; but it is also clear that as well as needing a change of environment they need a change of heart. How are these two deliverances to be achieved? The agent of the first is the world-conqueror, Cyrus, the Medo-Persian king. The agent of the second, greater, deeper deliverance is the unnamed servant of Yahweh, whose identity is progressively revealed in these chapters.

Isaiah 40 – 66 may be divided into three sections of nine chapters each, by observing the small refrain repeated at 48:22 and 57:21. In the first nine chapters (40 – 48) the focus is mainly on the deliverance from Babylon and how this will come about. Babylon is first specifically mentioned in 43:14, where Yahweh announces that he is about to break down the prison bars. It is probable that the Babylonian authorities found such prophetic utterances subversive and destabilizing. It is also probable that some of the Jewish refugees had settled down very comfortably in Babylon in the preceding decades, and thus that they were not at all enthusiastic about the prospect of returning to a devastated homeland. This is the broad context of the words of chapter 45. Now let us look in more detail at the passage before us.

a. Creator and Redeemer of his people (44:24–27)

As often in the Old Testament the language of creation and redemption is mixed together here. The word *Redeemer* reminds us of the Exodus, and the drying up of rivers (44:27) also reminds us of the Reed Sea and of the Jordan. But creation language predominates, and the language is generalized: it refers to what Yahweh is always doing. God says to Israel (44:24), I am the One who forms you, who makes everything, who stretches out the heavens, and who beats out the earth. I am also the Overturner (44:25), nullifying the omens of false prophets, driving fortune-tellers crazy, turning the wise back and overturning their knowledge. I am also the Confirmer (44:26), establishing my servant's word, bringing to pass what my messengers predict. And *in particular* Jerusalem will be reinhabited and the cities of Judah be rebuilt. I myself will be the Contractor!

b. Lord of Cyrus, the world-conqueror (44:28 – 45:8)

Now comes the surprising prophecy! Apart from Yahweh's direct intervention, who is to be his agent in the rehabilitation of Jerusalem and the Jews? The answer is Cyrus! Cyrus II, the Medo-Persian king, who came to the throne about 559 BC, who conquered Croesus of Lydia and marched through Assyria in 547 BC, who took Babylon in 539 BC, and whose limestone tomb at Pasargardae fascinated the late Shah of Iran. Cyrus is described in kingly language as Yahweh's shepherd, and Yahweh's anointed. His striking, whirlwind progress through western Asia is described in terms of Yahweh's initiatives. Who beats down the nations before Cyrus and strips their kings? Who opens the doors and gates of cities before him? Who levels the mountains? Who breaks down the gates and snaps iron bars? Who reveals the most securely hidden treasures? The answer to all these questions is 'Yahweh'. In all these activities, Cyrus is invited to detect Yahweh's hand and call.

In counterpoint to Isaiah's words we have Cyrus's own account of his conquest of Babylon on the Cyrus Cylinder in the British Museum. Here we read how the gods became furious at the Babylonians, and how Marduk, the god of Babylon 'scoured all the lands for a friend, seeking for the upright prince whom it would have to take his hand'. Later Cyrus describes himself as 'king of the world, great king, mighty king, king of Babylon, king of the land of Sumer and Akkad, king of the four quarters' and describes how he sought daily to worship Marduk, who was happy and duly blessed Cyrus and his son and his troops.[2]

Verses 4 to 7 reveal more of Yahweh's purposes in these earth-shaking events, in which Cyrus continued to be an unwitting instrument. Cyrus describes how he 'returned gods to their places and housed them in lasting abodes'.[3] He also describes how he 'gathered together the inhabitants [exiles?] in many places and restored to them their dwellings'. The Jews are not specifically mentioned by Cyrus, but what the Bible records is entirely congruent with this new, tolerant policy. What verse 4 affirms is that in the first place Cyrus's activity was for the sake of God's people, Jacob/Israel.

But Yahweh also had a wider purpose, described in verses 5 and 6. Because he is the only God, his desire and purpose is that from furthest east to furthest west people might come to know him. This is, of course, a fulfilment of the blessing made to Abraham right back in Genesis 12:1–3.

In a final dramatic statement in this section, Yahweh asserts his sovereignty over all that happens – light and darkness, prosperity and trouble – he makes; he forms; he acts. In the course of international wars combatants and non-combatants, the guilty and the innocent, are caught up in tremendous tides of trouble, wicked-ness, sorrows, heroism and, sometimes, miracles. In this passage Yahweh asserts that he (and by implication) not Marduk is in control. It is important to note that this assertion does not carry with it the promise that the meaning of these events will always be transparent to us, now or later.

It is not surprising that a prayer breaks out in verse 8; for in the course of war, justice and truth are early casualties. If righteousness and salvation (two of the Old Testament's most capacious words) are to be found and experienced, if they are to fall like rain from the sky (a joy that only those living on the edge of a vast desert can fully appreciate), or if they are to spring up from the ground like a harvest – then they are a sign that the Creator Lord is at work.

c. Lord of disappointed Israel (45:9–13)

The prospect of liberation that Isaiah describes meets with questions and incomprehension. It is perhaps unfair to call them quibbles.

[2] D. Winton Thomas, *Documents from Old Testament Times* (Thomas Nelson, 1958), pp. 92–93.

[3] Ibid., p. 93.

Sometimes the ways of God's sovereignty seem desperately unintelligible to us. But Israel's complaints meet with a robust response from God (v. 9): Who are you to complain?! A pot cannot criticize the potter, through which it came into existence! Two possible complaints are mentioned: 'What are you making?!' 'A handless person could have done better!' But a child should not insult those on whom his very existence depends! 'What are you (father) fathering? What are you (mother) giving birth to?' Will you question me about the future, about my Cyrus-plan? Will you question me about my children, my pots? After all, I am (only!) the Creator! It was I who made the earth; who created human beings. It was I – my hands – that spread out the heavens and deployed all their hosts. I am the Lord of history too. It was I who woke him up to begin his work (everyone knows who 'him' is – Cyrus!), to begin his saving work. It is I who direct his paths. And it is he who will build my city and liberate my exiles. It is *my* initiatives that accomplish all this, not your schemes, your payments and bribes, says Yahweh.

d. Lord of the wide world (45:14–25)

This final section of Isaiah 45 falls into two parts. In verses 14–19 Yahweh addresses Zion/Israel regarding the astonishing influx of foreigners which is to follow the rebuilding of Jerusalem. In verses 20–25 there is a direct appeal to the 'ends of the earth' to turn from their idols to the living and true God. The glorious prospect outlined here is filled in in much more detail in chapters 60 – 62. Derek Kidner's comment on the language used in this section is helpful for those who are worried by metaphors which may sound nationalist or even jingoist: 'Such names as Egypt etc. and the details of chains and homage depict God's triumph in terms of the contemporary scene, using the vivid colouring of human victories. In the fulfilment, these will be transcended, as verses 20–25 make plain.'[4]

Verse 14 pictures an astonishing procession coming towards Zion (that Zion is in mind is indicated by the feminine pronoun throughout the verse). Who are these supplicants and what do they want? They are from Israel's ancient enemy Egypt and from deepest Africa. ('Sabeans' means roughly 'the back of beyond, somewhere extremely remote'.) They are wealthy, businesslike and physically impressive. They have not been overpowered by military might;

[4] D. A. Carson et al., *New Bible Commentary: Twenty-First Century Edition* (IVP, 1994), p. 659.

they are not economic migrants; they are not grovelling or destitute or coerced. Their motivation (v. 14) is religious:

> 'God is with you alone, and there is no other;
> there is no god besides him.'

How is verse 15 to be interpreted? Does it express the astonishment of the converts who are turning from visible gods to the invisible God? Or does it express the surprise of Israel at God's topsy-turvy ways – changing Israel, Babylon's captive, into the object of a world pilgrimage? Or does it express the prophet's own amazement at the opaqueness of God's purposes? Can it be compared to Paul's confession at the end of his long and agonized review of God's purposes for his people: 'O the depth of the riches and wisdom and knowledge of God! How unsearchable are his judgements and how inscrutable his ways!' (Rom. 11:33).

However this may be, verses 16 and 17 set out alternative destinies. Those who carve idols (mere shapes of persons without any life or personality) are doomed to reap shame and disgrace. There is only one God and Saviour. But Israel, by contrast, including those who have just arrived for inclusion in the community of faith in the one God, will be saved by Yahweh for eternity. An explanation follows in verses 18 and 19. Far from being secretive, ambiguous[5] or meaningless, God's creation is clear; his speaking is clear. God the Creator forms, makes, creates, establishes the world. He does not create it a chaos. God the Speaker does not mumble and mutter, gibber and squeak. He is not to be found in the land of darkness and chaos. He speaks what is true and right.

Finally in verses 20–25 Yahweh addresses the wide world directly, and particularly the fugitives who have fled from idolatry to worship the true God. How tragic is the state of idolaters – they are mentally blind; they have to carry their idols, in contrast to Yahweh who carries Israel (Is. 46:1–4); they keep on praying to an impotent god. Who foretold this ingathering of the nations to Israel? Ask each other; assemble your case if you can. It was I, Yahweh – victorious, saving, unique. These assertions now bring us to verses 22 and 23, which, as already indicated, are the climax of the passage. Each person, everywhere, should turn, may turn, to the only God, for the salvation, the righteousness which only he can

---

[5] A classic case of ambiguous prophecy is the response of the oracle at Delphi to Croesus of Lydia's enquiry whether he should fight Cyrus. The oracle answered Croesus, 'If you fight there will be a great victory.' Croesus omitted to inquire whether it would be *his* victory or that of Cyrus, went into battle and lost his kingdom.

THE MESSAGE OF MISSION

give. As verse 24 says, Yahweh is the unique source of salvation, victory and strength. The anger of abusers subsides into shame. Victory hallelujahs ring out from the enlarged community of Israel.

4. A critique of idolatry

Many histories of Israel in Old Testament times have presented the evolution of Israel's faith as a long rise from polytheism through henotheism (the worship of one god, while not necessarily denying the *existence* of other gods) to the high point of ethical monotheism (only one, universal God) in these chapters of Isaiah. This view requires a considerable reconstruction of the story as it is presented canonically, because, as the Old Testament stands, belief in only one Lord and God is very early indeed, and the whole history of Israel is threatened constantly by a slide into the polytheism and idolatry of the Canaanites and surrounding nations.

How are we to interpret this chapter of Isaiah in our modern pluralistic times when it is assumed very widely that there are multiple ways of saving access to the divine or to the ultimately Real, all equally valid? In such a context, the strongly exclusive tone of Isaiah's invitation, and his mocking of idolatry are sharply dissonant.

First, it is helpful to distinguish idolatry, the worship of strange gods, and iconolatry, which is the use of images in the cult of God.[6] It is the former of these with which we are primarily concerned in Isaiah.

Secondly, we note that this opposition to idolatry is not a surprise outburst in an isolated chapter. There is a constant undertow of criticism of idolatry in these chapters, rising to a sarcastic climax in chapter 44. Some examples follow. It is important to choose for your deity a wood that will not rot; and to make an image that will not topple (40:18–20). The prophet pictures the artisans encouraging each other, and paying particular attention to the fastening of the images, so that they will not wobble (41:6–7). In 41:21–24 the protest is that Yahweh is the only one who can interpret the past; and the only one who can predict the future. The idols can *do* nothing; they *are* nothing.[7] The climax is reached in the doggerel about domestic idolatry in chapter 44: a man chooses a piece of wood that he considers suitable; on half of it he cooks his meal; the other half he makes into a god, bows down before it and prays for it

[6] *Encyclopaedia Judaica*, ed. C. Roth and G. Wigoder, vol. 8 (Keter, 1972), p. 1227.
[7] Similar criticisms are made in 43:8–13 and 44:7, 8.

to save him! As Christopher North says, 'there are portrayed in these chapters two irreconcileable concepts of reality'.[8]

Thirdly, we note that as a matter of fact, these chapters of Isaiah are prophecy from the underside: they are refugee theology, liberation theology. These are not the words of an all-conquering missionary religion. They are words applied to the theological crisis of the exile. Presumably it was not at all clear to many of the Jews who were taken into exile in Babylon that Yahweh was the Ruler of the ends of the earth. Would it not have appeared to them that the gods of Babylon were very much stronger? Dostoevsky wrote that his hosanna of praise ascended to God only through the dark clouds of doubt. To read these soaring prophecies of Isaiah in the context of utter defeat and exile is to be reminded of the songs and prayers of faith that arose among black slaves in the cotton plantations of the American South or from the uttermost depths of the concentration camps in the Second World War.

Fourthly, it is clear that the great fear that some critics have of such exclusive claims as Isaiah 45 makes is that they are the parent of incivility, intolerance and bigotry. This is especially clear, for example, in John Hick's book *The Rainbow of Faiths*.[9] Here are three quotations from that book. The exclusive absolutisms of the great religions 'have created communal conflicts and have been used both to validate war and to intensify its savagery'.[10] 'Human savagery has too often found Christian dogma tailored for its own self-justification.'[11] 'Absolutism in religion, preaching the unique superiority of one's own tradition over against others, continues to motivate young men to be willing to kill and be killed for what they regard as a sacred cause.'[12] Robert Bellah has edited a whole book on the dangers of uncivil religion in North America.[13] Curiously enough aggressive pluralism can also be extremely beastly: Frederick Buechner wrote about the factionalism, the political correctness and the intimidation he discovered amid the unfettered pluralism of Harvard students.[14] We must turn away absolutely from all inquisitorial methods of religious enforcement; we must renounce the use of force and coercion for religious reasons; we have to confess with sadness that the cross, an instrument of torture, has been used by

[8] C. R. North, *The Second Isaiah* (OUP, 1964), p. 140.

[9] J. Hick, *The Rainbow of Faiths: Critical Dialogues on Religious Pluralism* (SCM, 1995).

[10] Ibid., p. 44.

[11] Ibid., p. 100.

[12] Ibid., p. 134.

[13] R. N. Bellah and Frederick Greenspahn, *Uncivil Religion: Interreligious Hostility in America* (Crossroad, 1987).

[14] F. Buechner, *Telling Secrets* (HarperSanFrancisco, 1991), pp. 60ff.

Christians in the past as a sword to compel submission. But a truly free society must include the freedom to share deeply held beliefs about the most important things. In fact, an *index* of its freedom may be found in the possibility it contains for the rational opposition of goodwill, for the fruitful and pleasant marriage of convinced conviction and concern for the truth leading to enthusiasm and eagerness to share what we believe *plus* an attractive attitude of courtesy, politeness, respect and hospitality for the views and experiences of others. There have been discussions in the UK about an extension of the laws of blasphemy, to prevent writers and speakers making trouble and causing deep offence by gratuitous insults about different religious beliefs. But it is doubtful if this would be the right course. Religious sensitivity can itself become an instrument of tyranny if, instead of arguing a matter in a friendly and civilized manner, one party rushes to the police station complaining that they have been offended.

Fifthly, the belief in the uniqueness of Yahweh and of Jesus Christ does not rule out a priori the importance of a detailed knowledge of other faiths. The fear, therefore, that exclusivism is the parent of ignorance is unfounded. As a matter of fact many missionaries have become extremely well informed about the faiths of those they went to serve. The pious German Lutheran missionary Bartholomew Ziegenbalg, who arrived in India in 1706 at the age of twenty-three, did not believe that Hinduism could bring salvation to its adherents. But he became a pioneer in the study of South Indian Hinduism. One of his most notable works was entitled *Genealogy of the Malabarian Gods*, which he completed in 1713. When he sent this back for publication in Europe, A. H. Francke, the redoubtable director of the mission, criticized him strongly, and the manuscript lay unpublished for 150 years.[15] Johannes Gottlieb Christaller, a German member of the Basel mission, born in a poor home, of indifferent health, but with an extraordinary gift for languages, became a world expert on the beliefs, customs and languages of several groups in Ghana.[16]

The late Professor Adrian Hastings noted the evolution of many theology departments in British universities into departments of religious studies, a development entirely to be expected in the light of the religious diversification that has taken place in the country. But he resisted strongly the deadening effect of an imposed

[15] See S. C. Neill, *A History of Christianity in India 1707–1858* (CUP, 1985), pp. 32–33.
[16] See article on Christaller by Kwame Bediako in G. H. Anderson (ed.), *Biographical Dictionary of Christian Missions* (Simon & Schuster/Macmillan, 1998), p. 133.

pluralism, or the setting up of some sort of 'global theology' which no believer could recognize. 'I would suggest, on the contrary', he wrote, 'acceptance of the logically non-compatible claims of different religions, rather than the attempt to relate them all systemically within an imagined "world theology" which would be recognized by the believers of no tradition.'[17]

A sixth issue concerns how Christianity ought to be classified. It would appear that, from a phenomenological point of view, it may be classified as a species in the genus 'Religion'. This is how it has often been studied at school and elsewhere, in the West. It is a largely human project with the usual human combination of impressive and repellent aspects. Often only the superficial aspects are studied: the fasts, the feasts, the buildings, the sacred writings, marriage customs, rites of passage and so on. Emil Brunner protested against this taxonomic approach over fifty years ago.[18] He also noted that, contrary to the view that different religions grow closer together as they climb, by different routes, up the mountain towards Ultimate Reality, in history we find that the higher the intellectual development of religion, the more intense the debates and the disagreements. What if there really is a God after all? What if this God has actually revealed himself? What if a real lion's roar obtrudes into the children's game? Herbert Marcuse spoke of the 'repressive tolerance' of Western consumer society: people can believe anything they want, provided they do not insist on its everywhere, always quality; provided that they do not bring these beliefs into the public square. Jürgen Moltmann has noted this repressive tolerance also: 'Tolerant in allowing everything as subjective possibility; repressive in respect to scepticism about any objective reality being adequately mediated by religious symbols.'[19]

5. The weakness of God

In the seventh place, we may note that these chapters of Isaiah were addressed to a devastated and demoralized people: their temple destroyed, their social life in disarray, their hopes deferred, and their prospects bleak. It is astonishing to reflect upon the soaring faith which saw in international events the hand of Yahweh, when to all

---

[17] Adrian Hastings, 'Pluralism: The Relationship of Theology to Religious Studies', in Ian Hamnett (ed.), *Religious Pluralism and Unbelief* (Routledge, 1990), p. 236.

[18] E. Brunner, *Revelation and Reason* (SCM, 1947).

[19] J. Moltmann, 'Is Pluralistic Theology Useful?' in Gavin D'Costa (ed.), *Christian Uniqueness Reconsidered: The Myth of a Pluralistic Theology of Religions* (Orbis, 1990), p. 152.

intents and purposes it must have seemed to many Jews that he was not able to save.

But it is also striking to reflect that the invitation of Isaiah 45:22 is just that: an invitation. It is not an order nor an imposition. As we know from his own inscription, Cyrus did not see himself as an anointed servant of Yahweh. The Cyrus cylinder glorifies his achievements, with polite bows in the direction of Marduk. In contrast, although these chapters set out their belief in Yahweh as the Lord of the whole earth, they also make clear the divine humility which makes room for human responsiveness. At that time, and since, the appeal for human beings to turn for salvation to the only true God has fallen on deaf and disobedient ears. Even in chapters 56 – 66 of Isaiah we see how privileged Israel is repeatedly disinclined to trust the One who has prophesied everything that has come to pass.

This vulnerability is reflected in the lives of many pioneer cross-cultural missionaries who have taken the good news of Christianity to those who have never heard it. It is perhaps hard for those who have never experienced it to imagine how weak such people feel when they first arrive. Where will I live? Who will befriend me? How will I learn the language, the customs, the culture? What will happen if I get sick? Some of these missionaries have been part of a Western missionary movement. For example, there was Cyril Vasilyevich Suchanov (1714–1814) who 'believing that missionary work depended more on quality of life than on the spoken word, reduced his personal possessions to what he could carry about in a travelling bag, and moved ceaselessly among the nomadic Tungus people of Dauria in Eastern Siberia and won their whole-hearted affection'.[20] He learned their language, built churches and schools, and 'met with such success that for many years thereafter the descendants of those won by him were called "Suchanov Tunguses"'.[21]

But by far the majority of 'missionaries' have been natives of their own country or continent. When Christianity first began to spread in Japan, it was the *irmao* (brothers), *dojuku* (apprentice clergy) and *kambo* (local lay elders) who mostly did the work; it was people like the Japanese brother Laurenco, a partly blind musician, a great translator and songwriter, debater and evangelist.[22] It was people

---

[20] S. C. Neill, *A History of Christian Missions* (Penguin, 1964), p. 217.

[21] K. S. Latourette, *A History of the Expansion of Christianity*, vol. 3 (Eyre & Spottiswoode, 1940), p. 369.

[22] 'This form of popular grass-roots indigenization, often unplanned by the missionaries, is often ignored by historians and missiologists who tend to concentrate on the written records of the educated elites who accepted or rejected Christianity' (A. Ross, *A Vision Betrayed* [Edinburgh University Press, 1994]), p. 27.

like Vedanayagam, the first great poet and hymnwriter of the Indian church, and the catechist Sattianathan, of whom Christian Friedrich Schwarz wrote, 'I have to admit that in his discussions with non-Christians he has put me to shame. He has laid before them the whole doctrine concerning Christ, and not only one part of it, and is so comprehensive and impressive that I have found myself not a little astonished and put to shame.'[23]

6. Elenctics and power encounter

In his last discourse with the disciples Jesus talked about the gift of the Holy Spirit, one of whose functions would be 'to convict the world of sin, and righteousness and judgement' (John 16:8). Fifty years ago J. H. Bavinck devoted the entire second part of his book *An Introduction to the Science of Missions* to the topic of elenctics: its nature, place, task and methods. What is elenctics? When Christ comes into contact with a culture, sooner or later there is a moment, a point of confrontation. What have you done with God? In what ways, even under the guise of religion, may you be seeking to escape from him as well as to find him? From what do you need to turn away in order to find the true and living God? It is notable that Bavinck emphasizes (as Roland Allen did before him; and Kenneth Cragg, with special eloquence after him) that the task of elenctics, of confrontation 'can actually be exercised only in living contact with the adherents of other religions. Each generalization, every systemization, carries within itself the danger that one will do injustice to the living person. In practice I am never concerned with Buddhism, but with a living person and *his* Buddhism ... '[24] Bavinck also speaks of 'the repeated awareness that the sharpest weapons [of elenctics] must in the first place be turned against ourselves'.[25] There is no escape for us either from the searching work of the Holy Spirit.

Sometimes the confrontation between Christ and the powers, or the Holy Spirit and a particular culture and people, comes about in a dramatic way. Boniface, in his missionary work in Germany in the eighth century 'won fame for himself and repute for the Christian cause by his courageous act in felling the sacred oak at Geismar in Hesse'.[26] The people expected him to die, but he didn't; he survived, and used the wood to build a chapel in honour of St Peter. David Burnett tells how an African preacher in Bugongo in Uganda in

[23] Neill, *Christianity in India*, p. 54.
[24] J. H. Bavinck, *An Introduction to the Science of Missions* (Presbyterian & Reformed, 1960), p. 240.
[25] Ibid., p. 271.
[26] Neill, *Christian Missions*, p. 75.

1973 had difficulty in preaching to the congregation, or reaching out to the children because of the sacred rock, Nyamavuta, which was within 100 feet of the church. He dug the rock up with his helper. When he did not die, many of the local people turned to Christ.[27] John Williams, the nineteenth-century London Missionary Society missionary to the South Pacific, was once preaching on Isaiah 44 to a number of Polynesians, when suddenly the chief sprang up and stamped his foot on the deck. 'What fools we have been!' he shouted. 'We have confused the *moah* for the *noah* (the sacred for the profane). To the day of my death I shall never again worship an idol with eyes that cannot see and hands that handle not.'[28]

It is important to note that the agents of such dramatic actions should usually be the members, and preferably the leaders, of a community that is turning towards Christ. Sometimes if a foreign missionary acts prematurely in such a manner, he or she may just drive old practices underground, to surface in another form, rather than seeing a true and deep turning. What is the importance of this issue? Isaiah insists that Yahweh is the incomparable, unique, universal God. The invitation to turn to him is based on the claim that is made by him. It would be a very appropriate act of humility by the scholars who discuss theories and theologies of religions to listen to those *who have actually turned*! It would be very odd if their discussions of who should or should not turn, of the whole concept of turning, converting, were not at all influenced by those who have actually responded to the invitation, and have found in doing so the liberation they sought.

7. Crucified love

Gavin D'Costa has criticized John Hick's pluralism as being insufficiently pluralist, because it appears that Hick really believes that *his* way is the only valid way. But 'the outcome of this flight from particularity can only be to nothing in particular'.[29] D'Costa insists that Christian mission cannot relinquish the conviction that God has disclosed himself, and that this news is good news for all people. And how is this conviction to be demonstrated? 'Crucified love, in service to the community, is central to mission.'[30]

[27] David Burnett, *God's Mission: Healing the Nations* (MARC Europe, 1986), p. 80.
[28] A. Tippett, *Verdict Theology in Missionary Theory* (William Carey Library, 1973), p. 4.
[29] Gavin D'Costa, 'The New Missionary: John Hick and Religious Plurality', *International Bulletin of Missionary Research* (April 1991), p. 68.
[30] Ibid., p. 69.

In 1988 a number of scholars and missiologists revisited Tambaram, Madras, on the fiftieth anniversary of the famous conference of the International Missionary Council held there in 1938. The report of the meeting[31] makes sobering reading. Stanley Samartha suggests that 'exclusive religious claims are a colonial hangover in the realm of knowledge', and that 'plurality is a guarantee against religious fascism'. W. C. Smith fulminates against those who cannot accept 'God's mission to us through all traditions'. In Smith's view these people, who reject dialogue, are blaspheming God. Diana Eck quotes W. M. Horton's experience in Japan with a Buddhist priest: 'It would be a blasphemy against the Holy Spirit ... for me to deny my Buddhist brother his place in the Body of Christ.' However, the late Bishop Lesslie Newbigin struck a different note in his thanksgiving sermon: 'the church can only be obedient to the will of the Good Shepherd if it goes out to all men regardless of creed, or caste, or colour, to proclaim the Kingdom of God, to call people of all faiths by word and deed into the life of the Beloved Community ... this compulsion does not grow old; it remains until the end of time.'[32]

Finally, it would be a mistake to leave Isaiah 45 with its global, cosmic reach, without focusing on the personal effect this chapter may have on individual lives. Two examples follow.

On 6 January 1850 a young lad in deep spiritual trouble stumbled into a Primitive Methodist chapel in Cambridgeshire in a snowstorm. Since the preacher did not arrive, a poor, thin-looking substitute was found, a shoemaker or tailor or suchlike. The lad wrote later, 'He was really stupid, as you would say. He was obliged to stick to his text for the simple reason that he had nothing else to say. His text was: "Turn to me and be saved all the ends of the earth." ' Finally, after about ten minutes of desperation, the preacher looked towards where the lad was sitting under the gallery. 'Young man,' he said, 'you look very miserable. And you always WILL be miserable if you do not obey my text. But if you obey now, this moment, you will be saved.' Then he shouted, as only a Primitive Methodist can shout, 'Young man, look to Jesus! Look, look, LOOK!' The young man was C. H. Spurgeon, who went on to become the most famous preacher in nineteenth-century England.

Recently a student at theological college went through a time of deep personal trial. It almost seemed as if God had hidden himself (Is. 45:15). For his ordination a friend printed a small card full of squiggly black lines showing almost complete darkness. But if you

---

[31] *International Review of Mission*, 78.307 (July 1988).
[32] Ibid., p. 331.

looked carefully you could see some streaks of light moving towards a door. The ordinand wrote later, 'This has come to mean for me that in the darkness of pain, bewilderment and uncertainty God is there with treasures which I never knew existed or had ever experienced before. Isaiah 45:3ff.'

Chapters 2 and 3 of this book have reviewed the story of creation and one outstanding Old Testament example of God's sovereignty in history. Taken together the stories speak of the Lord of time and space, Creator and sustainer of all that is, active from the beginning to the end of history, which of course includes our day. These two chapters are themselves embedded in chapters 1 and 4, which speak of Jesus Christ, who is the Lord of creation and of the new creation, and who has wonderfully come down to share our human life and story. He is the one in whom creation and history find their true meaning, because 'all things have been created through him and for him. He himself is before all things, and in him all things hold together' (Col. 1:16–17).

John 1:1–18
4. The Word made flesh

The Danish philosopher Søren Kierkegaard (1813–55) tells a simple story about a king who falls in love with a humble maiden. We must imagine that we have a very unusual king, one who wishes in no way to embarrass or offend the maiden. Should the king go to her cottage to announce his love, with magnificent garments and a large retinue, he would utterly overwhelm her. And besides, should the maiden manage to rise to the occasion and respond to his love, it would never be clear to the king whether it was he whom she loved or his pomp and majesty. One solution to his problem might be for the king to disguise himself as a beggar and go secretly to the girl. But, then, suppose that he did succeed in winning her love in this way, in that case she would not really love him: he is a king, but she would love a beggar. It is no good to reverse the procedure and instead of lowering the king, elevate the maiden. For this would suggest that as a humble maid she is not good enough to be loved, whereas it is precisely as a humble maid that the king loves her.

The only way of enabling a loving union is for the king to descend and identify with the maiden, and share her lot, her suffering and her poverty. He must take the initiative and become equal to her if they are to be able to love one another. And this can be no pretence. It is not enough to have a beggar's cloak which flutters loosely in the wind and betrays the royal garments underneath; it must be the true form of the king. 'For this is the unfathomable nature of love, that it desires equality with the beloved, not in jest merely, but in earnest and truth.'[1]

---

[1] Søren Kierkegaard, *Philosophical Fragments*, tr. David Swenson (Princeton University Press, 1962), p. 39.

1. Beginnings

Mark begins his Gospel with the words 'The beginning of the gospel about Jesus Christ' and proceeds to narrate the public ministry of Jesus of Nazareth. Matthew launches his story with Abraham, and Luke starts even further back with Adam. But John sees that even this is not enough to understand the reality of who Jesus is and what he did. Before Abraham was, indeed before time began, God was. The starting point of the good news can be traced back before the *beginning* of the entire universe. It was by God's Word that all things came to be. He spoke and all things were created, and by his Word they exist. There is no point in time before which the Word was not.

The Word (*logos* in the original Greek) is pregnant with meanings. It can refer to a person's inner thought, hence 'reason' or even 'knowledge', or to the outward expression of that thought, hence 'speech' or 'message' (as in 1 Cor. 1:18). The Stoics understood Logos to be the rational principle by which everything exists, and which is the essence of the rational human soul. It was for them the ultimate, invisible reality permeating the visible universe. The nearest equivalents in ancient Indian thought would have been the principle of *dharma*, order, or *prajñana*, the primeval intelligence, or *cit*, consciousness – and these are how many South Asian biblical translators often translate the term. Readers of John's Gospel, from whatever background they came, could not have failed to recognize that the author is dealing here with the bedrock of existence.

The Fourth Gospel is steeped in Old Testament allusions and imagery. Therefore, that must be the point of departure for unpacking all that the Logos connotes. There, 'the word (Heb. *dābār*) of Yahweh' is connected with Yahweh's powerful activity in creation (Gen. 1:3ff.; Ps. 33:6), revelation (Jer. 1:4; Is. 9:8; Ezek. 33:7; Amos 3:1, 8) and salvation (Ps. 107:20; Is. 55:1). Another way of saying that Yahweh spoke to the prophet Isaiah (Is. 7:3) is to say that 'the word of Yahweh came to Isaiah' (Is. 38:4; cf. Jer. 1:4; Ezek. 1:6). When some of his people faced illness that brought them to the brink of death, God 'sent out his word and healed them, / and delivered them from destruction' (Ps. 107:20). It was by 'the word of Yahweh' that the heavens were made (Ps. 33:6), and that same word effects deliverance and judgment (Is. 55:11; cf. Ps. 29:3ff.).

In short, God's 'Word' in the Old Testament is his powerful self-expression in creation, revelation and salvation, and the personification of that 'Word' makes it suitable for John to apply it as a title to God's ultimate self-disclosure, the person of his own Son.

But if the expression would prove richest for Jewish readers, it would also resonate in the minds of some readers with entirely pagan backgrounds. In their case, however, they would soon discover that whatever they had understood the term to mean in the past, the author whose work they were then reading was forcing them into fresh thought.[2]

The Word was *with* God, distinguishable from God and enjoying a personal relationship with God. Moreover, the Word *was* God. That is the translation demanded by the Greek structure, *theos ēn ho logos* (John 1:1). He was God's agent through whom *all things*, that is, the entire cosmos, came into being. Thus all human beings owe their life to him, whether they acknowledge him or not. Here is the identical thought that we encountered in the Christological hymn of Colossians (Col. 1:16; see chapter 1). It is repeated by the writer of Hebrews (Heb. 1:1–2); and the Apocalypse speaks of the Son as the 'Amen, the faithful and true witness, the *archē* (origin, beginning) of God's creation' (Rev. 3:14). John may be the most straightforward of the New Testament writers, but what he has to say about the pre-incarnate Christ is fully consistent with early Christian thought.

The Prologue is the conceptual centre of John's Gospel from which all other dimensions radiate. The rest of the narrative amplifies what is stated so succinctly in its opening verses. Don Carson notes that

> The relationship between God and the Word in the Prologue is identical with the relationship between the Father and the Son in the rest of the Gospel (cf. 5:26). Both 1:4 and 5:26 insist that the Word/Son shares in the self-existing life of God. Later on Jesus claims that he is both the light of the world (8:12; 9:5) and the life (11:25; 14:6). Both Wisdom and Torah are commonly associated with life and light in Jewish sources; John ties them in with Christ, the Word.[3]

There are three ways, at least, in which the Prologue to John's Gospel present a powerful missiological challenge to us that is also relevant and exhilarating.

2. The incarnation of the Word

And the Word became flesh and lived among us (v. 14). John's

---

[2] D. A. Carson, *The Gospel According to John* (Eerdmans/IVP, 1991), p. 116.
[3] Ibid., p. 118.

language must have shocked his readers of whatever background. The Word of God which is the ground of truth and life, understanding and power, has stepped into the world in a radically new and unexpected way. The Word has, literally, 'pitched his tent among us'. For Greek-speaking Jews and other readers of the Greek Old Testament, the verb *skēnoō* that John uses would have called to mind the *skēnē*, the tabernacle where God met Israel in the wilderness before the temple was built. The tabernacle was built at God's command: 'And have them make me a sanctuary, so that I may dwell among them' (Exod. 25:8). The consonants of the Greek word are also those of the Hebrew *šᵉkînâ*, which denotes the presence and glory of God. The 'tent of meeting' was where God dwelt with his people in a special way and where his glory was made visible (Exod. 40:34–38). The same glory had filled the temple of Solomon (1 Kgs. 8:10ff.). After that glory had departed from the temple (Ezek. 11:22ff.), Israel was promised that Yahweh would once again visit his people: 'Sing and rejoice, O daugher Zion! For lo, I will come and dwell and in your midst, says Yahweh' (Zech. 2:10). John narrates the coming of Jesus of Nazareth as no less than the revelation of the glory of the *father's only son* (v. 14b), the unveiling of the One whom no eye has seen (v. 18).

Outside the mystical Sufi schools, Islamic theology so stresses the transcendence of God that it excludes the possibility of God ever revealing himself to humankind. We can never know God, for the most that can be said is that believers know God's will, which has been revealed to them in the Qur'an and also through the messengers God sent humankind before Muhammad. Thus, Isma'il al-Faruqi, for example, states emphatically, 'God does *not* reveal Himself. He does not reveal Himself to anyone in any way. God reveals only His will ... and we have it in perfection in the Qur'an. But Islam does not equate the Qur'an with the nature or essence of God. It is the Word of God, the Commandment of God, the Will of God. But God does not reveal Himself to anyone.'[4]

Thus, the gospel goes beyond Islam and that other great prophetic faith, Judaism: not only does God *speak* to humankind, but the divine speech has *become* a human person. The statement 'This is what God is like' has been translated into the specific words and actions of an actual human being who spoke a particular language, lived in a particular place at a particular time, and shared a particular ethnic identity. This particular human being now makes known to us the character and purposes of God in a way that no-one else does.

---

[4] Isma'il al-Faruqi, *Christian Mission and Islamic Da'wah: Proceedings of the Chambésy Consultation* (Islamic Foundation, 1982), p. 47.

It is this conviction about Jesus Christ that has impelled men and women over the centuries to cross geographical and linguistic boundaries, and to offer their lives in the self-giving service of their fellow men and women. It was this conviction that enabled them to recognize the human worth, as well as desperate need, of tribes and cultures long despised by their non-Christian compatriots. It motivated and empowered them to serve the 'dregs' of humanity: the destitute, the disabled and the dispossessed. And this is the continuing story of Christian witness and mission in many parts of the world. Far from the message of incarnation breeding any notion of religious or cultural superiority, it humbles human pride (for it is all God's doing, not ours) and ennobles our common humanity (for God has taken into himself our human condition).

In saying this we are not, of course, denying that the Christian message has often been linked to domination, arrogance and racism. Church history right up to the present day gives ample examples of this ugly and shameful story. But these are so obviously *betrayals* of the message; not its logical entailment. In fact those darkest periods of church history have been the periods when the gospel was least understood within the church itself.

a. Incarnation and avatara

The pinnacle of personal theism within Indian religion is found in the eleventh chapter of the *Bhagavad Gita*. The *Gita* itself was originally part of the great epic *Mahabharata*, which tells of the struggle between two families, the Pandavas and the Kauravas, representing the forces of *dharma* (righteousness, order) and *adharma* (unrighteousness, lawlessness) respectively. Krishna, the divine charioteer, is on the side of *dharma*, and he acts as the guardian and friend of the Pandava hero Arjuna. Just before the crucial battle with the Kauravas, Arjuna asks Krishna to reveal himself in his supreme form. Krishna obliges by giving Arjuna a 'celestial eye' with which to behold his transfigured form. As Krishna throws off his human appearance, Arjuna falls to the ground in terror, unable to bear the aweful splendour of the deity.

Krishna is the best known and most important of the *avatars* of Vishnu. The term *avatar* means a 'descent', a 'coming down', from the prefix *ava*, 'down', and the verb *tr*, 'to come over'. 'The *avatar* is an appearance of any deity on earth, or descent from heaven, but it is especially applied to the descents or appearances of Vishnu'.[5] The clearest statement of the doctrine is found in the Gita: 'For

[5] G. Parrinder, *Avatars and Incarnations* (Faber & Faber, 1970), p. 19.

whenever the law of righteousness withers away and lawlessness arises, then do I generate Myself (on earth). For the protection of the good, for the destruction of evildoers, for the setting up of the law of righteousness I come into being age after age'.[6] The Vaishnava tradition to which the Gita belongs recognized ten classical *avatars* of Vishnu, including various animal forms. The human manifestations, such as Krishna and Rama, are themselves the objects of popular devotional cults in India, and it has been an easy matter for the Hindu to regard the Buddha, Jesus, and even modern gurus such as Sai Baba as *avatars* of Vishnu in different generations.

It is often suggested, especially in Hindu–Christian encounter, that the concept of *avatara* is equivalent to the Christian doctrine of incarnation; just as in the early period of the twentieth century it was popular among New Testament students influenced by the 'history of religions' school to suggest that the incarnation was derived from the 'mystery religions' of the ancient Mediterranean world, with their myths of dying and rising gods (e.g. Adonis, Osiris) modelled on the familiar cycles of nature. But the similarities are only superficial.

First, the concept must be interpreted within the whole Vedanta framework, for, as Smart and Konstantine observe, 'The fact that in the Hindu tradition there is no clear dividing line between the human and the divine, as witness not just the multiplicity of *avatars*, e.g. Krishna and Rama; but also the tendency to treat gurus and other holy people as divine means that avatarhood is not an intense and unique divine commitment.'[7] It is also of a piece with the doctrine of *karma* and rebirth where different bodies (human and non-human) provide a temporary vehicle for the same immortal self.

Secondly, the historicity of the *avatars* is not crucial to belief in them. Indeed, there is a tendency both in popular devotion and in 'neo-Vedanta' (sometimes called 'modern Hinduism') to look on the *avatars* in a somewhat docetic manner. Neo-Vedanta, with its ascending levels of reality and truth, sees the *avatars* as mere manifestations of the divine, suitable for those not yet at the highest stages of spiritual growth. Hindu philosophers treat them as mythical illustrations of 'timeless truths'. In his commentary on the *Bhagavad Gita*, Professor Radhakrishnan discounts the historicity of Krishna and makes him a symbol of the higher self in every human being. Thus:

[6] *Bhagavad Gita*, 4:7–8, tr. R. C. Zaehner (OUP, 1973).
[7] N. Smart and S. Konstantine, *Christian Systematic Theology in a World Context* (Marshall Pickering, 1991), pp. 255–256.

It is of little moment so far as the teaching is concerned, whether the author is a figure of history or the very god descended into man, for the realities of the spirit are the same now as they were thousands of years ago and the differences of race and nationality do not affect them. The essential thing is truth or significance and the historical fact is nothing more than the image of it.[8]

This leads us into the third and most important difference between the concept of *avatara* and the biblical doctrine of incarnation. In the incarnation he who is the source and sustainer of our humanity has entered *once and for all* into our historical experience to take that humanity *for ever* into his own eternal life. The resurrection of Jesus was not a casting off of the human and the resumption of the divine nature. The human is the manifestation and vehicle of the divine, both in the earthly life of Jesus and in his glorified humanity. The incarnation, atoning death and resurrection of Jesus Christ *decisively changed* the relationship between God and humankind. It is not only that the mystery of the infinite God, discernible in the varieties of human experience in all ages and across cultures, has now come to be known personally and concretely in terms of a finite human life; but the humanity of the crucified and risen Christ is the locus of our union and fellowship with God for ever. The risen Christ remains, in heaven, the human face of God. Although we do not understand now the manner in which the risen Christ incorporates the whole redeemed humanity, it is through his crucified and exalted body that we continue to be embraced by the love of God.

Thus the difference between incarnation and *avatara* is profound. It is not as if Hindus in their magnanimity affirm many incarnations, while Christians, out of narrow-minded bigotry, limit it to one. The difference is logical and ontological. To translate *avatara* as 'incarnation' is to invite confusion. It is more accurately a 'theophany', the visual appearance of a deity to human beings, of which, of course, there are many examples in the Old Testament (e.g. Gen. 17; 18; 32:24, 28; Exod. 3:2–6; 19:18–19; 24:15–18; Judg. 13; 2 Sam. 22:8–16; Is. 6:1–4; Ezek. 1).

It is also true that a number of self-sacrificing men and women can manifest in their lives more divine qualities than most, but that doesn't make them God incarnate. In Austin Farrer's well-known words, 'A good man helped by grace may do human things divinely;

---

[8] S. Radhakrishnan, *The Bhagavadgita: Introductory Essay* (Allen & Unwin, 1949), p. 37.

Christ did divine things humanly.'[9] If God has expressed not only his qualities but *himself* in a particular individual and bound us in love to himself in a new, personal and eternal relationship, then that can only be once for all.

b. Incarnation and 'inculturation'

The missionary can only begin by using words which have some meaning for his hearers. He has to begin by assuming a common framework of language, of experience, of inherited tradition, of axioms and assumptions embodied in the forms of speech. He can only introduce what is new by provisionally accepting what is already there in the minds of his hearers.

But what if the new thing which he wants to introduce is so radically new that it calls in question all previous axioms and assumptions, all inherited tradition and all human experience, so that even language itself cannot serve to communicate it? What if the new thing is in fact the primal truth by which all else has to be confronted and questioned? How do you explain that which must in the end be accepted as the beginning of all explanation? That is the problem of the evangelist.[10]

The Kenyan theologian John Mbiti has written that 'Since his Incarnation, Christian theology ought properly to be Christology, for theology falls or stands on how it understands, translates and interprets Jesus Christ at a given time, place and human situation.'[11]

Given the uniqueness of the incarnation, it is remarkable that the church did not sacralize the place of its origins. Bethlehem, Nazareth and even Jerusalem swiftly recede from view, and the new Christian communities that sprang up recognized no fixed geographical centre. What is even more remarkable, especially in comparison with the great world religions of Semitic and Asian origin, is that the original language Jesus used in his preaching was quickly abandoned in favour of country (*koinē*) Greek and 'vulgar' Latin as the uniting media of communication. The entire New Testament was written in a language other than the one in which Jesus preached.

[9] A. Farrer, *Saving Belief* (Hodder & Stoughton, 1964), p. 75. Note also his wonderful description of the incarnation: 'What then did God do for his people's redemption? ... He set divine life in human neighbourhood. Men discovered it in struggling with it and were captured by it in crucifying it,' p. 99.

[10] Lesslie Newbigin, *The Light Has Come: An Exposition of the Fourth Gospel* (Eerdmans, 1982), p. 2.

[11] John Mbiti, *New Testament Eschatology in an African Background*; quoted in John Parratt, *Reinventing Christianity: African Theology Today* (Eerdmans/Africa World, 1995), p. 78.

That the eternal Word of God belonged to the commonplace, everyday speech of ordinary men and women was a view that was, and remains, revolutionary. It resisted the tendency in some parts of the early church to cast the gospel into an élitist, Gnostic-type discourse. Unlike the widespread 'mystery religions' (and the dominant ethos of traditional Vedic, Tantric and Buddhist religious thought and practice), no attempt was made to develop a professional cultic language or make a virtue out of élitist secrecy. The missionary thrust of the early Christians was a force for cultural awakening.

This openness of the gospel message, and its endless translatability into languages and cultures outside Palestinian Jewish soil, derives from the heart of its content. For, as Professor Andrew Walls reminds us, the central event on which the Christian movement rests is an astonishing act of divine translation: divinity translated into humanity.[12] This fundamental act of divine translation is now re-enacted in countless acts of retranslation into the languages, thought-forms and relational patterns of the world that constitute the history of Christian mission.

In fact, Walls points out that translation is an excellent metaphor and working model of Christian mission. We always receive new ideas in terms of the ideas with which we are familiar. In translation, the novel terms of the source language have to be expressed in the vocabulary of the receptor language, whose terms come pre-loaded within an alien context of meanings and connotations. In the process of translation, the receptor language is expanded and put to new uses, with old terms acquiring deeper meanings, some loadings dropping out altogether and some new terms making their way in. There is always the risk of distortion and miscommunication. We can never arrive at a final translation, but endlessly revise our translations in the light of changed meanings and expanded repertoires.

We see this translation process beginning within the pages of the New Testament. The first contact the gospel makes with the Hellenistic-Roman world is through a group of unknown Jewish Christians who made their way to the city of Antioch, the capital of the Roman province of Asia. This was not the result of some grand missionary strategy on the part of the Jerusalem church, but rather the result of persecution. These unnamed refugees, we are told by Luke, began to speak to their Greek pagan neighbours about 'Jesus, the Lord' (Acts 11:20). The term is *Kyrios*, not *Christos*, Messiah. In the Septuagint, the Greek translation of the Hebrew Bible, *Kyrios* is the term used to translate the Hebrew Tetragrammaton *Yahweh*,

---

[12] Andrew F. Walls, *The Missionary Movement in Christian History: Studies in the Transmission of Faith* (Orbis/T. & T. Clark, 1996), ch. 3. What follows is greatly indebted to Walls.

the personal covenant name of the God of Israel. But to the Greeks of Antioch, *Kyrios* would immediately have reminded them of the many cult divinities that were honoured in various parts of the empire: *Kyrios* Serapis, *Kyrios* Osiris, *Kyrios* Isis and so on. The biblical connotations would have been lost on them. In speaking of Jesus as *Kyrios*, then, these Christian evangelists were taking the risk of presenting Jesus as merely one cultic saviour figure among legions of others in the pluralist world of the Mediterranean.

The reason this did not happen, Walls points out, is undoubtedly because the new converts were brought into a community where the Greek version of the Hebrew Bible was constantly read, and so the biblical associations of *Kyrios* gradually permeated their minds. But as the word of Christ and the word about Christ now had a foothold in Hellenistic culture, it brought about a rich dialogue and confrontation with that culture. It marked a turning point in Christian history, the beginning of the conversion of the Greek-speaking world. The Graeco-Roman world, with its complex array of customs, ideas and belief-systems, was now being transformed from within as its inhabitants found a strange new message being delivered in a language recognizably their own. In a conversion process that lasted a few centuries, the gospel addressed the principal concerns, the peculiar anxieties and compulsions, and the shared traditions of the Hellenistic world, turning them all towards the Jewish Christ. And, in so doing, it also raised questions and problems for Christians living in this environment, which the Jewish Christians, including the apostles themselves, had never imagined.

Some of these questions surface in the Pauline letters. Indeed, it could be argued that most of Paul's letters are responses to questions arising from this new situation of Gentile Christians. In accepting Christ through faith they have been incorporated into the history of Israel without having become Jews. This was an extraordinary situation. To the Jewish mind it was unthinkable that one could become part of the covenant people of God without the sign of the covenant, circumcision. And it was unimaginable for obedience to God to lie outside knowledge and submission to the Torah. Paul vigorously combats any attempt on the part of Jewish Christians to impose their cultural patterns on the new Gentile converts. And it is here that we see the crucial difference between Christian conversion and religious proselytism.

c. Incarnation and conversion

Christian conversion, then, is not the substitution of something new for the old, any more than the incarnation was a substitution of the divine for the human. Nor is it the addition of something new to what was before, any more than the incarnation was the addition of something new to a deficient humanity.

In conversion, the gospel permeates the intellect, emotions and attitudes of an individual in such a way that everything that makes him what he is – his past, his network of relationships, his work, his thought-patterns and moral processes – are given a new direction; namely, towards Christ. Conversion is about a radical reorientation of life. It is a risky enterprise, especially in first-generation Christian communities where there is no precedent for what form discipleship to Christ should take in that particular context and culture. Conversion has a beginning, but no end. It's a lifelong process of discovery and transformation.

Such conversion is not limited to individuals. The transformation of the individual carries with it an injection of the gospel into that world of shared history and tradition, thought-forms and practices that make up our national identities.

> The commanding heights of a nation's life have to be opened to the influence of Christ; for Christ has redeemed human life in its entirety. Conversion to Christ does not isolate the convert from his or her own community; it begins the conversion of that community. Conversion to Christ does not produce a bland universal citizenship: it produces distinctive discipleships, as diverse and variegated as human life itself.[13]

3. The rejection of the incarnate Word

If the assertion that *the Word became flesh* was shockingly subversive in the ancient world of Graeco-Roman philosophy, no less shocking would have been John's statement about the world's response to that incarnate Word. He has already hinted at it in verse 5: *The light shines in the darkness, and the darkness did not overcome it.*[14] Here is an anticipation of the duality of light and darkness that dominates much of the Fourth Gospel.

In the context of modern interfaith dialogue, many readers take verses 5 and 9 to refer to the inner illumination that the indwelling

---

[13] Ibid., p. 51.

[14] The verb *katalambanō* means 'to seize', and hence, derivatively, 'to overcome'; or, alternatively, 'to seize with the mind', and therefore 'to understand' (as in NIV). John may be playing with the two meanings, but 'to overcome' is clearly the meaning in the only other place where the verb is used with the light/darkness metaphor: John 12:35. The ambiguity can be preserved by translating it 'the darkness did not *master* the light'.

Logos has brought to all people of all cultures and at all times. This inner illumination is then frequently identified with the dominant religious expressions of those cultures that accord with the reader's own. Now while it is clear from what John has said about the Word's creative role in all human (and non-human) lives, that whatever truth, beauty and goodness we perceive in the world and in human affairs has its source in that Word, we suggest that this is not the thrust of the Prologue, nor indeed the rest of John's Gospel. 'Light' in the latter is not primarily the general revelation of God available to all human beings through conscience and creation, nor even the theophanies of the Word in the Old Testament (and, perhaps, in other cultures and times), but rather, the specific revelation that has come into the world in the Messiah Jesus and that has at its goal the redemption of that world.[15]

In the context of John's Gospel the 'darkness' is not only absence of light, but positive evil (3:19; 8:12; 12:35, 46). And the illumination that the coming of the *true light* (v. 9) brings is, primarily, the objective exposure of the wayward human heart. What is unveiled in the self-disclosure of the Word includes the truth that human beings prefer the darkness to the light (3:20). Apart from the light, men stumble, because they do not have the light in themselves (11:9–10) and do not know where they are going (12:35). When the light does put in an appearance they hate it, because they do not want their deeds to be shown up for what they are. Yet the purpose of this coming is not to bring final condemnation, but to lead men and women out of that darkness and so to bring them salvation (12:46, 47).

He was in the world, and the world came into being through him; yet the world did not know him (v. 10). The world – here not the created universe (the *all things* of v. 3) but the whole human race that ought to have recognized the light by which alone it lives – did not acknowledge him. And the depths of the darkness are disclosed when we remember that although all the world belongs to him who is its Creator, yet one people had been chosen from among all the peoples to be his special possession (e.g. Exod. 19:5). The one true light came *to what was his own, and his own people did not accept him* (v. 11). Here, even the purest and loftiest form of 'religion' is found to belong to the realm of darkness. The first twelve chapters of John's Gospel are all about the rejection of the incarnate Word by

---

[15] For a clear and succinct account of how inner illumination in general revelation relates to the finality of Christ, and how the questions relating to the status of those who have never had an opportunity to hear the gospel should be handled, see Peter Cotterell's 'Ten Theses' in his *Mission and Meaninglessness: The Good News in a World of Suffering and Disorder* (SPCK, 1990), ch. 6.

the custodians of biblical religion. Not those who are blind but those who confidently say 'We see' are found to be in the realm of darkness (9:41).

The cross of Christ thus reveals the true tragedy of the human condition. It subverts the stories that have dominated the West for the past two hundred years – stories of human self-mastery, self-autonomy, self-realization and human perfectibility. These have also been exported to the rest of the world in the name of capitalism or Marxism or unlimited faith in education or science and technology to solve all our problems and bring about a universal peace. What gets in the way of such dreams? It is the awkward and bitter fact of human sinfulness. Sin is our enslavement to self, a radical bent to our human nature.

It is at the foot of the cross that we are given a different vision of ourselves. For God not only affirms our created humanity but exposes and judges our human sin. If the message of the gospel is true, it calls into question the common assumption that it is through the 'religions of the world' that God is known and that it is, therefore, 'religious' people (or at least 'civilized' societies) to whom we must turn in our quest for God.

The late Lesslie Newbigin starkly sums up the challenge:

The same revelation in Jesus Christ, with its burning centre in the agony and death of Calvary, compels me to acknowledge that this world which God made and loves is in a state of alienation, rejection and rebellion against him. Calvary is the central unveiling of the infinite love of God and at the same time the unmasking of the dark horror of sin. Here not the dregs of humanity, not the scoundrels whom all good people condemn, but the revered leaders in church, state, and culture, combine in one murderous intent to destroy the holy one by whose mercy they exist and were created.[16]

The message of the cross is scandalous, for it tells us that it is not the 'good Christian' or the 'sincere Buddhist' or the 'devout Muslim' or the 'men and women of good will' who are recipients of the vision of God. But, rather, that it is the bad Christian, the bad Hindu, the bad Buddhist – those who know themselves to be moral failures – who may be closer to the kingdom of God. This can be so, simply because salvation is through grace, mediated through Christ, received in faith. There is probably no statement more subversive

[16] Lesslie Newbigin, *The Gospel in a Pluralist Society* (SPCK/Eerdmans, 1989), p. 175.

81

of the 'world of religions' than Paul's description in Romans 4:4 of the Father of the Lord Jesus Christ as 'the God who justifies the ungodly'.[17]

The longing for forgiveness and atonement surfaces in the writings of some of the most sensitive non-Christian poets of every age. Thus the great bhakti poet Tukaram of Maharashtra (c. 1568–1650):

> I am a mass of sin;
> Thou art all purity;
> Yet Thou must take me as I am
> And bear my load for me.[18]

It does not surprise us to learn that the Marathi poet Narayan Viman Tilak (1862–1919) said that he had journeyed by the bridge of Tukaram to the feet of Christ. Many men and women can testify how Christ spoke to them out of their own religious traditions, initiating a break with idolatry and a restless seeking after the living God, before they came to explicit faith in him.

The second-century Christian apologists in the Roman West are often appealed to in defence of the idea that Christ as the *Logos Spermatikos* (the indwelling 'seminal reason', in the common philosophical language of the day) lies like a grain of seed behind the religious systems of pre-Christian peoples, sprouting forth in their sacred scriptures, rituals and acts of piety. Justin Martyr (c. 100 – c. 165), the best-known of the second-century Christian apologists, could write, 'Indeed, all writers, by means of the engrafted seed of the *Logos* which was implanted in them, had a dim glimpse of the truth.' But, far from this being a disincentive to share the gospel with wise pagans, Justin immediately goes on to say, 'For the seed or something and its imitation, given in proportion to one's capacity, is one thing; but the thing itself, which is shared and imitated according to his grace, is quite another.'[19]

While speaking enthusiastically of Christ as the Logos imparting wisdom to pagan philosophers such as Socrates and Heraclides, the early apologists retained the gospel understanding of sin and

---

[17] See also John 9:40 – those who are blind now are given sight, while those who claim to see are blind.

[18] Quoted in A. J. Appasamy, *The Gospel and India's Heritage* (Christian Literature Society, 1942), p. 125.

[19] Justin Martyr, *Apology* 2.13; quoted in Gerald Bray, 'Explaining Christianity to Pagans: The Second-Century Apologists', in Kevin J. Vanhoozer (ed.), *The Trinity in a Pluralistic Age: Theological Essays on Culture and Religion* (Eerdmans, 1997), p. 20.

spiritual slavery. Just as Paul suggested in his Areopagus speech at Athens (Acts 17:22–23) that all the insights of these philosophers amounted to, at best, an indictment on human idolatry, but that they could not bring us knowledge of the Creator God and the good news of the gospel, so the second-century apologists honoured those philosophers who had been persecuted because of their scorn for the pagan theological systems. These men were a preparation by the Logos for his fullest manifestation, not in philosophy or religion, but in the words and works of Jesus:

> For when it was all said and done, the philosophers lacked the spiritual perception needed to distinguish right from wrong, and so were corrupted even in their better moments. This was a far cry from accepting that paganism had something positive to offer, or that it was possible to become a Christian without renouncing one's former life. Christ came into the world to judge paganism, even among its noblest forms. Whatever differences of approach there were among the Apologists, their basic message was the same – only by repentance and rebirth could a human see the kingdom of God.[20]

4. Witness to the incarnate Word

The rejection of the Word-made-flesh is not, however, John's final word. He interjects another of those wonderful biblical 'Buts' – *But to all who received him, who believed in his name, he gave power to become children of God* (v. 12). As in Old Testament times, there remains a believing remnant. This is nothing less than a miracle, for they are born not of human descent or human decision, but *of God* (v. 13). Here in a world darkened because men and women turn away from the true light, the fresh creative act of incarnation has resulted in the birth of 'a company of men and women whose life is a kind of extension of his, a new life which is no achievement of human desire or human power, but a sheer gift of God'.[21]

Such a company of men and women bear witness to what they have seen and experienced in Christ. *We have seen his glory, the glory as of the father's only son, full of grace and truth* (v. 14). *From his fullness we have all received, grace upon grace* (v. 16). The God whom sinful human beings cannot see without being consumed has now been disclosed: *God the only Son, who is close to the Father's heart ... has made him known* (v. 18).

[20] Bray, 'Explaining Christianity', p. 25.
[21] Newbigin, *Light*, p. 8.

There is a treasure-house of theological wealth that needs to be unpacked, but to do so would be beyond our capability, let alone the scope of the present chapter. The numerous commentaries on John's Gospel, however, do this task for us. For example, Don Carson points out that the last three words of verse 16, *charin anti charitos*, frequently rendered *grace upon grace* (as in the NRSV quote above), is better translated 'grace *instead of* grace' or 'grace *replacing* grace' in keeping with the commonest use of the preposition *anti* in the Greek Old Testament. The covenant of Moses based on obedience to the Torah was given by grace, and anticipated the incarnate Word, Jesus Christ. Now that he has come, that same prophetic law-covenant is necessarily superseded by that towards which it pointed.[22]

John's Gospel resounds to the theme of witness and testimony. The language is that of a courtroom. It is required of a witness that he not only speak the truth but has a character such that his testimony can carry credibility before the court. The first to bear witness to the incarnate Word is John the Baptist (1:6–8, 15; 10:40–42); then there is the witness of the Samaritan woman (4:39); the witness of the works of Jesus (5:36; 10:25); of the Father himself (5:32, 37; 8:18), of the Old Testament (5:39–40), of the crowd (12:17) and of the Holy Spirit and the apostles (15:26–27). All these direct the world to Jesus, who himself bears witness to the truth (18:37), in conjunction with the Father (8:13–18).

Closely linked with the theme of witness is the notion of 'sending' and 'being sent'. John the Baptist is sent by God to testify about Jesus (1:6–8; 3:28); Jesus himself is sent by the Father to testify about the Father and to do his work (4:34; 17:4 etc.); The Holy Spirit ('the Paraclete') is sent by both Father and Son to teach the apostles what Jesus has taught (14:26), to testify on behalf of Jesus (15:26), to convict the world of sin and righteousness and judgment (16:7–11), and to guide the church into all the truth and so glorify Jesus (16:13–15); and finally, the disciples are sent by Jesus into the world as the Father has sent the Son (17:18; 20:21).The Father alone is not sent. He is the origin, the ground and the model of all the 'sendings' of the Fourth Gospel.

All these witness-bearing missions are accomplished in the arena of the 'world'. The 'world' for John frequently carries negative overtones. The world, or frequently 'this world' (e.g. 8:23; 9:39; 11:9; 18:36), is not the universe, but the present age: the society of human beings and human affairs in rebellion against the Creator

---

[22] Carson, *John*, pp. 132–133. Thus the two halves of v. 17 stand in a relation of prophecy/fulfilment, not one of antithesis.

(e.g. 1:10; 7:7; 14:17, 22, 27, 30; 15:18-19; 16:8, 20, 33; 17:6, 9, 14). All these missions involve a personal relationship between the sender and the sent. They have the salvation of the world as their goal. All revolve around Jesus: John the Baptist announces his coming, the Holy Spirit gathers men and women from everywhere into his presence and leads them deeper into the truth that is ultimately bound up with him (14:6), and his disciples proclaim his word in the world.

If the life, death and resurrection of the Word-made-flesh is the content of the church's witness, then the *content* must also determine the *form* that witness takes. We do not stand apart from the suffering and sin of the world, speaking an alien, detached message from a position of superiority or self-indulgent ease, any more than the Word of God chose to present himself in the style of some slick TV guru whose disembodied words are conveyed impersonally to all parts of the globe by satellite technology. The gospel has to be *seen* in the church as well as heard, *lived* before it can be proclaimed. This is a theme to which we shall return in chapter 11.

Incarnational witness is

a way of describing Christian vocation in terms of Jesus Christ as the messenger, the message, and the model for all who follow after him. To speak of the incarnation missionally is to link who Jesus was, what Jesus did, and how he did it, in one great event that defines all that it means to be Christian. We might put it in terms of the great creedal traditions of the church. An incarnational interpretation of Christian witness is an attempt to allow the Second Article, the doctrine of Christ, to define and shape the theology of the Third Article, the Holy Spirit and the church.[23]

5. Conclusion

All the dominant schools of Hindu, Buddhist and New Age philosophies offer us liberation – liberation understood as release from the shackles of our humanness. The way to ultimate trans-cendence lies in breaking free from our individuality, our physical embodiment, and from our entanglements in this meaningless world of historical existence, the ordinary, everyday world of work and home. Our humanness is what gets in the way of transcendence or of union with the divine.

[23] Darrell L. Guder, *The Incarnation and the Church's Witness* (Trinity Press International, 1999), p. 9.

The incarnation speaks of a God who *is* entangled with our world, who immerses himself in our tragic history, who embraces our humanity with all its vulnerability, pain and confusion, including our evil and our death. God is neither absent from nor irrelevant in our age, because he knows for himself the experience of unjust suffering and death. Here is a God who comes to us not as master but as a servant, who stoops to wash the feet of his disciples and to suffer brutalization and dehumanization at the hands of his creatures. In identifying with us in our humanity he draws the human into his own divine life. So what this means is that the closer we get to God, the *more*, not less, human we become. This is a unique vision.

We have observed how translation (which takes people's whole contexts seriously, but without idolizing them) provides an apt metaphor for our missionary calling. We shall see in subsequent chapters how the church is called to walk in the way of the cross, renouncing the use of power for its own security and protection, and instead embracing the pain and hopelessness of others, exposing every form of idolatry, falsehood and injustice and confronting the 'powers' of this age, whether religious or secular, with the crucified form of the Lamb of God who takes away the sin of the world (1:29).

The Latin American missiologist Orlando Costas summed up this trinitarian mission thus:

The gospel proceeds from the communal, missionary and uniting God. The gospel is the story of the Father sending Jesus Christ the Son to lay down his life for a godless, broken and death-prone world in order to redeem it, regenerate it and restore it to communion with God. Hidden in this wonderful story is the reconciling activity of the Holy Spirit uniting the world with Father and Son in the all-embracing love of their eternal communion. God is glorified by the telling of and obedient response to the gospel story.[24]

---

[24] Orlando Costas, *Liberating News* (Eerdmans, 1989), p. 77.

Part 2
The international purposes of God

Genesis 12:1–4
5. Chosen to bless

1. Models of the church

There have been many attempts to identify a key organizing concept of the Old Testament, under the umbrella of which the huge diversity of writings in the Old Testament may be arranged. It is possible that the idea of the 'story of the people of God' *might* be a suitable overall title for the grand narrative of the Old Testament (and indeed of the New Testament as well). At least one might argue that this is the underbedding literary genre of the Old Testament, into which all the other types of Old Testament literature (psalm, wisdom literature, prophecy, apocalyptic) are planted.

One helpful way of giving Christians an overview of the story of the whole Bible is to ask them about their model of the church. A very helpful model, first proposed in these precise terms by George Lings of the Church Army, is that of a 'community mandated to reproduce'.[1] One can then give a panoramic review of the biblical story of the people of God, beginning with God's choice of Abram to be an instrument through whose descendants the whole world would be blessed, right through to the fulfilment of this vision in Revelation 7. Here the full number of God's chosen people is gathered in, and around the throne of God is an enormous crowd of people, which cannot be counted, from every tribe and nation and people and tongue – the New Testament's non-technical way of

[1] Presentation on church planting and ecclesiology, 'Mandated to Reproduce', at Anglican National Church Planting conference, Holy Trinity Brompton, 17 May 1993. See also G. Lings, 'Anglican Church Plants, Church Structures, Church Doctrine, their Relationships', a sabbatical report sponsored by the Diocese of Canterbury, the Ecclesiastical Insurance Group and the Parish of St George, Deal, revised version July 1993, privately printed, pp. 110–123.

saying 'anthropologically universal'; that is, people from every conceivable category.

2. Chosen to bless

It is with this panorama in mind that we thought it appropriate to devote one chapter of this book to a consideration of God's promises to Abraham, beginning with Genesis 12:1–4. This is such an important passage that I offer here my own translation:

> [1]*Now the* LORD *had said to Abram,*
> '*Go out*
>   *from your country*
>   *and from your family*
>   *and from your father's household,*
>   *to the land which I will show you,*
>   [2]*so that I may make you a great nation*
>   *and so that I may make your name great,*
> *and be a blessing*
>   [3]*so that I may bless those who bless you*
>   *(and the one who despises you I will curse)*[2]
>   *and all the families of the earth will be blessed in you.*'[3]
> [4]*So Abram went ... and Lot went ...*

The repetitive structure of this passage indicates clearly where the author or editor intended that the emphasis should lie. The passage is framed by the command to go out, and by the indication in verse 4 that this is what Abram and Lot did in obedience. The three-times repeated *from* indicates with increasing intimacy the separations that obedience would involve for Abram: from his country, from his clan or kindred, and from his father's house, his immediate family. The goal of his going is a land he will be shown (its location is not divulged in advance).

God's purpose in his going is indicated by the three-times repeated *so that* climaxing in the last clause: God intends to make this childless old man a great nation, he intends to make Abram's

---

[2] Careful study of the Hebrew text indicates that 'the word about curse is clearly not set here as part of the divine intention'. The (single) slanderer is an exception. See P. D. Miller, 'Syntax and Theology in Genesis 12:3a', *Vetus Testamentum* 34.4 (1984), pp. 472–475.

[3] There has been much discussion as to whether this verb should be translated as passive (in my text) or as reflexive 'shall bless themselves'. The earliest translations of this passage into Greek, Aramaic and Latin, as well as Acts 3:25 and Gal. 3:8 suggest that a passive sense is more appropriate. See B. K. Waltke and M. O'Connor, *An Introduction to Biblical Hebrew Syntax* (Eisenbrauns, 1990), p. 395.

name great (changing it in the process), and he intends to bless those who bless Abram – in fact, he intends that all the families of the earth will be blessed in Abram. There is a sentence of judgment on the person who despises him, but grammar and syntax indicate that this is an exception.

> The God of biblical faith ... is clearly bent towards blessing ... that is the good report which the bible transmits to each generation.[4]

> The promise that Abraham will become a great nation, implying both numerous seed and land, must be understood as being subservient to God's principal desire to bless all the families of the earth.[5]

> von Rad and Clines' understanding of the promises as tripartite, descendants, land and blessing of Israel, fails to pay sufficient attention to the climax of the promise that 'in you all the families of the earth shall find blessing'.[6]

The five-times repeated words of blessing overwhelm the command Abram receives. They remind us of the creation story (1:22, 28; and 5:2); of the blessing of the seventh day (2:3); and of the new beginning God made with Noah and his sons (9:1). As God begins a new chapter of the biblical story of salvation the emphasis is overwhelmingly on the blessing of the whole world. This observation is significant for the reflections on the meaning of 'election' which follow later in this chapter.

It is instructive to observe how the themes of land, descendants, protection and worldwide blessing are developed or alluded to in the whole story of Abraham (and indeed, in the stories of the other patriarchs, and in the rest of the Old Testament). Abram is aged 75 in Genesis 12:4. By the time he is 99 in 17:24 and his wife 90 (17:17), the promise of a son has still not been fulfilled. And by the time he dies aged 175 (25:7, 8), the only part of the land he actually owns is the family burial plot. In this quiet way the narrative reminds us that God's timescale may be different from ours, kindling the steadfast-ness of our hope, and warning us against false presumption.

No sooner has Abram been told to go to the *land* than we are

---

[4] Miller, 'Syntax', p. 475.

[5] T. D. Alexander, 'Abraham Reassessed Theologically', in R. S. Hess, G. J. Wenham and P. E. Satterthwaite (eds.), *He Swore an Oath: Biblical Themes from Genesis 12–50*, 2nd ed. (Paternoster, 1994), p. 13.

[6] G. J. Wenham, 'The Face at the Bottom of the Well', in ibid., p. 203.

told that the Canaanites are in the land (12:6) with all the re-verberations that the word 'Canaanites' would have for the informed reader in later times. But in verse 7 the LORD appears to Abram and says, 'To your offspring I will give this land.' Never-theless, in the next episode of the story there is a famine in the land (12:10); Abram heads for Egypt to find refuge there, and, far from being a blessing to Pharaoh, causes him a lot of trouble (12:17). However, the upshot of the visit to Egypt is that Abram becomes rich (12:16) and his wealth (13:2) and his nephew Lot's wealth are the cause of the next episode: the land cannot support both of them dwelling together (13:6); the herdsmen quarrel, so Abram jeopard-izes his own interests by giving Lot the choice of where to go; Lot chooses the best portion of the land (13:10ff.) and departs. A reader might have expected Lot to be Abram's heir; so if Lot departs, who will be heir?

Nevertheless, this is the context for the renewal of the Lord's promises in 13:15–17: Abram is to have offspring as uncountable as the dust of the earth; he is to look as far as he can see, north, south, east and west, and then to get up and walk through the length and breadth of the land, because it will be his.

Chapter 14 introduces us to the wider world scene. In the clash of armies Lot and his family are captured (14:12) and rescued (14:16) and Abram is blessed again by the mysterious figure Melchizedek (14:19). But still at the beginning of chapter 15 there is no sign of an heir; so, despite the Lord's reassurance (15:1), Abram wonders if his servant Eliezer is to be the heir – after all, he says somewhat plaintively, he is a member of my household ...

Patiently, God renews his promise. Abram's descendants will be as numberless as the stars (15:5), and Abram believes this promise (15:6). But Abram questions the Lord's intention to give him the land (15:8), this promise is renewed, a curious night vision confirms it, and now for the first time in the Abram story we find the word 'covenant' (15:18). Abram is told the dimensions of the land which his descendants will receive (15:18), despite, dauntingly, being occupied by ten national groups. A period of 400 years is mentioned before the land will be possessed (15:13).

Abram's wife, Sarai, speaks for the first time in 16:2. Her frustration is palpable, and her contextually appropriate proposal is that Abram, now aged 86 (16:16) go in to her maid, Hagar, which he does. Predictably, stress erupts in the household and the maid is ejected. This is not how the divine plan will be fulfilled, although it gives the editor the chance to indicate that Hagar too will have innumerable descendants (16:10).

Thirteen years elapse between chapters 16 and 17 and the Lord appears to the 99-year-old Abram to renew the covenant of years before. We are not told the reason for this renewal. Abram falls flat on his face in 17:3 and says nothing; but his attitude is perhaps revealed in that the next thing he does is to laugh (17:17) and get into a muddle ('Can a 100-year-old man give birth?') at the prospect that he and his 90-year-old wife will have a son. Nevertheless, the covenant is renewed in richer terms than before: Abram is to be 'exceedingly fruitful' (17:6); the covenant is to be an 'everlasting covenant' (17:7); and the land is to be a 'perpetual holding' (17:8). Abram's name is changed to Abraham, 'for I have made you the father of a multitude of nations' (17:5).[7]

The covenant is now given a sign, circumcision; Sarai's name is changed to Sarah; and Abraham is told by God (translating the first phrase literally), 'I *have given* from her to you a son, and I will bless her, and she shall become nations; kings of peoples shall come from her' (17:16). Abraham's thoughts are still mainly focused on Ishmael (who will become a great nation); but God clearly indicates, 'I will establish my covenant with Isaac [which means "He laughs"], whom Sarah shall bear to you at this time next year' (17:21). Chapter 18 introduces three mysterious visitors to whom Abraham is hospitable. We are told of Sarah's laughter (18:12), sympathetically dealt with by the strangers, probably because it is the laughter of a long disappointment.[8] Whatever happens, there *is* to be a son, and he will be called 'Laughter'.

The narrative now slows to a crawl as Sodom is about to be judged. No other short period of Abraham's life is narrated in such detail. Does this represent a cancellation of the promise to bless the nations? No, for in the midst of the divine reflection, we are reminded that 'Abraham will surely become a great and mighty nation, and all the nations of the earth shall be blessed in him' (18:18). Lot is clearly *not* the chosen heir: in a degrading close to his story he becomes the father of Israel's ancient enemies. It is probably in contrast to his behaviour and that of Sodom that a new note creeps into the covenant with Abraham – he and his household after him are 'to keep the way of the LORD by doing righteousness and justice'. Election clearly has ethical consequences. Abraham is now involved in a second incident with a foreign

---

[7] The etymology is a popular one: 'Abraham' in Hebrew resonates with other words meaning multitude, covenant, multiply, be fruitful and exceedingly. See G. J. Wenham, *Genesis 16–50*, Word Biblical Commentary (Word, 1994), p. 21.

[8] I think the laughter was close to tears. C. S. Lewis pointed out in his famous essay 'Transposition' that the emotions have a wider range and register than the sensations; thus the sensations have to do double duty, and may easily be misinterpreted. C. S. Lewis, *Transposition and Other Addresses* (Geoffrey Bles, 1949).

king; this time Abimelech, king of Gerar. Because Abraham is afraid (20:11) he says that his wife is his sister, which is partly true, as she is his half-sister (20:12). Reproaches follow when his half-truth is uncovered; he prays for Abimelech's wife and slaves so that they bear children (20:17), thus blessing a foreign nation (a covenant is added in 21:22–34) – but there is still no sign of a son *for Sarah*!

Finally, in chapter 21, a son is conceived, born, named and circumcised, leading immediately to renewed tension with the maid Hagar. She is sent off into the wilderness, but does not die; and her son, Ishmael, is also, like Isaac, to become a great nation (21:13, 18). We are not told how many years elapse between chapters 21 and 22, but by chapter 22 Isaac is already a young lad.[9] Now Abraham is subjected to the supreme test: he is commanded to sacrifice Isaac as a burnt offering, in one of the Old Testament's most famous stories.

Here his obedience is subjected to its severest test, which, in the narrator's view, he passes with flying colours. A further renewal of the covenant follows, in even more generous terms, sealed with a divine oath (when God swears, since there is no greater than he, he swears by himself, 22:16): Abraham will have offspring as number-less as the stars in the sky, or the sand on the seashore (22:17). The phrase 'they will possess the gate of their enemies' (22:17; 24:60) seems to bring the promise of a land more sharply into focus, which is something very specific, realistic, and perhaps more imminent.[10] Because of Abraham's obedience, all the nations of the earth will be blessed (22:18).

Now the story is beginning to pass to the next generation. Sarah dies in chapter 23, and Abraham gets his first piece of land – a burial place; but this is a pledge of that which is to follow. In the long chapter 24 we are introduced to the question of whom Isaac is going to marry. There is repeated stress on how God has blessed Abraham (24:1, 27, 31, 35, 48, 60), and Rebekah is sent on her way with a blessing promising that her offspring will be 'thousands of myriads' (24:60). Finally, in chapter 25, Abraham dies aged 175, and the story of Isaac begins, paralleling in some respects that of his father and his son, as the rest of Genesis relates.

3. The wider context of this story

The wide, long and deep promises of the Abraham story are embedded in a wider context which we should observe briefly.

[9] The word used here is used elsewhere of young men old enough for military service.

[10] See Wenham, *Genesis 16–50*, p. 112.

Immediately before the Abraham story are the table of nations (Gen. 10:1–32) and the tower of Babel stories (Gen. 11:1–9). These two stories give complementary accounts of the state of the world before the patriarchs are introduced. They are linked too by a play on the words *mabbûl* (flood, Gen 10:1) and *bābel* (Babylon, Gen. 11:9). In Genesis 10 the unity of the ancient world is grounded in a common descent from Noah, through his sons. It is not necessary to assume that this chapter attempts to give an account of *all* the nations of the ancient world – it is probable that seventy nations are described to form a macrocosm in which the microcosm of Jacob's family of seventy souls (Gen. 46:27) is set. There are several other plays on the number 'seven' in the chapter. The chapter is an astonishingly wide survey of the ancient world, especially the major groups known to Israel, starting with the more distant nations, descendants of Japheth, coming closer to Israel with the descendants of Ham, and then concluding with the descendants of Shem, including what we would call the 'Semitic' peoples. In Genesis 9:1 God's blessing on Noah and his sons includes the command to 'be fruitful and multiply, and fill the earth'; and Genesis 10:32 indicates that this command is being fulfilled as the nations spread out in the world after the flood.

Genesis 11:1–9, a brilliant short story, gives a very different account, and focuses on the breakdown of language and communication: at the beginning of the story 'the whole earth had one language and the same words'; by the end 'the LORD confused the language of all the earth; and from there the LORD scattered them over the face of the whole earth'. Here the people come together (rather than spreading out); insecurity and arrogance breed a gigantic building project; but inferior building materials are used; and although *they* aspire to build a tower 'with its top in the heavens', it is so far from achieving its object that the LORD has to 'come down' even to see it! The object of this building programme is 'to make a name for ourselves'; the readers of this story will know that it is God who makes names great (e.g. that of Abram, 12:2), especially his own name (e.g. Is. 63:12, 14).

If we picture these two stories as two panels of a diptych, then Genesis 10, on the one hand, emphasizes the world's unity: it has a positive ring to it as the divine command of 9:1 is fulfilled gradually. Panel 2, Genesis 11, on the other hand, has a negative ring: here the unity of the human race is shattered as people become unable to communicate with each other; their search for security, unity and technological mastery founders in disarray, dispersal and divine disapproval. The human race has stumbled from *mabbûl* to *bābel*. Far from Babylon being the gate of the gods, as the Babylonians

95

conceived it, the verdict of this story is babble, jabberwocky, gabble, confusion![11]

'Babylon' is a word which reverberates powerfully through the rest of the Bible as a symbol of human economic enterprise, political power and military might organized without or against God. Isaiah predicts that such enterprises will come crashing down (Is. 14:13–15); and so does Revelation (ch. 18). This is not an anti-urban vision. Revelation pictures our final destination as a city – but it is 'the holy city, the new Jerusalem' not being built up to heaven by human beings; but 'coming down out of heaven from God' (Rev. 21:2).

So much for the precursors to the Abraham stories. On the *other side* of these stories are the cycle of Jacob stories (Gen. 25:19 – 35:29) and the Joseph cycle (Gen. 37:1 – 50:26). There are striking similarities between these cycles, and the book ends with Joseph as a plenipotentiary in Egypt, the superpower of the day; although, as he dies, his focus is on 'the land that he [God] swore to Abraham, to Isaac, and to Jacob' (Gen. 50:24).

Thus the passage in Genesis 12 which is the focus of this chapter is not like an alien meteorite landing in the Nevada desert. The blessing God pronounces on and predicts through Abram is part of the worldwide story which the book of Genesis introduces. We may now look at some of the specific mission issues which arise out of and are addressed by our Genesis 12 passage.

4. Mission and cultural identity

God said to Abram, 'Go!' and Abram 'went'. Without this habit of obedience to divine displacement there would have been no Jewish story, no biblical story, no international people of God. Mission begins with the 'displacement' of the Son of God from the bright land of the Trinity: 'God so loved the world that he *sent* his only Son ...' (John 3:16). And Jesus established a parallel between his own sentness and his sending of the apostles, when he said, 'As the Father has sent me, even so I send you ...' (John 20:21).

The history of the internationalizing of the Christian community is full of sending, going and receiving. Much of this movement has been *within* cultures as Anglican women travelled around danger-ous areas of Congo or Mozambique, while men were away at wars,

[11] Miroslav Volf reflects on the totalitarian architecture, the suppressing of differences, the homogenizing, controlling violence of Genesis 11, against which God's scattering is not only a punishment, but also a blessing. Babel stabilizes and aggrandizes the centre; the Spirit (in Acts 2) pours energy into the margins, thus bringing about a harmony of cultural diversity. See M. Volf, *Exclusion and Embrace* (Abingdon, 1996), pp. 226ff.

teaching, praying and caring; or as Chinese church leaders travelled, often at great risk, to minister to unregistered groups of believers, even in the dark days of the Cultural Revolution; or as Methodist preachers, many scarcely in their twenties, travelled all over England, Wales and Ireland in the eighteenth century.

But much of this travelling, this displacement, has been *between* countries and cultures. Miroslav Volf says that to be a child of Abram means exodus, voyage, pilgrimage, being a stranger: 'at the very core of Christian identity lies an all-encompassing change of loyalty ... departure is part and parcel of Christian identity'.[12] In our homogenizing, modern world many expatriates can travel around the world without ever leaving their English-speaking, air-conditioned, office-club-home bubble. But the Christian movement has been able to take root in an astonishing number of different cultures only because there have been some men and women who have been willing to leave home and family and children, sometimes for years at a time, to embed themselves in another culture, like a seed that falls into the ground and dies. This is the way Nestorian Christians, like Alopen, a Syriac-speaking Persian Christian, planted the church in China in the seventh century; this is the way Christianity spread from island to island in the Pacific; this is the way evangelists from Sierra Leone planted the church in remote areas, walking for weeks at a time.

5. The promise of the land

One of the components of God's promise to Abraham is the promise of a land, a territory. At first this is 'the land that I will show you' (Gen. 12:1). Later it is 'this land, from the river of Egypt to the great river, the river Euphrates', although at present occupied by ten nations (Gen. 15:18). Later Abraham is told that he will receive 'the land where you are now an alien, all the land of Canaan, for a perpetual holding' (Gen. 17:8). How are these promises to be interpreted?

Christians have watched the movement of Jewish people in the last hundred years, the horrors of the Holocaust, the formation of the state of Israel, the Six Day War in 1967 in which Israel regained access to the old city of Jerusalem, and all the developments of the last thirty years with amazement and trepidation. How are we to correlate the promises to Abraham and the events of recent times? What attitude should we take towards the continuing conflict between Israelis and Palestinians, which is so largely to do with land?

[12] Volf, *Exclusion*, p. 40.

There is no doubt that some of the territory now occupied by Israelis was rightfully purchased from the legal owners, during the early waves of Jewish immigration beginning in the nineteenth century. But since the establishment of the state of Israel, and especially since the war of 1967 and the extensive building programme of Jewish settlements in East Jerusalem and the West Bank, the issue has become hugely controversial. On the one hand, Israelis and their supporters claim that law is on their side: 'The bottom line here is that we Jews have the Biblical mandate to settle our land and we have the legal, moral and historical right as declared and recognized by the League of Nations in 1922. The United Nations demonstrates total disregard for its own predecessor, The League of Nations, by referring to any part of the Jewish homeland as occupied territory.'[13] On the other hand, the legal advisor to the Latin Patriarchate of Jerusalem, Fr Majdi al-Siryani, has insisted that under the law of extinctive prescription[14] 'the Israeli historic claim to the land of Palestine is not based on occupation and use, [and] lacks any legal validity under international law. On the other hand, the Arabs' historic claim has a stronger background of longstanding occupation and sense of territorial entitlement.'[15] He quotes a Professor Collins (whom I have been unable to trace) as saying that under the principle of 'historic rights', so often quoted by Israel's supporters, some present-day Romans might lay claim to Big Ben, Parliament and the white cliffs of Dover. Perhaps also some American Christians who support Israeli annexation of Palestinian land might be shocked if some native Americans were to expropriate *their* property by quoting 'historic right'.

It is probable that readers of this book are more concerned for theological arguments in the case. For some Christians there is no uncertainty: 'According to God's distribution of the nations, the Land of Israel has been given to the Jewish people by God as an everlasting possession by an eternal covenant. The Jewish People have the absolute right to possess and dwell in the Land, including Judea, Samaria, Gaza and the Golan.'[16] Earlier, Lewis Sperry Chafer, founding president of Dallas Theological Seminary, had set it out quite clearly in his theological textbook: 'Israel is an

[13] See <http://www.israelunitycoalition.com/israel_history/historic_right!.htm>.

[14] Defined as 'a mode of acquiring a right by continuous, uninterrupted, peaceable, open and unequivocal possession for a time specified by law'; see <www.mifsudbonnici.com/lexnet/articles/>.

[15] Majdi al-Siryani, *The Bible and the Israeli Claims to the Holy Land*, January 2001; to be found at <http://www.al-bushra.org/promisedland/majdi.html>.

[16] International Christian Zionist Congress Proclamation, International Christian Embassy, Jerusalem, 25–29 February 1996.

eternal nation, heir to an eternal land, with an eternal kingdom, on which David rules from an eternal throne.'[17]

It would appear that this certainty is misplaced because it is based on an erroneous method of biblical interpretation. In Leviticus 25:23 the Israelites are warned through Moses that the land is not absolutely theirs: 'The land shall not be sold in perpetuity; for the land is mine, and you are but aliens who have become my tenants.' If they do not keep God's laws, the land will 'vomit you out for defiling it, as it vomited out the nation that was before you' (Lev. 18:28).

In the teaching of Jesus there is no territorial focus. W. D. Davies pointed out that by his death on a cross Jesus polluted the land, and 'by that act and its consequences he shattered the geographic dimension of the religion of his fathers'.[18] Dr Christopher Wright has pointed out that the book of Hebrews sums up the fulfilment of Old Testament promises very comprehensively: the 'land' we receive is the promised rest in Christ; we have a High Priest, an altar, a final and complete sacrifice in the person and work of Christ; he is the tabernacle and temple where we may meet God. 'Indeed, according to Hebrews (13:14) the only thing we do *not* have is an earthly, territorial city.'[19]

When Paul enumerates the privileges of the Jewish people, which he acknowledges, he does *not* include the land (Rom. 9:4, 5). There *is* a future for the Jewish people in Paul's thinking, but it is not focused on the holding or retrieval of territory. In Romans 4:13 there is a very significant substitution of the word 'world' for the word 'land' in Genesis. According to Miroslav Volf, this involves 'the radical reinterpretation of the relationship between religion and cultural identity'.[20] According to Peter Walker, 'Jerusalem has lost whatever theological status is previously possessed. The way the Old Testament ascribes to Jerusalem a special, central and sacred status within the ongoing purposes of God is not reaffirmed by the New Testament writers.'[21]

Christ is the fulfilment of the genealogical promise to Abram; and the end of genealogy as the locus of privileged access to

[17] L. S. Chafer, *Systematic Theology*, vol. 4 (Dallas Seminary Press, 1975), pp. 315–323.
[18] W. D. Davies, *The Gospel and the Land: Early Christianity and Jewish Territorial Doctrine* (University of California Press, 1974), p. 375.
[19] C. J. H. Wright, quoted in Stephen Sizer and Neil Cornell debate 'Whose Promised Land?' at Guildford Diocesan Evangelical Fellowship, 18 March 1997, published on the Web at <http://www.virginiawater.co.uk/christchurch/articles/debate.html> (source not given).
[20] Volf, *Exclusion*, p. 50.
[21] Peter Walker, *Jesus and the Holy City: New Testament Perspectives on Jerusalem* (Eerdmans, 1996), pp. 319, 326.

God.[22] The Old Testament picture of the nations flowing in towards Jerusalem is superseded by Christ's command to his disciples to preach the good news to every creature, so that the church may take root in every culture: no particular territory is sacred any more; no pilgrimage is necessary except along him who is the Way, leading towards the heavenly city. It is clear that in Paul's thinking salvation is for Jews and Gentiles in the same way, through faith in Jesus Christ.[23] What then does he mean by 'to the Jew first and also to the Greek'? It is clear that the Jews had a certain historical priority in the unveiling of God's plan of salvation, because it was the Jewish people whom God chose and with whom he made his covenant in the first place, as I have set out in this chapter. It is also clear that as a matter of missionary practice Paul often began his evangelistic work in the synagogue. It is also clear from Romans 9 – 11 that Paul has a hope and vision for the final salvation of all Israel in the consummation of the purposes of God, because the gifts and calling of God are irrevocable (Rom. 11:29). But there is no special entry or 'fast track' into salvation for those of Jewish descent apart from faith in Jesus Christ.[24]

6. Mission and ethics

In Genesis 18:18 the Lord is pictured reminding himself that Abraham is to become a great and powerful nation, and all nations on earth will be blessed through him. At the very moment when the Lord is contemplating an obliterating judgment on the cities of Sodom and Gomorrah because their sin is so grave, we are reminded of the scope of God's intention and plan of salvation.

How is God's plan to bless the whole world through the descendants of Abraham actually going to come about? Verse 19 spells this out in a carefully structured sentence:

> I have chosen Abraham
> *so that* he may charge his children and his household after him
> to keep the way of the LORD by doing righteousness and justice;
> *so that* the LORD may bring about for Abraham
> what he has promised him.

[22] Volf, *Exclusion*, p. 45.

[23] '[The gospel] is the power of God for salvation to everyone who has faith' (Rom. 1:16).

[24] Tom Wright has written, 'The irony ... is that the late twentieth century, in order to avoid anti-Semitism, has advocated a position (the non-evangelization of the Jews) *which Paul regards precisely as anti-Semitic*' (*The Climax of the Covenant: Christ and the Law in Pauline Theology* [T. & T. Clark, 1991]), p. 253; his emphasis.

Here the fulfilment of God's promises to Abraham are causally linked to the behaviour of his children and household after him, which are themselves causally linked to God's choice of Abraham in the first place. 'The election of Abraham is for the purpose that he will establish a community with a God-shaped ethical life, and that in turn is for the purpose of enabling God to fulfil his ultimate redemptive goal. Ethics is here the middle term, the hinge, between election and mission.'[25]

Wherever the church pursues its mission, this matter is of central importance. The Christian message is not a disembodied piece of information that just needs to be circulated in massive campaigns, through print, film, video or broadcast media. It is the good news *embodied* and shared in the changed lives of individuals and communities that constitutes authentic witness. Without this embodiment, Christians are vulnerable to the charge of propaganda, with the resistance and distrust this commonly evokes. It is the *life* of a school teacher, day after day, that makes most impact on the pupils she lives among. In southern Sudan Christians commonly lack all the apparatus of modern communication; yet the church has grown as Christians have demonstrated a different quality of life in the midst of disaster, degradation and despair.

7. Mission for the whole human race

One of the insistent arguments of both Old and New Testaments is that Yahweh, or the Lord, is not just a tribal god, but has a universal claim. We have already observed the importance of Genesis 10 as a background to the Abraham story, and this anthropological survey is unique in the ancient world. Using a combination of linguistic ('tongues'), territorial ('lands') and anthropological ('nations', 'families') terms, this chapter asserts the common ancestry, and thus common humanity of a huge range of ancient nations.

What is meant by a 'nation' in the Old Testament? Clearly, the reference is not to the relatively modern idea of a 'nation state'. Daniel Block identifies ethnicity, territory, theology (deities), kingship (or not) and language as components of Old Testament ideas of national self-consciousness.[26] The fact that all nations are accountable to the Lord is reflected in the fact that several of the prophetic books have oracles concerning, or against, foreign nations, bringing them to the bar of divine justice, even though they did not profess

---

[25] C. J. H. Wright, Commentary in *Third Way*, September 1986, p. 7.
[26] W. A. VanGemeren (ed.), *New International Dictionary of Old Testament Theology and Exegesis*, vol. 4 (Paternoster, 1996), pp. 967–972.

allegiance to the Lord (e.g. Is. 13 – 24; Jer. 46 – 51; Ezek. 25 – 32; Amos 1 – 2; Hab. 2).

David Barrett has attempted the most detailed of all world ethnocultural classifications in the second edition of his *World Christian Encyclopaedia*.[27] In this remarkable survey he proposes that any human population has six defining characteristics: race, colour, ethnic origin, nationality, culture and language. The first two are inherited; ethnic origin is the hardest to define; nationality (citizenship) can easily be changed; and the last two are learned. His following classification attempts to assign codes for every significant group of people at 11 progressively detailed levels: 5 major races with 7 skin colours, 13 geographical races, 71 ethnolinguistic families, 432 peoples, 12,600 subpeoples, 13,500 languages and so on. His purpose is to offer this coding as an instrument for measuring cultural distance between different people groups, and he offers mathematical formulae for doing so. The usefulness of this anthropological algebra may be questioned, especially in the light of Barrett's own admission that no pure racial stocks exist because of human interbreeding; but the idea of paying sensitive attention to the needs of a huge variety of human groups (especially minority groups who may be overlooked), and their need to hear the good news in their own language and in a culturally sensitive way, is important.

It has been customary for a long time (at least since William Carey's *Inquiry* of 1792)[28] to consider the spread of Christianity and the needs of the world in territorial terms. Maps have pictured the waves of advance and recession of the Christian movement by colouring various areas at different times. In more recent times it has become necessary, since Christianity has gained at least a foothold in almost all countries, and in order to focus the evangelistic task more precisely, to pay closer attention to the nature and quality of this penetration. If we pay attention only to countries, we may, for example, overlook the need of some groups of people who have a clear cultural identity but no country to their name. An obvious example is 15 million Kurds. Here is a group of people spread through parts of Iraq, Iran, Turkey, Armenia, Georgia, Kazakhstan,

---

[27] David B. Barrett, George T. Kurian and Todd M. Johnson, *World Christian Encyclopaedia: A Comparative Survey of Churches and Religions in the Modern World*, 2nd ed., 2 vols. (OUP, 2001), pp. 15–241.

[28] Original full title: *An Enquiry into the Obligations of Christians to Use Means for the Conversion of the Heathens. In which the Religious State of the Different Nations of the World, the Success of Former Undertakings, and the Practicability of Further Undertakings, Are Considered*; first published in London in May 1792; a facsimile edition with an introduction by E. A. Payne was published in London by Carey Kingsgate in 1961.

Lebanon and Syria, but who do not have a country.[29] But also, within a country, Christianity may have penetrated unevenly: there may be whole groups of people whose needs are still unmet. Such groups may be defined ethnically (e.g. minority groups), sociologically (e.g. student groups or married women) or economically (e.g. the urban poor).

In the Old Testament, from the period of Moses and following, there are a number of Hebrew words to describe different units of a national grouping. The most general word is 'people'. Underneath this canopy are words denoting tribe, clan, family/household and individual.[30] These terms are used with some precision. But in Genesis there does not appear to be a usage of equal precision. In Genesis 12 the word 'nation' (gôy) is used in verse 2; and the word 'family' (mišpāḥâ) is used in verse 3. In Genesis 17:6 Abraham is told that 'kings will come from you'.

We conclude from these observations that it is not possible to link directly the exact terminology of the Bible (Old or New Testaments) with the current preference for identifying ethnolinguistic people groups as focal concerns for evangelization.[31] But it is clear from the Abraham story, and from the use that the New Testament makes of this story, that God's concern is for the entire created order. People from every conceivable human grouping are called into the people of God. Genesis 1 – 11 and Revelation 'form a great envelope structure'[32] into which is inserted the story of God's dealings with Abraham and his descendants, through whom he was going to bless the entire world.

There is one further aspect of the choosing of Abraham which is fruitful for our consideration under this heading. In Old Testament times the life of the individual was always firmly integrated into his family and thus into his people. Segregation and isolation because of accusations (false or just), persecution or sickness were horrors and miseries by all means to be avoided; loneliness was to be avoided if at all possible. From this point of view the call to Abraham to leave country, kindred and family might seem to be almost a curse! But here we are introduced to an alternative call to loneliness, and that is the calling to God's service, as representative, messenger, prophet,

---

[29] See the New Internationalist, *The World Guide 2001–2002* (New Internationalist, 2001), p. 295.

[30] See R. H. O'Connell in VanGemeren, *New International Dictionary*, vol. 2, p. 1141.

[31] As e.g. John Piper does in his challenging book *Let the Nations Be Glad! The Supremacy of God in Missions* (IVP, 1994), ch. 5.

[32] C. H. H. Scobie, 'Israel and the Nations: An Essay in Biblical Theology', *Tyndale Bulletin* 43.2 (1992), pp. 283–305.

servant. Jeremiah is the prophet in the Old Testament who feels this
loneliness most deeply, as he felt himself an outcast from the
community to whom he was called (Jer. 15:17, 18). Sometimes
following the call of God involves going against the tide, swimming
against the stream, separation from the crowd. Such a person 'with
the love of God that is directed towards him, with the divine
demand that is addressed to him, and with the invitation of faith that
applies to him is given the courage to say: *si omnes, ego non* –
though all, yet not I'.[33]

8. Mission as faith in God's promise

God promised Abraham, when he was old and childless, that
through his descendants the whole world would be blessed. In
Psalm 2 the Lord invites his anointed Son and Servant,

> Ask of me, and I will make the nations your heritage,
> and the ends of the earth your possession.
>
> (Ps. 2:8)

When the risen Jesus commanded his eleven unexceptional
followers to make disciples of all nations he also included a promise:
'I am with you always, to the end of the age' (Matt. 28:20). Later on,
Paul was reviled and opposed for testifying to Jews in the synagogue
at Corinth that the Messiah was Jesus, and so took to preaching in
the house of Titius Justus next door. We are not told directly of the
rumpus this must have caused, but we are told that the Lord
appeared to Paul in a night vision: 'Do not be afraid, but speak
and do not be silent; for I am with you, and no one will lay a hand
on you to harm you, for there are many in this city who are my
people' (Acts 18:9–10).

Walter Brueggemann says cogently, 'The threat and possibility
articulated in the narrative of Abraham and Sarah put a crisis before
humanity. It is the crisis of deciding to live either *for the promise*,
and so disengaging from the present barren way of things, or to
live *against the promise*, holding on grimly to the present ordering
of life.'[34]

The Christian missionary movement (from everywhere to everywhere, not just from the West to the rest, or from the North to the
South) has been criticized sharply for its imperial ambitions. We
have confused the kingdom of Christ with the kingdoms and

[33] Helmut Gollwitzer, quoted in H. W. Wolff, *The Anthropology of the Old
Testament* (SCM, 1974), p. 222.
[34] W. Brueggemann, *Genesis* (John Knox, 1982), p. 113.

projects of human beings. The good news has sometimes been proclaimed in tones of regrettable shrillness. Those who have gone to plant churches have stayed for too long and been too controlling. There have been plenty of signs and blunders.[35] But this is only one side of the story. Another side contains many stories of those who lived (and in some cases died) to spread the good news, often without power, without support, poor, living simply, often sick and in danger – these are the ones who lived and worked for the fulfilment of the divine promise that all the nations of the world are to be blessed by the descendants of Abraham.

Among all these debates, with the energy they consume and produce, sensitive Christians are conscious that they live in a disordered world, a world of great polarities. The disorders may be hard-to-understand personal tragedies or genocidal conflicts, aided and abetted by the great powers, on a mind-numbing scale. Because of the media and the Internet, even without travelling anywhere, we have more details about these events more promptly than ever before. Missionaries, with the Christians they seek to serve, or with those whom they are trying to win, often (not always) live in the border zone of conflict between 'the kingdom of our Lord and of his Christ' and 'the kingdom of this world' (Rev. 11:15). Often too they are conscious of the groaning of the whole creation: images spring to mind – of the killing fields of Cambodia; of bodies in their thousands clogging the rivers of Rwanda; of refugee tents and desperate people clinging to barren, volcanic rock; of a line of Zambian women hoeing soil in a cloud of dust, hoping for rain which never comes.

In reaction to these scenes some hopelessly, hand-wringingly, withdraw; others with anger and tears attempt to put a finger in the dyke of suffering. Others, more fortunate and at a greater distance, come up with ideas and schemes that have something genuinely beautiful about them: a millennial jubilee scheme for the remission of the worst debts of the poorest of the poor; a microcredit scheme that enables villagers to buy seeds that will help them grow some vegetables and thus put before their children food that is at least slightly more nourishing; a nine-hundredth anniversary walk through countries devastated by the First Crusade, to confess sorrow and to confess Christ.

Those who know something of what Dante called 'the thirst, which is instilled into us at our creation, and which never leaves us, for the kingdom whose maker is God' are inspired and energized to

[35] See Allan Anderson, *Signs and Blunders: Pentecostal Mission Issues at 'Home and Abroad' in the Twentieth Century*, at <http://www.martynmission.cam.ac.uk/Csigns.htm>.

love and serve this Lord by the conviction that the hopes of which we already have some foretastes of fulfilment will one day be fulfilled beyond our wildest dreams. For then the kingdoms of this world will become the kingdoms of our Lord and of his Christ; and he will rule for ever and ever.

Deuteronomy 10:12–20
6. A distinctive people

My wife and I recently received a letter from a friend working in the Mercy Ships ministries of the international Christian organization Youth With a Mission (YWAM). Describing the work of the ship's teams in the West African state of Benin, she wrote:

> Our construction teams are building in three separate sites while medical and dental teams work in four locations. Add to that our 'secret weapons' teams. That's what I call them – our crew who use their off-time to visit the lonely and hurting. Each week 120 of them in 27 teams visit orphanages, prisons, children's homes and hospitals in 18 different locations. I love this ministry. They paint or pray or hug, or clean or build or feed. Sometimes all there is to do is cry with the broken-hearted. The need is overwhelming, the finances, resources, people and time seems so desperately limited. Yet to share in the pains of the helpless, even for a short time, is to enter into the fellowship of our common humanity. It is to live as Jesus showed us, it is to please the heart of the One we call Father.

1. A missionary charter

The book of Deuteronomy can be read as the missionary charter of the Hebrew Bible. The people of Israel, a ragged, motley collection of squabbling tribes have arrived at the edge of the land of Canaan after a generation of aimless wandering in the Sinai desert, following their liberation from Egypt. They have been given, through their leader Moses, a unique law which, if practised diligently in the land they are about to enter, will form them into a distinctive people that will provoke the surrounding nations to curiosity and awe (Deut. 4:5–8). The book is largely Moses' exhortation to Israel to

107

remember the words of Yahweh, both for their own well-being and that they might be a light to the nations.

This short passage, which begins and ends with the command to 'fear Yahweh your God', is a wonderful summary of the whole book, if not the entire Old Testament! It declares who the God of Israel is, and what kind of nation Israel was called to be. It challenges the people of God in every age to rethink their vocation in the light of their own contemporary situations.

'The fear of Yahweh' is a phrase that resonates throughout the wisdom literature of Israel. It denotes not the cringing, servile fear we show before powerful men who can hurt us, nor the sheer terror we experience in the face of human and physical evil, and not even a generalized reverence towards the sacred and 'numinous', but rather an awed, grateful recognition of our absolute dependence on the One whose utterance spells the difference between life and death. In what must seem a paradox to modern ears, an ancient sage declares:

> The fear of Yahweh is life indeed;
> filled with it, one rests secure
> and suffers no harm.
>
> (Prov. 19:23)

Poetic parallelism in verse 12 defines the 'fear of Yahweh' as tantamount to 'walking in all his ways'. Chris Wright reminds us that this expression is the nearest equivalent in the Hebrew Bible to our modern notion of 'ethics'.[1] The answer to the question 'What should we, then, do?' was always 'Do what you see Yahweh doing.' All ethics is theological ethics, and the latter was not for Israel a matter of learning abstract principles but of imitating the historical outworking of the divine life as it impinged on their own. The true Israelite, in response to Yahweh's ways, loves and serves Yahweh with his entire being. Peter Craigie observes that the requirements summed up in verses 12 and 13 spell out the *positive* nature of total commitment to the one God. It is a 'positive sermon on the negatively stated first commandment [in the Decalogue] "You shall not have other gods besides me"'.[2]

What it means to love and serve Yahweh, and to walk in all his ways, is spelled out in the subsequent text. Some commentators

---

[1] Christopher J. H. Wright, *Walking in the Ways of the Lord: The Ethical Authority of the Old Testament* (Apollos, 1995); *Deuteronomy*, New International Biblical Commentary (Hendrickson, 1996), p. 145. We are deeply indebted to the latter commentary for much of our exposition.

[2] P. C. Craigie, *The Book of Deuteronomy*, New International Commentary on the Old Testament (Eerdmans, 1976), p. 204.

draw our attention to the poetic flavour of the passage, the six verses 14–19 falling neatly into a pair of triplets, with each verse of the first set corresponding to (or parallel with) a similar verse in the second. They form a symmetrical pattern, common in Hebrew hymnody. So verses 14 and 17 combine in proclaiming who Yahweh *is*. They give us a description of his character. Verses 15 and 18 declare something about what Yahweh *does*. They tell us about something extraordinary that he has done or is doing. Finally, the third verse of each triplet (vv. 16 and 19) spells out what Yahweh *requires* of his people.

2. The universal sovereignty of Yahweh

First, then, who is Yahweh (vv. 14, 17)? *Heaven and the heaven of heavens belong to Yahweh your God, the earth with all that is in it* (v. 14). This is a Hebrew way of saying that the whole of the cosmos, all of reality, belongs to Yahweh. He is not just another tribal deity. He 'is confined neither within the physical world nor even within the cosmic heaven of Near Eastern mythology'.[3] He is the cosmic owner and ruler of everything. Everything that *is*, owes its existence to him. In the parallel verse in the text we read that Yahweh is *God of gods and Lord of lords, the great God, mighty and awesome* (v. 17a). Not only all material reality but all spiritual reality falls under Yahweh's sovereignty. Whatever gods the nations surrounding Israel may worship, whatever astral powers may tyrannize them, they do not compromise Yahweh's sovereign rule. He has no rivals in the cosmos. In the early chapters of Deuteronomy Moses narrates how Yahweh has been at work in Canaan and the surrounding lands even before Israel appeared on the scene. He is sovereign over the migrations and transformations of other nations (Deut. 2:9–12, 19–23, 30–31; cf. Amos 9:7).

Furthermore, this verse announces that Yahweh *is not partial and takes no bribe* (v. 17b). He is utterly fair and just in his dealings with the nations. He is not the kind of deity who can be manipulated through religious techniques for our selfish purposes. It follows that the worship of Yahweh must be radically different from the sacrificial cults surrounding the local Canaanite fertility gods. The worship of the latter, like much religious worship in temples, shrines and churches around the world today, was a matter of learning the right postures and sacrifices which would ensure fertility for one's crops (and wife), prosperity and freedom from sickness. Yahweh is utterly different.

[3] Ibid.

The New Testament takes the exalted language that refers to Yahweh in these verses and applies it to Jesus of Nazareth. In Revelation 19:16, for example, the risen Jesus is described as the 'King of kings and the Lord of lords'. The New Testament writers see in Jesus the climax of the story of Israel. Israel was called to be a light to the nations, but they failed by disobeying Yahweh. Jesus comes as the true Israel to fulfil the filial obedience that Israel was called to. He lives in perfect loving obedience to his Father and so becomes that light to the nations. But the New Testament writers go even further: they speak of Jesus not only as the embodiment of Israel but as the incarnation of Israel's God. In Jesus, Yahweh himself entered the stage of human history in the form of an individual human life.

3. The particular love of Yahweh

Positively, however, what does Yahweh do? First, Yahweh stooped to love a particular people: *Yet Yahweh set his heart in love on your ancestors alone and chose you, their descendants after them, out of all the peoples, as it is today* (v. 15). It is remarkable that just before speaking of Yahweh's impartiality, Moses reminds the people of Yahweh's special concern and action towards Israel. Obviously, then, we are to conclude that Yahweh's particular acts of love towards Israel are not an expression of partiality, least of all favouritism. This is emphasized repeatedly in the earlier chapters of Deuteronomy (e.g. 7:7ff.). The implication is that he loves them for the sake of *all* that he has created. But who are these people on whom Yahweh has set his heart in love? They are the *ancestors* of Israel, a bunch of rather unattractive people introduced to us in the patriarchal narratives in Genesis, beginning with Abraham, the coward willing to sacrifice his wife to save his own skin; Isaac, the weak parent, manipulated by his wife and son; Jacob, the arch-schemer and deceiver. Yet these are the very objects of Yahweh's love. 'And you, rabble,' Moses seems to be saying, 'with all your complaining and grumbling and backslidings, are no different from them. Yet Yahweh has loved you, and loves you still!'

Why does God love the unlovely? Because that is the nature of love. But he also loves unlovely Israel for the sake of the rest of his unlovely world. We saw (in v. 14) that Yahweh's universal rule extends over the whole earth and that all human creatures belong to him, even in their disobedience. Verse 15, on the other hand, speaks of his particular redemptive love for a particular people. If God loves this people, it is because his gaze, so to speak, is on the whole world. It is for their sake that he is working with this family and their descendants. The calling of Abraham (Gen. 12:1–3) had as its ultimate goal the fulfilment of the promise that 'all peoples of the earth will be blessed through you'. So, while Yahweh is at work in all nations, in no nation other than Israel is he at work *for the sake of all nations*.[4]

Chris Wright, in his fine commentary on Deuteronomy, reminds us that, missiologically, we need to keep verses 14 and 15 together in a creative tension. If we were to stress the universality of Yahweh's rule to the exclusion of his particular love, we would end up with an *unbiblical universalism*. That would mean blurring the distinction between the redeemed, covenant people of God and the rest of the nations. But, on the other hand, if we so stressed God's particular love for his covenant people we could end up with an equally *unbiblical exclusivism*. It is possible to talk as if God is concerned only with his covenant people and, by implication, has turned his back on the rest of his world. Such talk fails to recognize that the covenant people of God are a sign and anticipation of God's transforming purposes for humanity. Both are distortions of biblical truth. We need to preserve the balance of truth, as embodied in verses 14 and 15.

Missionary practice compels us to maintain this balance. It is only in concrete encounters with people in their life-situations, in obedience to the call of God, rather than in theoretical reflection on the cultures of the world, that we discover the risen Christ in the most unexpected places. This is why all mission is an adventure of exploration. In the words of a famous twentieth-century missionary to the Muslim world, 'They who take Christ are in a state of perpetual discovery. The discoveries they make are through the discoveries they enable.'[5]

These verses, when viewed from the perspective of the New Testament, bring into relief one of the compelling challenges to mission in our contemporary world; namely, *the challenge of engaging with religious pluralism*. The challenge is how to acknowledge that God is at work in all nations and in their histories and yet that what he has done in the history of Israel, a history that reaches its consummation in the life, death and resurrection of Jesus Christ, is not only paradigmatic (of his work elsewhere), but *decisive* for the

---

[4] 'The purpose of God's particular action in the history of Israel is ultimately that God, as the saving and covenant God Yahweh, should be known fully and worshipped exclusively by those who as yet imperfectly know him as El' (John E. Goldingay and Christopher J. H. Wright, 'Yahweh our God, Yahweh One: The Old Testament and Religious Pluralism', in A. D. Clark and B. W. Winter [eds.], *One God, One Lord in a World of Religious Pluralism* [Tyndale House, 1991]), p. 39.

[5] K. Cragg, *The Call of the Minaret* (OUP, 1956), p. 183.

future of the whole world. How do we relate that 'once-for-all' sense of God's saving action in Jesus to what God has been doing and continues to do among peoples who have never heard of Jesus? This calls us to discern, in our missionary engagement, whatever is compatible with the gospel in all cultures and societies, affirming and nurturing their growth, but also exposing and confronting those things that are incompatible.

Our modern world, no less than the world of ancient Israel, is redolent with gods. These deities are to be found not only in the worlds of traditional religions and new religious movements, but also in much that is labelled 'secular'. Secular societies are no less religious than religious cultures. Only the worshipped gods are more sophisticated. They disguise themselves behind such fancy names as 'market forces', 'national security', 'economic growth' or 'technological progress'. It is a part of our calling as the Christian church to unmask these false gods that have taken over God's world. We need to expose their clay feet and show our nations that enslavement and dehumanization are the inevitable outcome of false worship. It is a task that calls for prayer, spiritual discernment and moral courage.

4. The scandalous justice of Yahweh

Cultural and ideological pluralism in the modern world is closely bound up with our understanding of social justice. It was no less so in the world of ancient Israel. The second part of the answer to the question 'What does Yahweh do?' is given in the parallel verse, 18. Namely, Yahweh is the God who *executes justice for the orphan and the widow, and who loves the strangers, providing them with food and clothing* (v. 18). This phrase 'the orphan, the widow and the stranger' recurs many times in the Old Testament. It denotes those people within Israel who had no natural protection within the community; and so becomes a kind of shorthand for all who are weak and vulnerable, the marginalized of society, who are most likely to be pushed to the wall when things get tough. Given their precarious situation, Yahweh has a special concern for them. It is this biblical vision that is enshrined in the slogan, first coined in a Latin American context in the 1960s, 'God's preferential option for the poor'.

The law Israel were to obey in the land of promise, which they were about to enter, had a particular 'bias' towards the weak and the vulnerable (in a sinful world where life is biased towards the wealthy and the powerful, God's actions will always be perceived as a counter-bias!). To the extent that they followed Yahweh's lead,

Israel would communicate a unique vision of God to the rest of the world. Among Israel's neighbours, as indeed in the ancient cultures of the world (including Indian, Chinese, African and South American civilizations), the power of the gods was channelled through the power of certain males – the priests, kings and warriors embodied divine power. Opposition to them was tantamount to rebellion against the gods. But here, in Israel's rival vision, it is 'the orphan, the widow and the stranger' with whom Yahweh takes his stand. His power is exercised in history for their empowerment.

The index of Israel's spiritual health as a society would be the way they treated the poor and vulnerable in their midst. 'God's people are to be known for their concern for those whose social and economic position expose them to exploitation and oppression.'[6] Worship and social justice went hand in hand. Whenever Israel forgot Yahweh and turned their back on him, running after the gods of the other nations, they inevitably forgot the weak and the vulnerable. Thus religious idolatry and social oppression were closely associated.

The biblical vision of justice springs from the conviction that God *loves* justice (e.g. Is. 61:8; Ps. 37:28) and that this love is an *active* love which issues in his putting right situations of injustice (e.g. Pss. 103:6; 140:12; 146:7–9). God's people follow him in doing justice; that is, restoring to the community all those who, through misfortune, calamity, deprivation or oppression have been hitherto excluded. For this to be achieved, resources and opportunities must be opened up to all. Justice is a necessary means to human re-creation and reconciliation.

The implication of this biblical vision is that growing disparities between rich and poor, and indifference to the plight of the latter, indicate that a nation is in the grip of gods other than Yahweh. Hence Christian witness to the character and purposes of Yahweh/Christ necessarily includes social and political action on behalf of the poor.

Christians from the earliest times have been known for providing for the material needs not only of their own community but also for their non-Christian neighbours. This practice of the early church, even in times of persecution, often dumbfounded contemporaries. Pagans received poor relief and hospitality at the hands of Christians who were often as poor as themselves. Eloquent testimony to this practice comes from an unlikely source, the ex-Christian emperor Julian ('the Apostate') who, finding it difficult in the 360s CE to

---

[6] Duane L. Christensen, *Deuteronomy 1–11*, Word Biblical Commentary (Word, 1991), p. 208.

THE MESSAGE OF MISSION

reinstitute paganism as the official religion of the Roman Empire, complained against Christians that it was 'their benevolence to strangers, their care for the graves of the dead and the pretended holiness of their lives that has done most to increase their atheism [what Christians were accused of] ... the impious Galileans support not only their own poor but ours as well'.[7]

5. A global challenge

In an interview with *Newsweek* magazine, Jimmy Carter, the former US president, called the growing disparity between rich and poor the 'ultimate challenge of the twenty-first century'. He remarked, 'there is an insensitivity even an unawareness in the rich developed world about the plight of people in the poverty stricken, under-developed world. It is a chasm that's growing and I don't see any encouraging movements in the US or Europe or Japan or other rich countries to address it.'[8] This, then, is the second challenge to contemporary mission that the Deuteronomic text presents to us; namely, *the challenge of global economic justice.*

Some figures from recent United Nations Human Development Reports[9] lend support to Carter's lament. What kind of world are we living in at the beginning of the twenty-first century? Growth in inequalities between rich and poor countries is actually worsening, with 20% of the world's population accounting for 86% of global consumption. The income gap between the fifth of the world's population living in the richest countries and the fifth in the poorest was 74 to 1 in 1998, up from 60 to 1 in 1990 and 30 to 1 in 1960. The rich nations with 20% of the world's population controls 71% of global trade in goods and services, 58% of foreign direct investment, and has 91% of all Internet users.

According to these reports, the three richest people on the planet have assets that exceed the combined gross national product of the forty-eight least developed countries. The income of the richest 1% added up to that of the poorest 57%. Among the 4.6 billion people in developing countries, almost three-fifths lack basic sanitation, one-third have no safe drinking water, one-quarter have inadequate housing, while one-fifth are undernourished, and the same proportion have no access to modern health services. One-fifth of the

[7] Cited in A. Kreider, 'Worship and Evangelism in Pre-Christendom', *Vox Evangelica* 24 (1994), p. 16.
[8] *Newsweek*, 24 May 1999, p. 25.
[9] Taken from *UN Human Development Report 2001: Making New Technology Work for Human Development* (OUP, 2001) and *UN Human Development Report 1999: Globalization with a Human Face* (OUP, 1999).

world's population are not expected to live beyond the age of forty. Eleven million children under the age of five die every year from malnutrition or easily preventable diseases – more than 30,000 on average a day. The Director General of the World Health Organization, Hiroshi Nakajima, called this 'the silent genocide on our planet',[10] and castigated Britain and America in particular for cutting back on their giving to organizations like UNICEF and the World Health Organization.

Some of the poorest countries in the world are reducing their spending on education and health care in order to buy more arms from rich countries or to pay interest on loans. The North – Europe, America and Japan – receive in debt repayments every year roughly between $20 billion and $40 billion more than what is given out in so-called 'aid'. (So-called 'aid' because 'aid' is a misnomer; it is actually a commercial loan, often given with political strings attached.) And if we were to add to this figure the loss to the developing world created by the brain drain to the West (often encouraged by Western corporations and universities), and also the massive amounts of money siphoned from poor economies and stashed away in European and American banks by corrupt developing-world politicians, businessmen and army generals, it becomes clear that the rich countries actually live on the backs of the global poor. The financial flows in the world are not from the rich to the poor, but from the poor to the rich.

Inequalities run within nations as well as between them. In cities in India, China, Russia and Pakistan magnificent private mansions and millionaires' clubs are surrounded by public squalor and deteriorating municipal services. Nations that boast of nuclear weapons and satellite technology are unable to feed and shelter their own people. Even in rich industrial nations, more than 130 million people are income poor, 34 million are unemployed and adult functional illiteracy rates average 15%.

The scandal of poverty cannot be captured in statistics alone:

In vivid terms it means precarious housing (frequently destroyed by fire, flooding or earthquakes), with large families sharing one or two rooms and sleeping together on the same bed (or adjacent piece of floor), no running water, no proper toilets, open drains, scanty health services (e.g. dental and eye care), unaffordable medicines and a meagre diet. Over one billion people go to bed at night hungry and undernourished. Poverty hits children

---

[10] Quoted in Noam Chomsky, *Powers and Prospects: Reflections on Human Nature and the Social Order* (Pluto, 1996), p. 106.

115

particularly hard (and in many societies especially girls); they are prone to disease, stunted in their physical and mental growth and often destined for an early death. If they survive into their early teens they may be forced into prostitution or hard and monotonous labour in order to scrape together a miserable income for their families.[11]

The global spread of a culture of capitalism that sees all land, water and natural resources simply as profit-making commodities, has served both to enrich some sectors of developing countries and to impoverish others. Often the hardest hit are indigenous tribal peoples whose ancestral lands are taken over by foreign multinational corporations (with inadequate compensation), farmers with smallholdings or the landless, rural poor. Global 'big business', opportunistic local politicians and international 'aid' donors often combine in projects that, while they may increase economic productivity for a nation, also deepen the misery of the poor and widen social inequalities.

Wherever we live, the challenge before us is multipronged:

i. Despite the torrent of innovation in communications technology, those with the most amount of information technology at their fingertips are often the most ignorant of what is happening in our shrinking world. Stories and statistics about the impoverishment of peoples need to be told in schools, in churches, at shareholders' meetings, and on TV in the affluent nations of the world. The church in these nations has an educational and political role to play, raising awareness of how the practices of wealthy corporations and governments may be affecting the livelihoods of communities and biological diversity in other parts of the world. Just as Jubilee 2000 awakened the public in the West to the terrible plight of chronic developing-world indebtedness, and other NGOs have challenged the pharmaceutical corporations over their indifference to HIV patients in southern Africa, so we need to bring pressure to bear on Western governments and global institutions to formulate and enforce a code of ethics for multinational corporations. Christians can also collaborate across nations to highlight cases of fraud or corruption involving local politicians and foreign business interests.

ii. We need to encourage Christian businessmen and development agencies to invest in job-creation in some of the poorest countries of the world, and in the poorest regions of better-off countries. They

[11] J. Andrew Kirk, *What Is Mission? Theological Explorations* (Darton, Longman & Todd, 1999), pp. 97–98.

need to be convinced that long-term investment for the benefit of the poor is a much better way to use capital than to look for quick short-term profit. Many local churches and NGOs in the developing world have a good track record in providing low-interest credit to sustain small-scale enterprises run by the poor. These need to be multiplied, in combination with programmes to educate women, to develop indigenous skills and knowledge systems, and to provide greater access to new technologies.

The conflict of interest in the development of new technologies between public benefits and private profits is becoming more intense due to the concentration of research in a few megacorporations of the developed world. According to the UN Human Development Report 2001 (*Making New Technologies Work for Human Development*), 'Public research, still the main source of innovation for much of what could be called poor people's technology, is shrinking relative to private research. Gaining access to key patented inputs – often owned by private firms and universities in industrial countries – has become an obstacle to innovation, sometimes with prohibitive costs.'[12]

iii. We need to work, alongside others with like concerns, for a more participatory democracy in all our nations. Economists such as Amartya Sen have argued cogently that there is a strong link between democracy and the elimination of poverty (even though the former remains a goal worth pursuing in itself). Politicians and CEOs of corporations must be held accountable to the people who are affected by the decisions they make. We need to strengthen those groups in civil society that can demand of governments that they meet the basic needs of all their citizens (the needs for adequate nutrition, shelter, health care, literacy and safe drinking water) before they spend on military defence, prestigious technologies and showcase 'development' projects. Markets too need to be democratized, made more accessible and accountable to all people and not just those involved in the import–export sectors.

One of the more imaginative social thinkers in Europe, George Monbiot, argues that true market freedom requires effective government regulations and that governments stop rescuing large corporations whenever they get into trouble. He suggests that we remove such dispensations as limited liability (which allows corporations to wriggle out of their responsibilities) and ever more generous property rights (which grant them control over such fundamental commodities as knowledge, the genome, plant varieties, land and water). Companies should be subject to freedom of information

---

[12] *Report 2001*, p. 98.

laws of the kind that permit United States citizens to scrutinize the state.

> The scale of some corporations has become an impediment to democracy, dwarfing the power of citizens and competitors. We should perhaps set a global limit, forcing all companies above a certain size to divest parts of their business. A global maximum wage, restricting managers and directors to a multiple of the salary of their lowest-paid employees, would restrain the coercive power of the rich and provide an incentive to raise the wages of the poor. And if a single corporate tax rate were set worldwide, companies would no longer be able to force governments to let them off the hook.[13]

iv. We need Christian economists, politicians and lawyers from all sections of the global church who will be more outspoken in pressing for greater transparency, democratic accountability and stronger social and environmental clauses in the World Trade Organization (WTO). Such an organization may well be the only form of protection for weaker nations from the savagery of the more powerful. International trade requires a framework of just rules to prevent bullying and evasion by the big powers. Some communities may need to be compensated by the WTO for decisions that destroy their livelihoods and/or habitats.

Why has 'globalization' become a dirty word in many poor nations? A major reason is because it cloaks the fraudulence of the US and the European Union, who preach a hypocritical rhetoric of 'free trade' to the poor while erecting barriers (in the form of quotas and tariffs – effectively taxes on trade) to imports from the poor. When, say, Ghanaian farmers export raw cocoa beans into the European Union, they face a tariff of 3%. If they tried to export processed chocolate, the tax would rise to 27%. Moreover, between them, the US and European governments subsidize their farmers by a massive $350 billion a year (six times what they give in foreign 'aid'), which allows their agricultural surpluses to flood cheaply into poor countries, depress world prices and undermine local farming.

Christian economists and politicians should argue also for alternative models of development that respect the decision-making capacity of native peoples, as well as ensure that such people have access to seeds and medicines developed from their lands. Further,

---

[13] George Monbiot, 'Freedom Through Regulation', *Guardian Weekly*, 3–9 May 2001, p. 21.

why can Christian churches and the various non-governmental organizations not put pressure on European and American banks to give back the billions of dollars they have received from developing-world politicians and military generals – money stolen from the poor? (If the Jewish lobby could do this in the case of Swiss banks and Nazi gold, why not Christians, who far outnumber Jews in Europe?)

v. We need to challenge those cultural and religious beliefs, values and social practices that imprison people in numbing poverty and give them little incentive to struggle for change. While the centuries-long oppression of the caste system is responsible for much of the rural poverty in India, in many parts of the developing world Christians have been the pioneers of education and health care for women and other marginalized groups. In oppressive communities – where the dominant religious world-views justify the domination of some by others, or encourage a passive resignation in the face of social evils and natural calamities, a fear of demons and astral forces, a disparagement of the material world and of human innovation, or the subjugation of women and foreigners – the proclamation of the gospel is economically and politically transforming.

It is, therefore, both incoherent and hypocritical to argue, in the name of a spurious 'religious tolerance', that while serving the poor may require converting their understanding of sickness and disease, or of work and gender roles, we must, under no circumstances, encourage them to change their religious world-views or cultural values. Cultural relativism is incompatible with social justice.

6. A global perspective

We return to our text in Deuteronomy. We have seen who Yahweh is, and what Yahweh does. Our third couplet (vv. 16, 19) introduces us to what Yahweh requires: *Circumcise ... your heart, and do not be stubborn any longer* (v. 16). In one word, repentance. Circumcision was the sign of covenant membership, and so it is noteworthy that from the earliest days of their national formation it is the inner disposition of the heart, shown in loyalty to Yahweh's word, that marks out the true Israelite. It is amazing that on the heels of a verse that declares how much Yahweh has set his affection on them and their forefathers – just when we expect the text to continue, 'therefore, celebrate, sit back and sing hymns and songs of praise all day' – Israel is summoned to repentance. Centuries later, Yahweh announced to the northern tribes of Israel, through the prophet Amos:

119

> You only have I known
>   of all the families of the earth;
> therefore I will punish you
>   for all your iniquities.
>
> (Amos 3:2)

God's judgment begins with his people. His grace calls forth a decisive break with sin.

One specific, practical outworking of repentance is now spelled out in the parallel verse *You shall also love the stranger, for you were strangers in the land of Egypt* (v. 19). The verbal form 'You (sg.) shall love' occurs only four other times in the Hebrew Bible: twice it used of loving God (Deut. 6:5; 11:1), once of loving your neighbour (Lev. 19:18), and once of loving the resident alien or stranger (Lev. 19:34). Here the plural 'you' is used uniquely, and it reinforces 19:34.[14]

This is the other side of Yahweh's impartiality: the people of Yahweh must have a special sensitivity towards the vulnerable non-Israelites in their midst. They are the most likely to be scapegoated and to suffer xenophobic violence when national fortunes decline. It is important too to observe the logic behind the command. We saw, in verse 18, that Yahweh's character is to take delight in loving the 'other'. Israel was a nation of 'others' in Egypt. So Yahweh, true to his character, loved and rescued them from their oppression. Having experienced Yahweh's love for the alien, they now reflect Yahweh's character by loving the aliens among them. Repentance is shown in learning to imitate Yahweh in his actions.

Jesus expanded this commandment to loving one's enemies – both one's personal enemies and one's national enemies. We shall see in chapter 9 that this was what made Jesus unpopular among his contemporaries and eventually led to his crucifixion. He distanced himself from their nationalist aspirations, their obsession with the land and the temple. He challenged them to renounce violent confrontation with Rome, and instead to love their enemies; and when he demonstrated this himself in Gethsemane and on the way to the crucifixion, he was showing them a new way to be Israel, God's counterculture, a light to the nations.

In the Deuteronomic command to love the stranger, we thus see a third challenge for our contemporary mission: it is the challenge of *overcoming nationalism*. Nationalism defies easy definition, having both an attractive and ugly side to it. The attractive side is love for

---

[14] Wright, *Deuteronomy*, pp. 150–151.

one's nation and one's culture. God wills linguistic and cultural diversity. However, the ugly side of nationalism, experienced so often in the history of the past century, is when our nation (understood either as a political entity, a nation state, or as an ethnic group within a pluralist state) so defines our identity that we cease to be critical of our nation's values and actions. The nationalist is one who speaks only of the harm that other nations or ethnic groups have inflicted on him, never of the harm that his nation has inflicted on others. The nationalist is the one who says, 'Whatever is good for us must be good for the whole world,' or 'As long as *we* are doing fine, to hell with the rest of the world.'

'It seems to me a true Christian instinct', remarks the political theologian Oliver O'Donovan, 'to defend small and imperilled cultural and linguistic communities liable to be overwhelmed by the homogenizing pressures of Western technological culture ... To justify such measures we should reflect on the loss to everyone if all such communities should disappear from the face of the earth.' But he goes on to add:

> Yet it is undoubtedly true that self-protective, xenophobic communities can be, and often have been, tyrannical to their members and threatening to their neighbours. The church has witnessed to their humane claims, allowing them neither to be overridden nor to be exaggerated ... It is the creator's will not only that human beings should live in communities and cultural homes, but that from their homes they should be able to engage peaceably with those of other communities.[15]

It would be a grave mistake to identify nationalism only with the worst examples of xenophobia, as in Pol Pot's Cambodia in the 1970s or in the Balkans and Rwanda in the 1990s. When the United States, the world's only superpower, effectively sabotages all internationally agreed treaties designed to save the planet from the ravages of human greed and selfish ambition (whether in the form of nuclear stockpiles, fossil fuel emissions, anti-personnel landmines or the trade in small arms), Christian leaders in that nation must publicly confront such dangerously narrow definitions of what constitutes America's 'national interest'. We are called to witness to God in the midst of our national insularities.

Poor immigrants and refugees in affluent Western societies are particularly vulnerable to exploitation and discrimination. Apart

---

[15] Oliver O'Donovan, *The Desire of the Nations: Rediscovering the Roots of Political Theology* (CUP, 1996), p. 267.

121

from their relative poverty, which they may share with many native citizens, they often have to grapple with colour prejudice, ignorance and feelings of cultural alienation. Christians from the majority culture must then grapple with the question 'What does it mean to love the strangers in our midst practically?' It would surely involve taking initiatives to protect immigrants from discrimination and harassment, educating them as to their civic rights (including the right to have their own places of worship), challenging the caricatures and stereotypes of such people in the popular media, and generally helping to build bridges of mutual understanding.

Today, the majority of Christians live in the countries of Asia, Africa and Latin America. The majority of these Christians are economically poor, socially marginal. The global church, then, doesn't only stand *with* the poor or even *for* the poor. It *is* the poor. As Christians our primary loyalty is to each other in the global family of Christ. It is this family that defines who we are.

Imagine the political reverberations of Christians waking up to this global perspective, of being freed from their national insularities. What if American and European Christians would publicly challenge the hypocrisy and double standards of their governments' rhetoric on 'free trade' or 'human rights'? Or, if they were to speak out on behalf of those 30,000 children who die every day, and speak with the same passion that they do for aborted foetuses in the West? Or if Tamil Christians living in self-imposed exile abroad were to show solidarity with Sinhalese churches destroyed by anti-Christian mobs in Sri Lanka? Or for Malaysian Christians to defend the rights of native Indians in Brazil against the destructive practices of Malaysian logging companies? Or for Singaporean and Japanese churches to speak out on behalf of the tribes suffering 'ethnic cleansing' in Burma – and to oppose all Japanese and Singaporean business deals with the Burmese regime?

The biggest challenge of globalization for affluent churches, then, is not how to use the Internet or satellite technology for the evangelization of the world. It is, rather, to become more self-critical about their *local* practices; for, in a globally interconnected world, what we do in our backyard may have global repercussions. But this interconnectedness also means that to tackle local problems we may have to look for global solutions. This challenges us to work at strengthening global mechanisms of governance, such as international courts of law. National sovereignty has become an idol that, in the interests of global well-being, Christians in the affluent nations need to unmask.

7. Conclusion

They stand as one people before one God in the land. They must do everything in their power to maintain justice and right relationships, and to guard equality and equity, so that the relationships for which they have been set apart can be enjoyed in all its fullness … In the light of his redemption, they cannot treat one another in a way which is incompatible with the way he has treated them. Now that they have become an exodus people, a people of journey, they are destined to keep moving forward with Yahweh, their redeemer God.[16]

In conclusion, mission is not primarily about *going*. Nor is mission primarily about *doing* anything. Mission is about *being*. It is about being a distinctive kind of people, a countercultural, multinational community among the nations. It is modelling before a sceptical world what the living God of the Bible really is like. Whether we remain all our lives in the towns of our birth or travel to the slums of Calcutta or the wastelands of Madison Avenue, we are all called to mission. For mission is to put our lives on the cutting edge where God is at work. And we have seen in this passage that God is at work challenging the false gods of culture, religion and the market-place; God is at work seeking justice for the widow, the orphan and the alien; and God is at work freeing men and women, giving them new identities that transcend those of class and tribe and nation.

What was true of Israel's calling is also true for our calling as the church of Jesus Christ: 'They are to be a people set apart, different from all other people by what they are and what they are becoming – a display people, a show-case to the world of how being in covenant with Yahweh changes a people.'[17]

---

[16] J. Gary Millar, *Now Choose Life: Theology and Ethics in Deuteronomy* (Apollos, 1998), p. 146.
[17] J. I. Durham, *Exodus*, Word Biblical Commentary (Word, 1987), p. 263.

Jonah 1 – 4
7. A resentful servant

In this central section of our book we have chosen passages which set out, in different ways, the international purposes of God. In chapter 5 we chose the classic passage which spoke of God's call of Abraham to be a blessing to the whole world. In chapter 6 we traced in Deuteronomy the character of the people of Israel as instruments in the wider world of God's sovereignty, love and justice: the people of God are to *be* a distinctive people, through whom God's character can be clearly seen. In chapter 8 we shall see, through one of the so-called 'servant songs' of Isaiah, the character of God's servant-people more clearly delineated, and the deep and wide ministry to which they are called because of the incomparability of God and his universal purposes. This chapter also reflects on these themes, but in a surprising way, because Jonah is a surprising book.

1. A wonderful story

Like so many Bible stories, Jonah is a wonderful story. It is clearly connected with a historical prophet, Jonah, son of Amittai (2 Kgs. 14:25) in the time of King Jeroboam of Israel, but we are not given any more details about Jonah than the book of his name reveals. The story shows similar features and language to the stories about the famous prophets Elijah and Elisha. The book's position in the Bible, near Hosea, Joel, Amos and Micah suggests it is *not* one of the latest books of the Old Testament (and arguments about whether the specific language of the book is 'late' or not are inconclusive). The references to Nineveh, in great concentration in Jonah 3, remind us of the time of the world-gobbling Assyrian Empire,[1] one of the

[1] Pritchard has pages of Assyrian historical texts, in which successive Assyrian kings speak in great detail of armies conquered, captives taken, booty piled up, subject kings kissing their feet, or having their heads cut off and impaled on pikes, of

cruellest and most rapacious empires of the ancient world. It is perhaps difficult for us to feel the resonances the word 'Nineveh' had for a pious Jew. We need to think of some words, names of people or places, which arouse in our minds and hearts today horror or revulsion; possible words may be Hitler, Pol Pot, Stalin, Hutu/Tutsi, Auschwitz, Cali, Srebrnica, Chechnya, Saddam Hussein ...[2] All these details about Jonah (the man and the book) connect the story with real-time life and history; it is not a fantasy, like *Winnie the Pooh*, or a parallel world as in *Lord of the Rings*.

On the other hand the story is artfully and vividly told with puns and wordplays, and there are careful structural elements too, even to the parallel use of exact numbers of words. Nearly half the book is in direct speech which adds liveliness – it needs to be *heard*, not just read. It includes elements which make you gasp and stretch your eyes – fourteen times we are told that something is *big*![3] Another striking feature is the number of questions in the book:[4] the story begins quietly 'Once upon a time ...' but the quietness only lasts for about a sentence. Again and again the questions in the story address the reader, as if to say, 'So, here and now ... what?' And Jonah is most unusual – he must be the most successful failure of all the prophets!

But how is one to *interpret* the message of the book of Jonah? One might say that the ocean of interpretations has almost capsized the book.[5] It is striking to notice the tendency of interpreters to import their own preoccupations into the text. The Fathers of the early church were fascinated by the Jonah–Jesus typology[6] (almost, but not always, forgetting how importantly *unlike* Jesus Jonah is in

---

corpses spread across vast plains and cities burned to the ground. J. B. Pritchard (ed.), *Ancient Near Eastern Texts Relating to the Old Testament* (Princeton University Press, 1955), pp. 274–317.

[2] We had better not forget that for some people, in other parts of the world, other names might come to the front of their list, which would be shocking for us – which is perhaps precisely part of the point of the book of Jonah.

[3] Big city, big wind, big storm, big fear, big fish, big (i.e. important) people, big anger, big joy. The translations of the same Hebrew word ($g\bar{a}d\hat{o}l$) vary in the different English translations.

[4] Thirteen or fourteen, depending on how you count (Hebrew has no question mark). A few of the questions are rhetorical, and one is in Jonah's prayer in ch. 2.

[5] The most brilliant, rollicking, confusing survey of interpretations over the centuries must be Y. Sherwood, *A Biblical Text and its Afterlives: The Survival of Jonah in Western Culture* (CUP, 2000). This is a jambalaya, a bouillabaisse of a book, warning us against the danger (does she avoid it herself?) of making a text a mirror in which we just see our own preoccupations, our own prejudices.

[6] Typology is a particular type of parallelism between (usually) Old Testament and New Testament, whereby an earlier event or person (the 'prototype') provides a pattern which is filled out or fulfilled by its later parallel (the 'antitype').

125

some respects); Calvin interpreted the book as a warning to submit to God's discipline; Bishop John Hooper used the book to preach before King Edward VI a warning against sedition.[7] Professor Pusey in 1860, the year after Darwin's *The Origin of Species*, spent pages on whale science. More recently some interpreters have insisted on the historical character of the book, suggesting or implying that uncertainty about this reflects disbelief in the miraculous or a failure to follow Jesus in his interpretation of the 'sign of Jonah'. But it may be that this concern for historical 'accuracy' reflects relatively modern ideas about historical truth being the only 'real' truth.[8] We can't escape the influences of these predecessors, but we can try to open our hearts to the book's questions in a fresh way.

There are elements of comedy in Jonah (laughter often helps understanding)[9] in the pious sailors, the shivering ship, the sack-clothed cattle, the fabulous plant and the militant worm, but the book as a whole quickly punctures our curiosity and quietens our amusement. Three life-and-death questions hover over the book:

- What will Nineveh do?
- What will Jonah do?
- What will God do?

Surprises lurk round each of these corners. The reader is provoked to ask, 'Where is the Lord God of Jonah?' She is also invited to consider her own life as God's representative and to see the skyline of her own city.

2. The story summarized

What notes does the story of Jonah strike that are of interest and relevance for the theme of this book? We shall summarize them by overviewing the progress of the story.

---

[7] 'Don't Rock the Ship of State!' P. Jenson, *Reading Jonah*, Grove Biblical Series B14 (Grove, 1999), p. 4.

[8] Sometimes such commentaries suggest that there are well-documented cases of people surviving long periods of time inside sea creatures. One of these stories, involving a mariner named James Bartley, has been amusingly shown to have no historical basis: E. B. Davis, 'A Whale of a Tale: Fundamentalist Fish Stories', available (August 2002) at <http://www.asa3.org/asa/pscf/1991/PSCF12-91Davis.html>. The big fish occupies a very small part of the book of Jonah (1:17 and 2:10), and needs to be kept as a minor 'bit part'.

[9] Some deny this, as if something 'funny' can't be inspired or instructive. But is this the case? And, anyway, 'comedy' is here used to mean more than just 'amusing'. Dante's *Divine Comedy* is not all amusing: it is called a comedy because it has a happy ending and is written in accessible language.

In chapter 1 Jonah is called to be a prophet, a carrier of the word of God, but the nature of his commission is utterly surprising! Unlike any other prophet he is called not just to speak *of* or *about* foreign nations, but to go *to* Nineveh. The size of Nineveh is mentioned[10] and so also is her wickedness (although we should not miss the fact that this word also has overtones of 'calamity, disaster'). Just like Elijah, or any other obedient prophet, Jonah 'sets off' in response to the divine call – but (unlike the obedient prophets) in the opposite direction. Nineveh is to the east, so Jonah heads off towards 'Tarshish', which is mentioned three times. We are not exactly sure where 'Tarshish' was, except that it was apparently in the extreme west, practically off the map of the known world, like modern English-speakers use 'Timbuktu'. The narrator quietly notes that the key thing about Tarshish is not its geographical location, but its spiritual location: *away from the presence of the LORD.*

A prophet is meant to be a person who rises up, up, up into the council and counsel of the Lord God. But this prophet goes down – down to Joppa, down into the ship's hold, and later *down to the* [bottom of the sea, the] *land / whose bars closed upon me forever* (2:6) from which he is miraculously delivered. Thus the author of the story uses narrative space as well as narrative time to unfold his story.

We are all familiar with the great wind and furious storm, and we even see the storm from the ship's point of view – the ship *thought it would break up* (1:5).[11] But the impressive aspect of this part of the story for our theme is that while Jonah is travelling away from God's presence, the sailors seem to be travelling in the opposite direction: at first they are afraid and all cry to their gods; the captain brusquely wakes Jonah and tells him to call on *his* god! When they question Jonah he tells them about the Lord, whom he worships, which makes them even more afraid. Jonah tells them what to do (throw him overboard), but they try hard to bring the ship back to shore. When this fails, they cry out to the Lord in 1:14, and then throw Jonah overboard as he has said. The storm abates and the sailors fear the Lord even more, offer sacrifice to the Lord (the phrase *to the LORD* is repeated) and make vows.

The sailors fear the storm; they are even more afraid when Jonah

[10] This is emphasized again in 3:2, 3; 4:11 and is obviously important, because 3:3 mentions that Nineveh was gigantic – it took three days to walk across it. But one possible interpretation of these words focuses not so much on size as importance: 'Nineveh was so big that it took three days to make a proper visit.'

[11] Sherwood remarks, humorously, 'the ship became a nervous wreck'! *Biblical Text*, p. 251.

tells them his story; and they are petrified (but now the word 'fear' is used with a more religious tinge) of the Lord when there is a great calm. We may compare Mark 4:41. A prophet is meant to be a man of prayer; but in this story the prophet sleeps and it is the heathen sailors who pray. Jonah has an orthodox theology (1:9) but his conduct does not match his confession. How is his advice to the sailors to be interpreted? Is it a death wish (in which case it is not the last – see 4:3, 8) or is it heroic self-sacrifice? E. J. Young thought that

> Jonah being cast into the depths of Sheol and yet brought up alive is an illustration of the death of the Messiah for sins not His own and of the Messiah's resurrection. Jonah was an Israelite and servant of the Lord, and his experience was brought about because of the sins of the nations. The Messiah was *the* Israelite and true Servant of the Lord whose death was brought about by the sins of the world.[12]

We shall discuss a little later the meaning of the 'sign of Jonah'.

In chapter 2 (which begins at 1:17 of the English Bible) the narrator of the story quietly introduces the big fish at the beginning and the end of the section: God *appointed* the big fish to swallow Jonah (a death-like deliverance); and the Lord *spoke to* the fish and it spewed Jonah out upon the dry land.

The *big* fish appears briefly, subject to God's stage directions one might say, at the beginning and end of this scene. It is a sign of Bible readers' eccentricity (off-centredness) that the fish in history has expanded to fill the whole horizon – paintings, windows, diagrams and even a pulpit in Poland. An Israeli artist has depicted Jonah disembarking from the fish in Haifa, with two suitcases, in a shtetl coat, looking tired and nauseated like a new immigrant. We'll see the same eccentricity again when scholars try to measure Nineveh with their trundle-wheels or visit Kew Gardens to check the taxonomy of the gourd plant.

The rest of the chapter is a thanksgiving psalm for the deliverance or salvation only the Lord can give (2:9). The Jews were not a seagoing people and 'the deep' stood for the precreation chaos, the valley of deepest darkness that lay at the bottom of the world. Jonah had sunk, soaking and desperate into this dark world, and from it, when he prayed, God rescued. Jonah had confessed God as Creator in 1:9; now he climaxes his thanksgiving with the acknowledgment that God is Saviour (2:9). He casts a sidelong glance at those who worship *vain idols* in verse 8, but his focus is on thanksgiving for

---

[12] E. J. Young, *Introduction to the Old Testament* (Tyndale, 1964), p. 263.

salvation. It is sobering to note that this orthodoxy produces some remarkable preaching, but it doesn't apparently moderate Jonah's later xenophobic anger or pathetic self-pity.

Chapter 3 speaks of revival in Nineveh. The plot rewinds: the Lord repeats his commission to Jonah and this time the prophet obeys. Nineveh fills the horizon. Jonah preaches an astonishingly short sermon, reported in Hebrew in five words: *Forty more days and Nineveh – overthrown* (v. 4). The writer has cleverly used a word ('overthrown') that can be taken in two ways: either it means 'flattened by judgment'; or it can mean 'turned upside down' and refer to an astonishing change of heart and life. There is an amazing response: the whole city, world-centre of evil and violence (*ḥāmās*, v. 8) repents, from the unnamed king downwards, including the animals. The king of Nineveh speaks in perfect Hebrew (like a Gestapo officer speaking English with a BBC accent), and all the Ninevites fast and pray and drape their animals in sackcloth. Finally, God 'repents'! This refers to God's unalterable commitment to change his mind when people repent, because judgment is his strange work, He is 'slow to anger and plenteous in mercy' (Ps. 103:8) and does not desire that evil persons be rewarded in kind.[13]

Subversion, terrorism and social instability threaten the world's big cities today. Can I imagine this violence being subverted by a prophetic word? Can I imagine people, large numbers of people, in these cities believing in (3:5) and all calling out mightily to (3:8) a God whom they scarcely know, from the greatest to the least? This story does not gratify my curiosity and has left no trace in Assyrian records: not many revivals are reported in the media.

Chapter 4 is another roller coaster of surprises. When God sees the Ninevites turn from their evil ways, he decides not to bring down on them the evils of his judgment. What sentence might we expect to follow such a wonderful turn of events? A rough paraphrase of the writer's wordplay in 4:1 is *And it was evil to Jonah – a big evil – and he was angry!*

Earlier, in celebrating his own deliverance (2:9), Jonah has cried out, *Deliverance belongs to the LORD!* but when this extends to the Ninevites, Jonah is furious. He complains to God that this is what he said back home; this is why he headed for Tarshish instead of Nineveh in the first place; this is what he knew about the Lord – that he is merciful – and he pours out his confession about the

---

[13] 'God does not want to be angry, and his wrath only happens when people remain stubbornly impenitent, when they leave God no alternative but to act in judgment. But even then God would much rather do them good, because he is compassionate by nature' (Clark Pinnock and Robert Brow, *Unbounded Love: A Good News Theology for the Twenty-First Century* [IVP, 1994]), p. 69.

character of God in word-perfect, orthodox terms. And then – to our surprise – he follows up his confession with a death wish which God quietly questions. Jonah does not answer, marches angrily off stage, makes himself a farmer's shack of branches and leaves, and, sweltering in the heat of the desert and of his own anger, he waits to see what will happen *now* to the city.

More surprises and wordplays follow. The Lord who appointed the big fish to swallow Jonah now appoints a plant, which rapidly grows up to give him some shade; we had better not inquire the genus of the plant: let us call it a *qîqāyôn*. What was the purpose of the *qîqāyôn*? The writer uses an ambiguous phrase which can mean 'to relieve him from his distress'; but the phrase can also mean 'to deliver him from his wickedness'. Jonah's *big* anger is supplanted by a *big* gladness for the bush. But the gladness is not to last, for the next day God makes two more appointments: a worm which attacks the *qîqāyôn* so that it withers away, and a scorching desert wind which, with the sun, troubles Jonah so badly that he again asks to die. God questions Jonah again about his anger and receives an abrupt reply which repeats his death wish.[14]

The book ends with a contrast and a question. Jonah evidently cares deeply for the *qîqāyôn*, for which he has not toiled, which he has not grown, and which comes and goes in a day. A fortiori, should not God care deeply for the huge city of Nineveh, the teeming crowds of people and children, and animals galore? Every shelter Jonah has sought (ship, hut, plant) has failed. God's question to Jonah is thirty-nine words, exactly the same number as Jonah's earlier confession. There seems almost a tit-for-tat quality about God's trumping of Jonah's complaint, or, to change the metaphor, God seems almost to be saying 'Checkmate' to Jonah. But the question hangs in the air: Can Jonah – can we – be more merciful than God? Does not his mercy abound over all creation?

3. Great is the Lord

This chapter enlarges on the themes of our preceding chapter, but in unexpected directions. The readers of Deuteronomy were reminded that the heaven, the heaven of heavens and the earth with all that is in it belonged to Yahweh (Deut. 10:14), but there was a constant danger in Israel of Old Testament times, especially because of her consciousness of being particularly chosen by God, for this view to shrink into something more ethocentric and tribal.

---

[14] 'Of course he was right to be angry, damned angry,' says Allen, and refers to an article by D. Winton Thomas on the phrase 'to death' with the force of an expletive (L. C. Allen, *Joel, Obadiah, Jonah, Micah* [Eerdmans, 1976]), p. 233.

The book of Jonah challenges these diminished views of God, not by distancing him to some untouchable, transcendent remoteness, but by unsettling our complacency that human beings can predict with certainty, and even control, the actions of God. There are uncomfortable angularities in the picture of God the book of Jonah paints for us. He is the Lord from whose presence there is no escape (1:3). He hurls a great wind and a mighty storm upon the sea (1:4), which sends experienced mariners crying fearfully to their gods. It is these sailors who come to the recognition that he does what pleases him (1:14). The Lord appoints the great fish, first to swallow Jonah down and then to vomit him up. The God whose fierce anger burns against the violence of the Ninevites (3:9) responds to their repentance by withholding his judgment (3:10). The Old Testament does not shrink from using these anthropopathic phrases to describe a God who is a living God, not some distant, impassible abstraction.[15] The Lord God appoints a *qîqāyôn* to give Jonah some shade. But hardly has this bush grown up before God appoints a worm to attack it, and a hot desert wind to make Jonah's plight even worse than before. Finally, the rhetorical question with which the book ends presupposes the narrowness of Jonah's heart and view of God; one may suppose that his unspoken protest, which lies behind God's question, is, 'How is it that God is so free and undemanding in the mercy and forgiveness he offers to the Ninevites?'

The discovered Jonah responds to the barrage of questions from the sailors by answering one of them, *I fear the LORD, the God of heaven, who made the sea and the dry land* (1:9). Structurally, this confession is the very heart of the paragraph in which it is embedded. Later in chapter 4 Jonah's description of the Lord's character corresponds exactly to what he has been taught like any pious Jew. Jonah's thanksgiving for deliverance climaxes with the resounding *Deliverance belongs to the LORD!* after a 'sideswipe' at those who worship vain idols and forsake their true loyalty (2:9, 8). But the unsettling thing for the reader of the book (and it ought to have been more unsettling for Jonah too) is that the sailors and the Ninevites seem to have grasped something about God which the orthodox Jonah has not reached. Furthermore, as the reader can quickly appreciate, the God whose mercy is so rich and wide that it covers the repentant Ninevites is also the God of the storm, the fish, the worm, the wind. He is not a God whom we can tame and box into our own neat theological kennel.

Those who move from one culture to another, especially if they

---

[15] See A. Heschel, *The Prophets*, vol. 2 (Harper Torch, 1962), chs. 1–5.

are moved by missionary loyalty to the One whom they believe to be the true and living God, often have to struggle with this largeness and surprisingness of God. Sometimes this struggle is not revealed in their biographies, which major on their victories and their confidences; but it is revealed sometimes in their diaries and private letters. In their home environment they enjoyed peaceful certainties, buttressed by the fact that these were widely shared. But travelling away from this homeland (sometimes they may have to travel only a few streets) to another culture, and especially to another religious environment, they find looming questions which they have never even considered. And the hardest questions may be the religious questions, especially in an environment where people are following one of the world's more ancient religious traditions: 'What is the significance of all this religious commitment, this spirituality, which people have been practising here since time immemorial?' Answers which seemed so clear and certain back home, shrivel up as the weight of this religiosity presses down upon the one who witnesses it.

4. Pious pagans

Attention has already been drawn to the conduct of the sailors in chapter 1. We ought to notice particularly the carefully calibrated use of the word 'fear' by the narrator in this chapter; a usage rendered particularly significant because the same word can refer just to the human emotion, but it is also used with the sense *worship* as in 1:9. At the beginning of the great storm, we are simply told *the mariners were afraid* (v. 5), a natural reaction one might think. When Jonah reveals to them that he 'fears' the Lord, the God of heaven, who made the sea and the dry land, then, we are told *the men feared a great fear and said to him, 'What is this that you have done?'* (v. 10). Finally, after further conversation with Jonah, and desperate attempts *not* to do what he has advised, they pray and throw him into the sea, whereupon there is a great calm. Then, the story says (literally), *the men feared with a great fear the* LORD (v. 16). They also offered a sacrifice to the Lord and made vows. It is unclear if we are to understand that they did this there and then; probably they did not, but instead, unaware of what had happened to Jonah, they did this at their journey's end. Thus as God's appointed but disobedient messenger is swallowed up in the storm, which is a symbol of divine anger, these sailors, never known for their sincere practice of religion, appear to be more devout and serious than the preacher!

It is also instructive to pay close attention to the use and distribution of divine names in Jonah.[16] The word Yahweh (LORD) is used 25 times; and *'elōhîm* (God) 15 times, the latter 7 times in conjunction with 'LORD'. 'Yahweh' is the covenant name of the God who revealed himself to the Israelites; 'Elohim' is a generic word for God in the Old Testament. In Jonah the name 'Yahweh' comes 19 times in the early episodes (1:1 – 3:3), which concern the prophet's adventures. But in the story of the amazing events in Nineveh (3:5–10) the more general word 'God' is used 5 times. When Jonah again comes to the forefront (4:1–5) the name 'Yahweh' occurs 4 times. But then, in the remaining verses, the pattern breaks up as 'Yahweh', 'Elohim' and 'Yahweh Elohim' all occur.

Can we make any steady inferences from these curious facts? Some earlier scholars, using the different divine names, proposed identifying different sources, a process which had been used to produce an elaborate source analysis of the Pentateuch. It is very uncertain that this is a fruitful procedure, especially with Jonah, and anyway scholars these days are more interested in the final form of biblical narratives than in highly speculative source criticism. It seems likely that the author is partly moved, like any writer, by the desire for stylistic variation. But we may also be stimulated by his usages in chapters 1 and 3 to ask questions about the spirituality of the pagan sailors and the Ninevites. How much knowledge of the Lord God did the sailors have? Jonah's reported message to the Ninevites is not expressed in covenantal terms. We have no detailed knowledge of what he said to them, other than his warning that the city was about to be turned upside down. When they repented with such startling thoroughness, how much knowledge of the true God, Yahweh, informed their repentance? It is Jonah in this story who makes the careful orthodox confessions about God's nature. And yet it seems as if there is something more than admirable about the sailors' 'fear', their desperate generosity to Jonah, and their urgent prayers that they may not be 'guilty of innocent blood'. Similarly the extraordinary city-wide repentance in Nineveh, the world-capital of evil (as one might think) seems to contrast favourably with the hard-heartedness of Jonah the prophet of the true God. The author of the book does not *spell out* his views on these matters in any explicit way; so we had better avoid constructing elaborate theories about different paths to God from his hints.

But we may all receive this story of Jonah and his mission as an instrument by which we can review our own knowledge and under-standing of God *and also* the implications of that understanding for

[16] See F. D. Kidner, 'The Distribution of Divine Names in Jonah', *Tyndale Bulletin* 21 (1970), pp. 126–128.

those outside the pale of Christianity who may be seeking God in their own way, under the canopy of their own culture and religion. Some commentators on the book of Jonah have become almost anti-Semitic in their harsh comments on the hard-hearted self-centredness of Jonah.[17] Perhaps they have not experienced the stress involved in living in the centre of a society and culture strongly hostile to Christianity. In such circumstances it is possible for one's own reserves of fascination, hospitality and love for such people to be replaced by pessimism, weariness and a responsive hostility. For obvious reasons this is not what one reads about in missionary biographies, but it does exist.

Henry Frost was Hudson Taylor's best friend until near the end of Taylor's life. He was born in January 1858, was involved from the very beginning in 1888 in the setting up of the North American component of the China Inland Mission (CIM), of which he was the leader for over forty years, and he died in 1945. In 1932, when he was seventy-four, he wrote his autobiography, 900 pages of double-spaced typing, in 81 chapters, which was never published. It is certain that Geraldine (Guinness) Taylor consulted this story in writing her book about Frost, called *By Faith: Henry Frost and the CIM*, published in 1938. One of the strongest principles of the CIM was in no way to ask for money, and Frost was one of the most rigorous appliers of this principle. He collected some early missionary boxes but refused to use them. If money was designated to China, it all went to China; if a gift was designated for ice cream, ice cream was bought – even if other things were badly needed.

Often when there were recruits at home, supplies went down; Frost interpreted this as an opportunity for the new recruits to exercise faith and to pray. (With the quick insight of a child, Frost's young son Inglis, aged ten, when faced with another miserable meal, asked, 'Have we got some more candidates?' On another occasion the same year, facing nothing but potatoes, the same child looked round at the glum faces and said, 'Well, let us gird up our loins and be cheerful!')[18] When Taylor later, in undoctrinaire fashion, suggested that information about the $6,000 needed for the purchase of a new mission home might be mentioned in *China's Millions*, Frost wrote a long letter explaining how he couldn't possibly do this. 'This was the first difference of opinion which I had had with Mr Taylor, and I greatly grieved over its occurrence.'[19] Even Geraldine Taylor suggested that Frost may have shown 'undue

---

[17] Yvonne Sherwood gives a catalogue of horrible adjectives: *Biblical Text*, p. 65.

[18] H. Frost, 'Years That Are Past: The Story of a Life and Work' (unpublished typescript held at OMF UK office), ch. 43.

[19] Ibid., ch. 48.

sensitiveness' in money matters. There was an all-or-nothing, very black-and-white side to Frost's thinking, which may have become more pronounced as he grew older.

By late 1890 Archibald Orr-Ewing, an independently wealthy CIM missionary, visiting America, thought Frost looked worn out and offered to pay all expenses for a visit to China, the first of many benefactions. Thus Frost left in January 1891, returning in July, the first of four long trips. He doesn't say much about his wife in his memoirs, except one long paragraph of tribute; but she must have been an outstanding woman of faith and prayer. Frost's first view of the Chinese was on the lower deck of his steamer: 'dressed in soiled garments, eating common looking food, smoking opium, gambling and disputing over things great and small ... however much one wanted to think well of the Chinese, one could not but conclude that they were a dirty and low-living lot'.[20] It is possible that this may be an accurate description of one group of people, but it is a pity to have to report that, despite Frost's long-continued passion for mission to China and to the Chinese, there is not a single sharply focused picture of an individual Chinese in all his memoirs, nor any passages showing critical understanding or culturally sensitive sympathy with Chinese practices and customs. Heathen darkness is the whole story; Chinese New Year is diabolism let loose; only the scenery is occasionally beautiful: 'the land was fair beyond portraying; but heathenism was dark beyond describing'.

5. Great cities in need of God

It is hard to read the story of Jonah and his mission to Nineveh without thinking of the needs of the great cities of the world, and especially of their need for God. Even the story of Jonah tells us much more about Nineveh than about Jonah's message to these people. And it is not difficult to imagine that the very *word* Nineveh chilled the hearts of Jonah and his compatriots. Nineveh was the denial of everything Jerusalem, its polar opposite, stood for.

Two hundred years ago only 5% of the world lived in cities;[21] the world's largest city was Beijing, which had reached one million inhabitants in 1770. In 1800 two of the world's largest cities (London and Paris) were in the 'Christian' world. In the following century (the so-called 'Great Century' of missions) many of the

[20] Ibid., ch. 30.
[21] The data in the following paragraph are taken from David B. Barrett and Todd M. Johnson, *World Christian Trends AD30–AD2200* (William Carey Library, 2001), Global Diagrams 21 and 54, amplified by data from David B. Barrett, *World-Class Cities and World Evangelization* (New Hope, 1986).

world's large cities were evangelized, so that by 1900 the five largest cities – London, New York, Paris, Berlin, Chicago – had become strong resource centres for Christian mission. At that time about 14% of the world lived in cities and there were twenty cities of one million inhabitants. Since 1900 the number of megacities[22] has multiplied twenty-fold to 402; and the number of urban inhabitants has gone up almost tenfold, from 233 million to 2,882 million (48% of the world's population). It is predicted that by 2050 there will be 7 billion urbanites (80% of the world's population), 900 megacities, 220 cities of over 4 million, and 80 cities over 10 million. By 2050 the world's five largest cities will be Shanghai, Mexico, Beijing, Mumbai, Calcutta. What these numbers summarize and simplify is the most massive migration of people in the whole of history – from the countryside into cities. These numbers also show that the significant successes of Christian urban mission in the nineteenth century have not been continued in the twentieth century: the number of Christian disciples as a proportion of all urban dwellers has been decreasing. Christians also need to note that while in the West a significant amount of de-urbanization has been taking place, people are still moving in vast numbers to the cities of the developed world, some of which are or may be strongly hostile to Christian missionary witness in the coming decades.

It is not suggested that we should raise our voices about these massive trends or try to throw our weight around in international power plays. But it does seem that there is a massive imbalance in the proportion of Christian resources devoted to Christian presence, witness and mission in the huge and growing cities of the South. It is suggested that this context may give a special resonance to God's final, quiet question to Jonah, *Should I not be concerned about Nineveh, that great city?* (4:11).

6. The sign of Jonah

Matthew and Luke both record an incident in which Jesus talks about the 'sign of the prophet Jonah' (Matt. 12:38–42; 16:1–4; Luke 11:16, 29–32). According to Matthew some Jewish leaders approach Jesus,[23] address him politely (although a hint of threat may be implied) as teacher, and indicate a wish to see a sign. Luke sets the scene more generally, with a mention of 'others' who wanted to test Jesus, and Jesus' reply being given amid increasing crowds. Jesus is being invited, despite the readily available evidence of works of

---

[22] A 'megacity' is a city of one million or more inhabitants.
[23] Matt. 16:1 says that they intended 'to test him'.

healing and deliverance he has already done, to 'confirm his own credibility in some miraculous way'.[24]

The robust response Jesus gives indicates clearly that he interprets the request in a negative way. He indicts his questioners and the people they represent as 'an evil and adulterous generation' (Matt. 12:39). This language does not refer to their sexual habits; it is language that harks back to the disobedience and infidelity of Israel to Yahweh in Old Testament times, which ended up with them being sent into exile in Assyria and in Babylon. Jesus indicates that *this* generation of Jews, who are privileged to experience in their own towns and villages the personal visitation of God through Jesus himself, are no better than their Old Testament counterparts. The signs Jesus has already done have not aroused the response of faith they deserve; instead, more 'evidence' is being demanded – and some are even attributing Jesus' power to Satan!

To such unbelievers no sign will be given except the sign of Jonah. Both Matthew and Luke indicate that the sign of Jonah for 'this generation' involves a contrast. The contrast is between the Ninevites who repented at the preaching of Jonah and Jesus' contemporaries who do *not* repent (i.e. turn from their sins in trustful commitment to God) at the preaching of Jesus who is a 'greater than Jonah'.[25] Matthew alone records that Jesus made a comparison as well as a contrast: in 12:40 Jesus says, 'As Jonah was three days and three nights in the belly of the sea monster, so will the Son of man be three days and three nights in the heart of the earth.' Here there seems to be an explicit parallel between the experience of Jonah in the heart of the sea for 'three days and three nights' and Jesus' own experience in the heart of the earth before his resurrection.

So what exactly *is* the 'sign of Jonah'? The parallel drawn here between Jesus and Jonah has spawned a huge and confusing variety of interpretations, so much so that a French scholar, Yves-Marie Duval has written a 748-page book summarizing some of these interpretations from Jerome onwards.[26] Sherwood admits that Jonah gains from keeping such superlative company; but she

---

[24] I owe this form of words to my colleague John Nolland, in his forthcoming commentary on Matthew.

[25] Matthew and Luke both indicate that Jesus also spoke of the Queen of Sheba in this conversation. She came from the ends of the earth to hear the wisdom of Solomon and 'something greater than Solomon is here'. The foreign men who repented at Jonah's preaching, and the foreign queen who travelled a great distance to hear the wisdom of Solomon, both put the unresponsive, undiscerning contemporaries of Jesus in an unfavourable light.

[26] Y.-M. Duval, *Le Livre de Jonas dans la littérature chrétienne grecque et latine: sources et influences du commentaire sur Jonas de saint Jérome* (Etudes Augustiniennes, 1973).

complains that the twinning of Jonah and Jesus acts like a huge magnet gathering interpretations, especially those focusing on the passion of Christ, and that Jonah himself loses his voice, his script and his outline, becoming instead a ventriloquist for Christ. Specifically, Jonah's rebellion against God's call is lost; so also is the messiness of the book and the uncertainty whether Jonah is to be viewed as a hero or as a narrow nationalist, the grudge, glowering over God's too-easy forgiveness of the Ninevites.[27]

We should not treat the story of Jonah allegorically and look for parallels in every detail between the life of Jonah and the life of Christ. This sort of arbitrary treatment gives results which are misleading (e.g. drawing a parallel between Jonah asleep in the ship's hold and Jesus asleep in the boat in the storm-tossed lake) or bizarre (as when the sailors may be compared to the apostles or the Romans or the Jews or Pontius Pilate washing his hands of responsibility for Jesus' fate). It is better to stick to the simple, unelaborated references in Matthew and Luke, and to conclude that the 'sign of Jonah' points in two directions. In the first place, it points to the resurrection of Jesus as the sign which points above all others to the fact that 'a greater than Jonah is here'. Jonah's extraordinary deliverance from death precedes his preaching in Nineveh with the astonishing results which followed. Jesus will also experience an even more extraordinary deliverance – after a similar short time 'in the heart of the earth' he will be raised from the dead, in vindication of all his mighty words and works, and of all he claimed to be. Thus, as with many New Testament interpretations of the Old, the focus is Christological. Just as all rivers flow towards the sea, so the Old Testament scriptures point towards Christ. In the second place, the 'sign of Jonah' lies in the repentance of the Ninevites. In the judgment Jesus constantly foretells in his parables and teaching, the Ninevites will 'rise up'[28] in condemnation of Jesus' contemporaries because they (the Ninevites) repented at the teaching of Jonah, whereas the Jews, who were favoured by a visit from the 'Son of Man' himself, were unbelieving and sceptical towards his teaching and claims. Thus the special privileges the Jewish people had because of their election, described in previous chapters, will not mean their exemption from God's judgment; rather, it will mean that they will be more severely judged, because the greater the revelation received, the heavier the penalties for rejecting it.

Two questions from the final chapter of Jonah linger in the air as

[27] Y. Sherwood, *Biblical Text*, pp. 17ff.
[28] In biblical court scenes, the deliberations were conducted while participants were seated; the judge stood up to deliver his verdict.

we finish this reflection on his book and its implications for mission. One is the twice-repeated question *Is it right for you to be angry?* (4:9). Jonah is angry about God's treatment of the Ninevites, and angry about God's treatment of him and the bush sheltering him. The second question is *Should I not be moved to tears about Nineveh?* (v. 11). The picture of Jesus moved to tears over Jerusalem and Paul's picture of God's stretched-out hands towards his own people, come to mind (Luke 19:41; Rom. 10:21). Professor Limburg finishes his commentary on this book with a reference to the Jonah window in Christ Church cathedral in Oxford, England, where Jonah is sitting under the *qîqāyôn*. 'His focus – and the focus of the viewer – is on the city of Nineveh. We see the houses, the shops, and the streets, and cannot but recall the words: "Should I not care about Nineveh, that great city … ?"' [29] Can we see? Do we care?

---

[29] J. Limburg, *Jonah* (SCM, 1993), p. 98.

Isaiah 49:1–26
8. A ready servant

In AD 177, for reasons which are unclear, a ferocious persecution broke out against Christians of Asiatic, Greek and Gallic background in Lyons, France, and Vienne, a town 20 miles away down the river Rhône. There were forty-eight known martyrs, and the story of what happened, told in a letter sent by an anonymous survivor to the churches of Asia and Phrygia, is described by W. H. C. Frend as 'for simplicity, sincerity and for the sheer horror of the events it describes ... unmatched in the annals of Christian antiquity'.[1] First, the Christians were banned from baths and market; then excluded from all public places; then hounded and attacked openly, assaulted, beaten and stoned. Finally, they were dragged to the forum, accused, and, after confessing to be Christians, were flung into prison. There, under torture, about ten gave way and recanted; others had red-hot brazen plates applied to their most tender parts; some were scourged, thrown to wild beasts, or sat in a red-hot iron chair (the 'frying-pan') which fried their bodies and choked them with smoke; finally a 15-year-old boy, Ponticus, and a young woman, Blandina, were brought into the forum: the boy died without yielding; Blandina was scourged, thrown to the wild beasts, put in the frying pan, and at last thrown into a basket and presented to a bull which tossed her to death. The bodies of the victims were left unburied for six days, then burnt, and their remains cast into the river, a stratagem, it appears, by which the pagans hoped to hinder their resurrection.[2]

This is just one of the stories from those times. Throughout the

---

[1] W. H. C. Frend, *Martyrdom and Persecution in the Early Church* (Basil Blackwell, 1965), p. 1.

[2] The text of these events is to be found in H. J. Lawlor and J. E. L. Oulton, *Eusebius: The Ecclesiastical History and the Martyrs of Palestine*, 2 vols. (SPCK, 1927). The text is found in Eusebius, Book 5.1.1–63.

history of the advance and recession of the global Christian movement, there are stories of persecution, suffering and martyrdom. In 1989 my wife and I walked in a park in Beijing with a Christian Chinese professor who had been exiled for 22 years to the far north of China, only being released soon after his wife had died. 'One should not speak evil of the Communists,' he said. 'When you open your mouth you should bear witness to God.' Repeatedly the good news has been spread by those on the underside, those of no account, those who have been despised, underestimated and rejected: Filipina housemaids in the Gulf; Sudanese refugees in other parts of Africa; black students in Russia or China; and by Christians in Western churches who are again and again pushed to the margins of society.

Isaiah 49 is a message about mission from the underside, a refugee project. The church is not necessarily strongest when it is most powerful. The situation presupposed and addressed by these chapters in the second half of the book of Isaiah is that the Jews, after the destruction of Jerusalem in 587 BC, are in exile in Babylon. Structurally, these twenty-seven chapters of Isaiah fall into three groups of nine (note the refrain in 48:22 and 57:21). In the central group, where our chapter falls, the emphasis is shifting from a vision of Cyrus as God's agent to deliver the Jews from Babylon (a topic discussed in chapter 4 of this book) to a vision of the Servant as God's agent for the restoration of Zion.

The main themes of these chapters are the incomparability of God and his universal purposes: he is the Holy One of Israel and of the nations; he is the Creator and Ruler of time and space. His intention is to fulfil his purposes through his servant, and there is emphasis on the themes of obedience, witness and endurance as the characteristics of the servant. Who is the servant? Apparently it is Israel to begin with; but the nation Israel proves unbelieving, reluctant, stubborn and rebellious. So God's purposes narrow down to a remnant and, finally, to one individual. These chapters, and especially the so-called 'Servant Songs' within them, deeply influenced the mind, the life and the teaching of our Lord. He is the Servant above all; he is the Israel for Israel; all that Israel wasn't, he is; all that Israel was, he transcends.

1. Components of God's call (vv. 1–6)

In verse 1 the servant himself speaks (unlike 42:1ff. where the servant is spoken of in the third person). *Listen to me* ... indicates his authority; it is not traditional prophetic phraseology: the prophet usually says, 'Thus says the Lord ... '

What is immediately striking about the servant's self-description is the range of his vision, described in the framework of the song (vv. 1a, 6b) and of primary relevance to the theme of this book. The servant is called to a far-reaching, international ministry; call and designation are matters of international significance. Coastlands, distant peoples, nations and the ends of the earth are summoned to pay attention. The word translated 'coastlands' characteristically appears in these chapters with other phrases or names describing distant places: Tarshish, Put, Lud, Lebanon, the nations … (see e.g. 60:3; 66:19; 40:15; 41:1).

The servant is conscious that God's purposes for him stretch back to the time when he was still within his mother's womb. God's call reached back far behind any decisions, any choices, any mistakes that he, the servant, had made. God was at work prenatally and personally, calling him, designating him by name.

From verse 2 it is clear that God had protected and prepared him for an arduous and difficult task. Since he was called to a prophetic ministry, God made his mouth like a sword, a sharp sword that did its job; God made him a polished arrow, which flies straight and fast to its target. When God calls a person to a prophetic ministry, he equips that person for the task. Later in Isaiah it is said:

> my word …
>> shall not return to me empty,
> but it shall accomplish that which I purpose,
>> and succeed in the thing for which I sent it.
>
> (Is. 55:11)

Coming out of metaphorical language into direct speech in verse 3, the speaker is called 'my servant, Israel' and told that he will display God's beauty. Christopher North translates, 'God points to Israel as his crowning achievement', and suggests that the meaning is almost 'Yahweh will show himself off by means of Israel'.[3]

The wide and long loveliness of this commission is lost on the servant, who initially replies in self-centred pity[4] in verse 4: I have toiled for nothing; I am exhausted; I have spent my strength for emptiness, chaos, vapour; it all amounts to nothing. But then, with a sudden and strong change of tone he says, 'But for sure …'[5] and

---

[3] C. R. North, *The Second Isaiah* (Clarendon, 1964), p. 143.

[4] In the Hebrew text the first person pronoun is in emphatic position.

[5] An adversative particle denoting strong contrast is used. See B. K. Waltke and M. O'Connor, *An Introduction to Biblical Hebrew Syntax* (Eisenbrauns, 1990), p. 671.

recalls that his cause and reward are with his God. What do these words mean? The first word, *mišpāṭ*, is a very common word, with judicial connotations, used 425 times in the Old Testament, most frequently in the prophets, and especially in Isaiah. The second word, *pe'ullâ*, is used 57 times in the Old Testament, 17 times with God as subject, and it is an exclusively poetic word, meaning wages, punishment, reward, payment. Together these words indicate that 'Yahweh will assuredly declare his confidence in me';[6] that the servant will in due course be vindicated, whatever he has to suffer in the meantime.

Words of commissioning follow in verses 5 and 6. First, although the servant is called 'Israel' in verse 3, here his task includes that of bringing Jacob back, gathering Israel again; these words describe a shepherd's pastoral ministry. It may be that the last two phrases of verse 5 reflect that a shepherd's work was characteristically despised as an unclean task – but the servant finds it an honour, and realizes his need for divine strength to carry it through. In verse 6 Yahweh enlarges his commission: re-establishing the tribes of Jacob, restoring the offshoots of Israel (a quick change to a horticultural metaphor) are too light a task. The Lord says, *I have set you for a light to nations, to* be *my salvation to the ends of the earth!*[7] Only time will reveal who can most accurately be described as the *embodiment* of God's saving power to the ends of the earth.

2. Transformational ministry (vv. 7–12)

a. Universal homage (v. 7)

In these verses we have an elaboration of some of the implications of the servant's calling. In verse 7 he is apparently the object of international derision and contempt, a 'slave' with all the age-long reverberations of misery that word contains. But to our surprise, in the presence of this person, kings rise up and princes prostrate themselves (both actions being signs of respect and even subordination). Why should this be so? Because in some unexplained way the presence of the Lord is discerned in this person, the Lord, the Redeemer, the Holy One, the faithful One and the Choosing One.

---

[6] C. R. North, *Second Isaiah*, p. 55, a translation later (p. 189) explained as meaning 'Yahweh will give a favourable verdict'.

[7] My own rather literal translation of the text at the end of v. 6. 'The vocabulary of salvation is more abundant in Isaiah than in any other prophet' (J. A. Motyer, *The Prophecy of Isaiah* [IVP, 1993]), p. 383, n. 3.

b. A new covenant (v. 8)

Yahweh pays the closest attention to his servant, who is the object of his favour, answering him, helping him, keeping him – for what purpose? He is to be, in his own person, a covenant for the people.[8] What people? In the first instance the reference must be to Israel, for the promise includes re-establishment in the land God gave Israel years before (Deut. 4:21), and the repair of its ruins. But, as the following verses show, Yahweh has much wider purposes in view. A covenant usually implies a special relationship, from which others are excluded; but from the very beginning of the Old Testament, when God called Abraham, he was intended to be, in his descendants, a means of blessing to the whole world (Gen. 12:1–3).[9]

c. The release of prisoners (v. 9a); the return of exiles (vv. 9b, 10)

The servant is to call prisoners out of their dungeons,[10] and the returning exiles are pictured as a flock of sheep, feeding safely, wandering peacefully, led by a caring shepherd, protected from the scorching desert sun, and brought to drink at fresh springs.

d. Ingathering from all corners of the earth (vv. 11, 12)

The prophet sees in his mind's eye (Lo!) a much wider multitude on the high road to Zion. No word for east is found in verse 12, because the returning refugees (from Babylon) have already been mentioned. But people are coming from the north and the west and also from the land of Syene. Most probably this points south, towards the area in Egypt we know today as Aswan (note the shared consonants), and not to China, as some missionaries once hoped. But the unique word may be used in the way we today might use the word 'Timbuktu' to mean 'the back of beyond', 'the outermost fringes of the inhabited world'.

3. Contrasting responses (vv. 13–14)

An unknown cantor invites nature to break out in praise at this wonderful work of the Lord. It is as if the joy of his redeeming work overflows into the inanimate world (see also 42:10–12; 54:23; 52:9;

---

[8] The expression is an unusual one, literally 'a covenant of people'. It is similar to the expression 'a light to nations' in 42:6.

[9] See further W. A. VanGemeren (ed.), New International Dictionary of Old Testament Theology and Exegesis, vol. 1 (Paternoster, 1996), p. 752.

[10] 'Sitting in darkness' was a metaphor for imprisonment: see 42:7; 47:5.

55:12–13). It is a sharp surprise and sadness (though not unprecedented)[11] that the only dissenting voice, the only one who refuses to join in this song of praise, is Zion herself. She remains disbelieving; forsakenness and forgottenness fill her horizon. But the Lord refuses to be disappointed.

4. Renewal of the divine promises (vv. 15–26)

In these words the earlier promises of the Lord are renewed and reinforced. Even a nursing mother may come to neglect the children she has borne, but the Lord will never forget Zion.[12] Although self-mutilation is forbidden in Israel, the Lord has tattooed on his palms sketches of the city he loves. In verse 17 the destroyers and demolition experts are disappearing as the children return;[13] and in verse 18 the picture merges and changes from a mother delighted at her reappearing family to a bride excitedly putting on her wedding ornaments.[14] Verses 19–21 picture a city seething with returning refugees, children of Zion's period of *bereavement*. Zion, the mother, is almost scratching her head and saying, 'Where have all these come from?' and the returnees are saying, 'Get out of my way!'

The Lord signals to the nations[15] and the wider family continues to gather. Zion's children, formerly slaves, are now carried in by kings and queens, who show their respect in elaborate gestures.[16] An impossible rescue has been achieved (vv. 24, 25) because the Lord himself was leading the rescue project; and, in the graphic and ghastly language of verse 26, Zion's enemies will self-destruct.[17] The purpose of this tremendous drama is summarized in two phrases:

[11] See the way the complaint of 40:27 follows the assurances of 40:1–26.
[12] 'All the commentators remark that nowhere in the Old Testament, except in Jeremiah 31:20, is the love of Yahweh for his people so poignantly expressed as here' (North, *Second Isaiah*), p. 194.
[13] The Hebrew text (and NRSV margin) read, *Your children come swiftly; your destroyers and those who laid you waste go away from you*. There is an obvious play on the words *bānāyik*, which means 'your children', and *bonāyik*, which means 'your builders'.
[14] The picture of Zion as the Lord's wife appears a little later, in 50:1; 54:1–8.
[15] It seems as if the Lord himself is the standard-bearer at the head of his 'troops'!
[16] Similar abandon is shown by the gestures of the Shunamite woman to Elisha (2 Kgs. 4:27); and by Mary to Jesus (Matt. 28:9). Motyer says, 'The picture is of political subservience but the reality is the recognition of spiritual indebtedness' (*The Prophecy of Isaiah* [IVP, 1993]), p. 395.
[17] The language could possibly refer to Zion's enemies being reduced, in siege conditions, to literal cannibalism to avoid starvation. North suggests that it means, 'the panic-stricken Babylonians will consume one another in internecine strife' (*Second Isaiah*), p. 196.

Zion will know (v. 23) and *all flesh* will know (v. 26) that *I am the* LORD.

5. Following Jesus the servant

Four passages in Isaiah which share a similar character have been given the title 'The Servant Songs' because of their common themes and focus. The passages are Isaiah 42:1–4; 49:1–6; 50:4–9; 52:13 – 53:12. Christians have always found Isaiah 53 an extraordinary preview or prediction of the redemptive sufferings of Jesus. In his earliest sermons after Pentecost, Peter several times uses the term *pais* (servant or child) to describe Jesus (Acts 3:13, 26; 4:27, 30). It is clear that the teaching of these 'Servant Songs' profoundly influenced Jesus' own understanding of his person and mission.

It seems that some Jewish writers by New Testament times interpreted these passages of a forthcoming Messianic figure, although the Targum, in particular, is careful *not* to entertain the idea of a *suffering* Messiah.[18] The evidence that these songs influenced Jesus' self-understanding and thus the Gospel writers' understanding of him also, includes the following:

- At his baptism Jesus heard the words from heaven 'You are my beloved Son, with whom I am pleased' (Mark 1:11). This seems to be an echo of Isaiah 42:1. In Mark 10:43–45 Jesus defines greatness for his disciples in terms of service, adding for reinforcement, '*For* the Son of Man came not to be served but to serve, and to give his life a ransom for many.' It seems that the language of ransom and the phrase 'for many' echoes Isaiah 53:11, 12. The striking thing about this particular saying is that 'Son of Man' language is associated with exaltation, victory and power in Jewish thinking; but Jesus uses *this* language with reference to his redeeming death.
- At the Last Supper Jesus specifically refers to the text 'He was counted among the lawless' as 'this scripture must be fulfilled in me' (Luke 22:37; Is. 53:12).
- We may also refer to Jesus' repeated teaching that he would fulfil his mission through rejection, suffering and death, thus fulfilling the role of the servant portrayed in Isaiah 53.
- But it is not only with reference to his death that these Servant Songs are used. In his famous early message at the Nazareth synagogue Jesus seems particularly to refer to Isaiah 61:1–2;

[18] See J. Jeremias's article on *pais theou* in G. Kittel and G. Friedrich (eds.), *Theological Dictionary of the New Testament*, vol. 5 (Eerdmans, 1964–), pp. 654–717.

there are many common themes between this later chapter of Isaiah and the Servant Songs.

- Matthew indicates that Jesus' healing ministry was a fulfilment of the prophetic saying (Matt. 8:17; Is. 53:4), and also quotes Isaiah 42:1–4 in full with reference to Jesus' general demeanour.
- John quotes Isaiah 53:1 with reference to Jewish unbelief in Jesus (John 12:38).

Michael Green has identified utter obedience, fearless witness and the endurance of innocent suffering as especially relevant themes from the Servant Songs, which run through the ministry of Jesus.[19] To these we may add that the Servant Songs envisage that the Servant's ministry has worldwide repercussions. One of Jesus' profoundest parabolic actions was to take a towel and basin at the Last Supper and wash his disciples' feet, fully conscious of who he was, and what he was going to do. He drove home the lesson with the words

if I, your Lord and Teacher, have washed your feet, you also ought to wash one another's feet. For I have set you an example, that you also should do as I have done to you. Very truly, I tell you, servants are not greater than their master, nor are messengers greater than the one who sent them. If you know these things, you are blessed if you do them.

(John 13:14–17)

The lesson could scarcely be clearer – we who follow in the path of Jesus the Servant need to be identified by our humble and quiet service.

6. Mission from the underside

It is an extraordinary fact that the far-ranging visions and hopes expressed in this chapter of Isaiah did not arise among one of the world-conquering superpowers of the day: the hopes were nurtured and developed among an exiled, refugee people, battered and bruised by successive waves of aggression and punishment.

In some circles today it has become commonplace to criticize the Western missionary movement as a collaborator with, or even an instrument of, the juggernaut of Western imperial and economic expansion. This criticism has been something of a blunderbuss,

---

[19] Michael Green, *Called to Serve* (Hodder & Stoughton, 1964), pp. 12–13.

scattering grapeshot over a wide area, and Brian Stanley has rendered a helpful service in demonstrating some of the places where the criticism has hit the target, and some of the places where it has missed.[20] In Sabah, East Malaysia (formerly called British North Borneo), the widespread mission work of the Australian missionary Hudson Southwell was so effective that, over a wide area of the rural areas, Christianity was known in Malay as *agama Tun Southwell*, 'the religion of Tun [an honorific] Southwell'. His credibility may have been enhanced because he was imprisoned in Borneo during the Second World War, when he might have escaped to safety in Australia.

Andrew Walls has noted that 'Of all the transformations of Christianity which have taken place since 1789, perhaps the most remarkable is the shift of its geographical and cultural centre of gravity.'[21] It has not always been remembered that the huge majority of those who have worked to bring about this shift are unknown and unremembered natives, not foreigners. A few examples may be helpful, while still remembering that these are far outnumbered by those who have not risen to the dignity of being historically noted and recorded.

William Carey saw clearly that if Christianity were to spread in India, it would be through Indian Christians. For this reason, he wrote of the importance of 'the forming of our native brethren to usefulness, fostering every kind of genius, and cherishing every gift and grace in them; in this respect we can scarcely be too lavish in our attention to their improvement. It is only by means of native preachers we can hope for the universal spread of the Gospel through this immense Continent.'[22]

In West Africa, Bishop Samuel Ajayi Crowther (1806–91), the first African bishop in the Anglican communion, bishop of the Niger territories, was an able, devoted and humble figure, both gracious and heroic and a legend in his own lifetime, together with his hundreds of co-workers.

Regarding East Africa, Raphael Akiri has written a doctoral thesis on the role of indigenous agents in the growth of Christianity in central Tanzania.[23] In this dissertation he criticizes the tendency of

[20] Brian Stanley, *The Bible and the Flag* (Apollos, 1990).

[21] Tim Dowley (ed.), *The History of Christianity* (Lion, 1977), p. 546.

[22] These words come from the eighth principle of 'The Bond of the Missionary Brotherhood of Serampore', originally printed at the Brethren's Press, Serampore, in 1805; conveniently available in A. H. Oussoren, *William Carey, Especially his Missionary Principles* (A. W. Sijthoffs, 1945), pp. 279–280.

[23] Raphael Akiri, 'The Growth of Christianity in Ugogo and Ukaguru (Central Tanzania): A Socio-historical Analysis of the Role of Indigenous Agents' (PhD thesis, Edinburgh University, 1999).

scholars to be obsessed with what is written down, because this de-privileges those societies where important traditions have been handed on by word of mouth for generations. He tells many stories of those who spread Christianity in Tanzania: Yohana Makeela, a rainmaker turned pioneer missionary; Danieli Mbogo, a trumpeter; Canon Andrea Muraka (c. 1871–1935) a trusted leader and great pastor, an exceptionally energetic man, but calm, compassionate and a much-loved, good listener. He also mentions Damari Vigowa Sagatwa (1875–1960), a Kaguru Bible woman who was baptized in 1902. In 1903 she married a teacher, Nuhu Sagatwa, was itinerant between Mamboya, Itumba and Nyangala between 1903 and 1914, and, with her husband, was a missionary to Ugogo from 1921 onwards. After her husband's death in 1927 she went to Mpwapwa, where she was a church leader. She was also a leader in revival from the 1930s onwards.

In 1997 I read of a 76-year-old Ethiopian evangelist, Mahe. Imprisoned twenty times, he planted 160 churches south-west of Addis Ababa in his first twenty-five years of ministry. In his fifties his vision turned towards the unreached peoples in the mountains and deserts towards Kenya. Obstacles he faced included the ferocious heat, man-eating crocodiles, virulent cerebral malaria and meningitis, and warring tribes who included man-killing as part of their puberty rituals. He wrote, 'God will not let me die until the gospel reaches the Kenya border. I have been praying that God will get me over the Omo River six times to take the gospel there.' He also wrote, with touching gratitude for modern technology, 'I am thanking God for the MAF plane because the 25-day walk to Walyata when I am so old, is hard with my bags and pots.'[24]

Dissertations have been written on the Anglican women of western Mozambique who kept the church going and growing all through the years of the civil war, when most of the men were away fighting; and also on how much of the evangelization and leadership of the church in the unstable eastern regions of the Democratic Republic of Congo has been done by women. There will be more and more writings of this nature as scholars study the mission of the church from the point of view of the missionized as well as from the point of view of the missioners.

7. Mission and martyrdom

It is common knowledge that the Greek word for witness (*martys*) and the English word martyr are closely allied. A diagram in the

---

[24] *Jesmond Newsletter*, September 1997 (back cover).

World Christian Encyclopaedia portrays in visual form the cost of
Christian witness, under the title 'The phenomenon of martyrdom:
70 million Christians killed for their faith in 220 countries across
20 centuries'.[25] It is sobering to observe that a great majority of
the seventy-six worst martyrdom situations, including eight of the
fifteen with over a million martyrs each, occurred in the twentieth
century. A map in the same volume,[26] entitled 'Religious liberty,
safety or persecution, and martyrdom in 150 countries, AD1900 –
AD2000' shows a wide swathe of countries coloured red, signifying
'highly dangerous'.

Recently the *Biographical Dictionary of Christian Missions* was
published.[27] In the appendix of this large volume is a review of the
nearly ninety martyrs mentioned in the book, noting their name,
country and year of death. A survey reveals that they died in a huge
variety of incidents: some deaths were random, criminal perhaps,
and not strictly martyrdoms as such; sometimes they were caught
up in local tribal disputes; sometimes they suffered because of
suspicion of foreigners. But when the longer articles are read we can
see that these named persons are only the tip of a huge iceberg.
There were 150,000 martyrs in Vietnam between 1820 and 1880, not
including some 500,000 who died in the countryside (see under
'Hemosilla'); 205 Japanese martyrs were beatified in 1867 (see under
'Spinola'); thousands of Catholics were executed in Korea in 1866
(see under 'R. J. Thomas').

Alexander Solzhenitsyn has written of the Christians he met
and knew in the vast archipelago of Soviet Union prison camps; and
Malcolm Muggeridge sardonically observed that Stalin was to be
thanked for the evangelization of Siberia because he sent so many
Christians there with one-way tickets. In New Testament times
early attempts to stamp out the nascent Christian movement
resulted in the movement spreading as the sparks jumped from
place to place. Chinese Christians will record, when the story of
Christianity's expansion in China since the 1950s is more fully told,
that there has been a similar phenomenon there as innumerable
Chinese Christians have been exiled to far places for many years,
there to plant and nurture new groups of Christians.

David Killingray has recounted many stories of Christian
martyrs in twentieth-century Africa in an article in a 500-page book

[25] David B. Barrett, George T. Kurian and Todd M. Johnson, *World Christian Encyclopaedia: A Comparative Survey of Churches and Religions in the Modern World*, 2nd ed., vol. 1 (OUP, 2001), Global Diagram 6, p. 11.
[26] Global Map 7, p. 856.
[27] Ed. G. H. Anderson (Simon & Schuster/Macmillan, 1998).

on martyrs and martyrologies from all periods of Christian history.[28]

We do not know the state of mind in which all these martyrs died, and it is probable that only the more heroic last words have been preserved. Who wants to remember the words of those who cracked under the strain? In Isaiah 49:14 Zion complains that the Lord has *forsaken* her. This testimony, says Walter Brueggemann, 'places at the centre of Israel's life a *massive Holy Problem*'.[29] Here Israel's faith confronts hiddenness, ambiguity, negativity. Is there any possibility that the Lord is fickle? How are we Jews to interpret that catastrophe of the exile in the light of God's promises to be with us forever? This chapter of Isaiah, however, confronts this doubt about God's faithfulness, with the most radical promises of God's steadfast love to be found anywhere in the Old Testament. What could be more constant than a mother's love for her own child? Yet even if this fails, God's love for his people will never fail.

Generations of martyrs have died with this certainty. Tertullian made this a key point in his *Apology*. Who can be found to embrace persecution like Christians? A Christian woman is so unafraid to die that a persecuting judge, with refined cruelty, sentences her to be raped rather than to be eaten by lions. This is how we conquer, says Tertullian: by dying. 'The oftener we are mown down by you, the more in number we grow; *the blood of Christians is seed*' (my emphasis).[30]

8. The geography of mission

This chapter of Isaiah pictures the homecoming of Jewish exiles from all points of the compass. Their ruined city will be rebuilt, and their community will be restored, either brought back by the subservient (vv. 22–23) or rescued from the tyrannical (vv. 24–26).

These hoped-for transformations were expressed in terms which would have been intelligible at the time. The Jews were in exile, away from home; the monarchy, the priesthood and the temple had been destroyed. Some Jews must have wondered whether God's covenant with them had been revoked for ever. It is perhaps hard for those of us who have never been uprooted from our homes and dispossessed of our land and property to imagine the tingling

---

[28] '"To Suffer Grief in All Kinds of Trials": Persecution and Martyrdom in the African Church in the Twentieth Century', in Diana Wood (ed.), *Martyrs and Martyrologies*, Studies in Church History 30 (Basil Blackwell, 1993), pp. 465–482.

[29] *Theology of the Old Testament* (Fortress, 1997), p. 310; his emphasis.

[30] A. Roberts and J. Donaldson (eds.), *The Ante-Nicene Fathers*, vol. 3 (Eerdmans, 1957), p. 55 (*Apology*, section 50).

expectancy with which some of the exiles must have received the promises of a homecoming.

As things turned out, God's purposes for and through Israel have been fulfilled far beyond the terms in which they are expressed here. There was a return of Jews from exile in Babylon, but it never matched the expectations painted here. At Pentecost men and women from all over the biblical world heard Peter preach the good news of Jesus' death and resurrection, with astounding effects. But as the Christian movement spread, it became clear that it was different from other religions which have a definite geographical centre. There is no city for Christians which corresponds in significance to Jerusalem for the Jews, or Mecca for Muslims, or Varanasi for Hindus, or Amritsar for Sikhs.[31] No part of the globe is reserved as the particular residence of Christians. Instead, the expansion of Christianity throughout the world has taken place in a series of tidal waves: there have been advances followed by recessions, but fundamentally, Christianity is not a territorial religion. The city Christians seek, and the home to which they aspire, is neither a geographical nor a political destination. Curiously, this has enabled Christians to be at home, to be resident aliens, in all sorts of ethnic, linguistic and political situations; and the translation of the Bible into hundreds of languages has encouraged local forms of Christianity to become deeply rooted in local cultures, while still remaining part of the universal Christian movement.

Similarly, the liberation of which this chapter speaks has sometimes come as wonderful good news to slaves. Andrew Walls has noted that 'the modern Church of tropical Africa did not begin by missionary agency at all; it arrived, a ready-made African Church'.[32] He is referring to the arrival of 1,100 men and women, Africans or of African descent, who arrived in West Africa in 1792 and marched ashore singing 'Awake and sing the song of Moses and the Lamb'. The settlement had many problems in the early years, but in later years Granville Sharp's 'Province of Freedom' (as it was called) became the source of a large and highly mobile missionary force, whose influence spread far beyond West Africa.

Just as the fulfilment of these Old Testament hopes has far exceeded the geographical terms in which they are expressed, so

---

[31] In chapter 5, pp. 97–100, we have written more about the fulfilment of the promise of a 'land' to Abraham; and in chapter 15 we write more about the 'better country' and the 'city that has foundations, whose architect and builder is God' (Heb. 11:16, 10), which is the new Jerusalem.

[32] A. Walls, 'A Christian Experiment: The Early Sierra Leone Colony', in G. J. Cuming (ed.), *The Mission of the Church and the Propagation of the Faith*, Studies in Church History 6 (CUP, 1970), p. 108.

the liberation of which the Bible speaks has been experienced by huge numbers of people in all sorts of different situations.

The universal ingathering (v. 12) and the vision and hope that *all flesh shall know that I am the* LORD *your Saviour* (v. 26) have already been fulfilled far beyond what could possibly have been realistically expected in Old or New Testament times. The family of Christian believers has become a global community. The Christian faith has taken root in hundreds of cultures. And yet, because of the population explosion, there are still millions of men and women and children who have not had the opportunity of a life-saving personal encounter with the good news of Jesus Christ. For this reason there is still a need for those who will follow in the steps of Jesus the Servant, who will preach and live out the good news, who will plant and establish evangelizing churches and who will hope and pray for the new heavens and the new earth, for the new holy city coming down out of heaven from God, whose temple is the Lord God Almighty, and whose light is the Lamb, who look forward to the time when the nations will walk by its light, and the kings of the earth will bring their glory into it. Then at last these Servant Songs will be fully and finally full-filled.

Part 3
Three-in-one mission

Luke 4:16–30
9. The freedom Jesus brings

Toyohiko Kagawa (1880–1960) was an outstanding Japanese Christian leader of the last century. A social activist (pioneer of labour unions and an anti-imperialist campaigner who was frequently imprisoned), mass evangelist and lay theologian, Kagawa found his central motivation in the freedom of the cross of Jesus Christ. He wrote about his spiritual journey in these words:

> I am grateful for Shinto, for Buddhism, and for Confucianism. I owe much to these faiths. The fact that I was born with a spirit of reverence, that I have an insatiable craving for values which transcend this earthly life, and that I strive to walk the way of the golden mean, I owe entirely to the influence of those ethnic faiths. Yet these three faiths utterly failed to minister to my heart's deepest need. I was a pilgrim journeying upon a long, long road that had no turning. I was weary. I was footsore. I wandered through a dark and dismal world where tragedies were thick ... Buddhism teaches great compassion ... But since the beginning of time, who has declared, 'this is my blood of the covenant which is poured out for many unto remission of sins?'[1]

1. Jesus at Nazareth

Luke introduces Jesus' public ministry as one that will manifest the power and the presence of the Spirit of God (4:14). His ministry begins in the Galilean countryside, where peasant resentment against rich landlords and revolutionary ferment against Roman occupation simmered not far from the surface, and occasionally erupted in violence. The capital, Sepphoris, had been destroyed by

[1] Toyohiko Kagawa, *Christ and Japan* (SCM, 1934), pp. 99–100, 113.

Roman armies in AD 6 after an anticensus revolt led by Judas the Galilean (Acts 5:37) who seems to have been viewed as a messianic leader. Pagan cultural influence in Galilee was strong, and the more religious Jews must have felt embattled to preserve their distinctive religious-cultural identity. Perhaps more so than with their compatriots in Jerusalem, loyalty to the Torah became the rallying point of national identity, and the Pharisees especially were rigid in their fixing of, and adherence to, boundary markers.[2]

By the first century synagogues had come into prominence as the locus of Jewish religious instruction and worship.[3] But Luke's account of the synagogue in Nazareth is the earliest description we have of a synagogue service. We know from later writings that a lectionary was followed, but in this early period it is likely that the reader chose the passages from the Law and the Prophets. Synagogue services were more informal then than most churches and Jewish synagogues are today, with free interaction on the sermon among those gathered. After an opening prayer, the Scriptures would be read in Hebrew, the reader normally standing, and often an Aramaic paraphrase was also given. The synagogue authorities would sometimes invite a distinguished visitor to read and expound the scripture. Luke records that Jesus had quickly acquired a reputation in the synagogues of Galilee as a skilled Bible teacher.

Now he comes to Nazareth, a small town 4 miles from Sepphoris, where he spent his childhood and early youth. News of his preaching and powerful acts of deliverance have already preceded him (v. 23) and the townsfolk gather expectantly. This is to be a celebratory homecoming. Perhaps they plan to take him out on the town the moment the Sabbath is over. Like every small-town hero he has put his town on the nation's map. Imagine the mayor and the local journalists, who might never otherwise grace the interior of a synagogue, jostling to enter. Will he preach a fiery sermon against the Romans? Will he do a mighty miracle in Capernaum?

As was his custom (v. 16b), Jesus goes to the local synagogue on the Sabbath, and gets up to read from the Prophets. The synagogue attendant hands him the scroll, opened at the book of Isaiah. Jesus turns to the opening words of the sixty-first chapter and begins to read aloud. When he has finished, he returns the scroll to the

---

[2] For general political and religious background see e.g. Everett Ferguson, *Backgrounds of Early Christianity*, 2nd ed. (Eerdmans, 1993), pp. 480–502; N. T. Wright, *The New Testament and the People of God* (SPCK, 1992), pp. 159–214; J. Julius Scott, Jr, *Customs and Controversies: Intertestamental Jewish Backgrounds of the New Testament* (Baker, 1995), pp. 200–228.

[3] For information about early synagogues see e.g. Ferguson, pp. 539–546.

attendant and sits down to teach. The eyes of the congregation are transfixed. His opening words are *Today this scripture has been fulfilled in your hearing* (v. 21b).

2. Jesus' sermon

What is this scripture that Jesus has just read? The thrust of the passage is lost in most English translations; so I give below a more literal rendering of the Greek which highlights the emphases of the text:[4]

> *18The Spirit of the Lord is upon* me,
> *For he has anointed* me,
> *To bring good news to the poor,*
> *He has sent forth* me
> *to proclaim for the captives release,*
> *and to the blind sight;*
> *to send forth the oppressed in release;*
> *19To proclaim the year of the Lord's favour.*
> (Luke 4:18-19; emphasis added)

Observe, first, that the anointing of the Holy Spirit is for the purpose of 'bringing good news to the poor'. This is the primary mission. It is not as if bringing good news to the poor was one among other activities ('release for the oppressed', 'sight to the blind' etc.), but the latter expand on what it means to bring good news to the poor.

But, who are 'the poor'? Some read the term as referring to Israel in her suffering and need, as indeed it is sometimes used this way in Isaiah and the psalms. But this doesn't account for the way it is used throughout the Lukan narrative. It is more common in scholarly circles today to identify 'the poor' with the economically destitute, what Marx dubbed the *lumpenproletariat*, a people so trapped in a culture of poverty that they could not organize themselves to transform their material condition. In Old Testament usage 'the poor' are the economically weak and vulnerable, but who live in utter dependence upon God and look to him for help. Jesus, in Luke's Gospel, does indeed have many challenging, even harsh, things to say about the rich and their greed, and Luke has culled the tradition that has come down to him to bring out Jesus' special concern for the dispossessed. For instance, unique to Luke is the

---

[4] This is a slightly adapted version of Joel Green's rendition in his *The Gospel of Luke*, New International Commentary on the New Testament (Eerdmans, 1997), p. 206.

159

woe-saying on the rich (6:24), the parable of the rich fool (12:16–21), the story of the rich man and Lazarus (16:19–31), and the exemplary conduct of Zacchaeus the chief tax-collector of Jericho (19:1–10). He is the only evangelist who has John the Baptist spell out in practical terms what it means to 'bear fruits that befit repentance' (3:8), and he does this in terms of economic relations (3:10–14). The term *ptōchos* (poor) occurs ten times in Luke, compared to five times each in Matthew and Mark.

But, in Luke's gospel *ptōchos* (poor) often appears to be a collective term for all those who are disadvantaged. As David Bosch points out, whenever Luke gives a list of people who suffer, he either puts the poor at the head of the list (as in the Nazareth sermon; but see also 6:20; 14:13; 14:21) or at the end, as a climax (as in 7:22). 'All who experience misery are, in some very real sense, the poor. This is particularly true of those who are sick. Lazarus, the exemplary poor person in Luke, is both poor and sick. Primarily, then, poverty is a social category in Luke, though it certainly has other undertones as well.'[5]

The New Testament scholar Joel Green has rightly drawn attention to the importance of grounding our understanding of 'the poor' in 'the ancient Mediterranean culture and the social world of Luke-Acts'.[6] In that culture, as indeed in many Asian and African societies today, a person's social standing in a community did not depend only on economic realities. A Buddhist monk in South-East Asia, or a forest hermit in India, may well be economically destitute, but he enjoys considerable social honour and sometimes political 'clout'. In strictly financial terms a man like Gandhi was poor, but in social terms he was not. Education, gender, occupation, ethnicity, family connections, religious purity and performance, these – with or without high income – are what for the most part determined in Jesus' culture (and determine, now, in ours) assessments of human worth. As Green observes, ' "poor" would serve as a cipher for those of low status, for those excluded according to normal canons of status honour in the Mediterranean world. Hence, although "poor" is hardly devoid of economic significance, for Luke this wider meaning of diminished status honour is paramount.'[7]

So Jesus' mission embraces all those who for, whatever social, cultural or religious reasons, are marginalized, relegated to a place outside the boundaries that hitherto define the covenant nation. He categorically states God's intention to break down those boundaries.

[5] David J. Bosch, *Transforming Mission: Paradigm Shifts in Theology of Mission* (Orbis, 1991), p. 99.
[6] Green, *Luke*, p. 211.
[7] Ibid.

These 'outsiders' are the objects of divine grace and so the focal point of Jesus' mission. 'Others may regard such people as beyond the pale of salvation, but God has opened a way for them to belong to God's family.'[8]

Observe, secondly, that the clause *to send forth the oppressed in release* is an addition from Isaiah 58:6. Whether this is Jesus' original reading, interspersing Isaiah 61:1–2 with 58:6 or, as is more likely, Luke's clarification of what characterized the ministry of Jesus, it coheres with the proclamation of the *year of the Lord's favour* (v. 19). This echoes the Jubilee legislation of Leviticus 25 – the year, after every seven sabbatical years, when slaves were to be released, the debts of the poor cancelled, the land to be left fallow and also returned to the original distribution among families and clans as decreed by Moses. (Indeed, the Hebrew word *yôḇēl*, translated in English as 'Jubilee', means 'release'.) Whether Israel ever practised the Jubilee instructions is uncertain. But scholars are agreed that both Isaiah 58 and the opening verses of Isaiah 61 hold out the prospect of eschatological deliverance for Israel in Jubilee language. The prophecies were originally addressed to the Jews who had returned from Babylonian exile, and who were 'mourning' (61:3), distressed because of their lost freedom and the destruction of their land. Isaiah 61 promised these former exiles a reversal of their present wretched conditions. Israel would recover, the prophet said, since the Lord will turn their dismal present into a new and permanent Jubilee.

Also, Isaiah 58:5–9a spoke to the upper stratum of the community immediately after the exile, in the midst of a severe national crisis. The prophet criticizes the social discrepancies in Israel, the oppression of the poor by the rich. Even on a day of fasting the latter pursue their own interests, making their employees work harder (v. 3), and wrangling with those who owe them money (v. 4). The social background to Isaiah 58 is reflected in Nehemiah 5, where we are told of poor Jews who, in order to pay the taxes levied by the Persian king, have to mortgage their vineyards and homes and even sell their children into slavery to rich fellow-Jews who have grasped the opportunity to exploit the predicament of the poor. Given this setting, the 'oppressed' or 'bruised' or 'broken victims' of Isaiah 58:6 are to be understood as those who were economically and socially ruined, those who had become bonded labourers with little hope of deliverance from their plight. Only the restoration of Yahweh's reign, a 'year of Yahweh's favour', can bring them release.

Among the Dead Sea Scrolls of the ascetic Qumran community there has been found a document known as 11QMelchizedek. Here

[8] Ibid.

Melchizedek, the ancient king of Salem who makes an enigmatic visit to Abram in Genesis 14, is portrayed as an agent of Yahweh who will appear in the end-time to destroy Israel's enemies and restore the fortunes of Israel. The text weaves together Sabbath and Jubilee themes in its presentation of the eschatological restoration of Israel. So, clearly the use of Jubilee imagery to express the hope of divine deliverance and renewal of the covenant was not unfamiliar in intertestamental Judaism.

Given this rich interpretative tradition, it is unnecessary to propose that Jesus was calling for an immediate implementation of the Jubilee in Israel.[9] He was, rather, announcing the dawning of the long-awaited epoch of salvation. In his mission God's eschatological purpose to bring release and restoration to 'the poor' was being put into effect. The curtain was going up on the final act in God's drama of salvation.

The primary release Jesus brings is release from sin – so that Jesus is the Saviour who forgives sins (1:77; 3:3; 5:20, 21, 23, 24; 7:47, 48, 49; 24:47). Indeed, 'to forgive', *aphiēmi*, is also the word for release, and is the translation used in the Greek Old Testament for the Levitical Jubilee (Heb. *yôbēl*). The Greek term *aphiēmi*, can mean 'to let go, loose, set free, acquit, dismiss, remit'. Note that by forgiving we set the other free. How? By removing from her or his shoulders the burden of our enmity. It is surely significant that the Levitical Jubilee was to be proclaimed in Israel on the Day of Atonement. Forgiveness for the nation implied not only her restoration to covenant relationship with God but also the restoration to the community of all who had been estranged. The righting of relationships in the whole community was inseparable from the experience of forgiveness from God. So Jesus' mission of 'release' would have important personal and social implications (5:27–32; 7:36–50). Also, the 'release' made available in Jesus' ministry is in opposition to the binding power of demonic forces. In almost all of Jesus' healing ministry 'healing is not only physical but also signifies wholeness, freedom from both diabolical and social restrictions'.[10]

Jesus' words about bringing sight to the blind (in v. 18b) is both literal and symbolic. In Luke's two-volume narrative Jesus and his apostles perform acts of physical healing, restoring sight to the visually handicapped (e.g. 18:35–43; cf. Acts 9:18–19); but the recovery of sight has also been presented in this Gospel as a metaphor for receiving God's revelation and experiencing his salvation in their midst (e.g. 1:78–79; 2:9, 29–32; 3:6; also cf. 10:21–24).

[9] *Pace* John Howard Yoder, *The Politics of Jesus* (Eerdmans, 1972), pp. 34–40, 64–77.

[10] Green, *Luke*, p. 212.

Observe, thirdly, that Jesus' reading of Isaiah 61:1, 2 departs from the prophetic text in a particularly significant way. The prophet not only predicts 'the year of the LORD's favour', but also 'the day of vengeance of our God' (v. 2); namely, vengeance on Israel's enemies. The two phrases stand together, not only stylistically in Hebrew parallelism, but theologically. It was unthinkable to anticipate a salvation for Israel that did not entail damnation for the enemies of Israel. The words of the prophecy anticipated a reversal of national fortunes such that the foreigners who now dominated them would in turn be dominated by the people of Israel and become their servants in a new sociopolitical order (61:5-7). But Jesus omits all references to Israel and Zion in the prophecy, as well as all elements hostile to the Gentiles.

3. From admiration to rage

How would Jesus' congregation in the synagogue have expected him to proceed? We saw that anti-Roman resentment was rife in Galilee, and Nazareth was no exception. The audience would expect him to apply the theme of 'release' in Isaiah 61 in such a way as to inflame their religious nationalism. He would announce the day when God's Messiah would lead his armies into battle against Rome, defeat Israel's enemies and restore the golden age of Solomon's reign. After all, even for the Qumran sect the Jubilee imagery was used to show how God's agent Melchizedek would not only deliver God's people (the sect themselves) but slaughter everybody else (including the corrupt Jerusalem priesthood). A sermon with a revolutionary thrust would have made Jesus the hero of the hour.

This may explain the initial positive response to him: *The eyes of all in the synagogue were fixed on him* (v. 20). His opening words, *Today this scripture has been fulfilled in your hearing* (v. 21), further fan these expectations. They are impressed both by the text he has chosen to expound and his attractive manner of speaking. They are astonished that one of their own can speak with such authority. Their words *Is not this Joseph's son?* (v. 22) do not necessarily imply scepticism, as many commentators have understood them. Unlike the readers of Luke's narrative who already know that Jesus is not Joseph's son, the people of Nazareth know him only as such. He is 'one of us', a local boy made good, and the whole town (indeed the nation) stands to gain from him. Surely he will perform for them, his own kith and kin, the deeds of power he has been doing for strangers (v. 23)?

But their admiration is short-lived. For Jesus develops his sermon in an utterly unexpected direction. He quotes two maxims (vv.

23–24) drawn from their everyday social world, and reminds them of two incidents from their own Scriptures (vv. 25–27). In doing so, he elaborates on his own self-identity and vocation.

The first maxim, *Doctor, cure yourself!* (v. 23a), was employed rhetorically in antiquity 'to insist that one must not refuse to do to one's own relations the favours one does to others, or that one must not benefit others while refusing the same benefits to one's own relations'.[11] Jesus is confronting head-on the parochial vision of his townspeople. Their assumptions about who he is and what he is to do constrict their outlook. They can receive God's favour only if they are open to recognizing that Jesus' mission is, according to 4:18–19, to all those who have no claim to status or favour with God. And he will go on to show that these include the Gentiles; indeed, they include their national enemies. God suspends his judgment on the nations that he might draw them out of their wickedness and into his family. If the people of Nazareth, and the rest of Israel, are offended by the lavishness of God's grace, they exclude themselves from experiencing that grace.

Thus his second maxim, *No prophet is accepted in the prophet's hometown* (v. 24), foreshadows the fate that will befall Jesus. His prophetic mission is so out of step with his hometown's expectations and desires both for him and for themselves, that conflict is inevitable. And this conflict, as Luke's narrative reveals, soon embraces the leaders of the nation (9:21ff.; 11:53–54; 19:41–44, 47).

But despite this resistance – indeed, because of it – his credentials as a prophet are not invalidated. For his mission to 'the poor', in the spirit of Isaiah 61:1–2, is anticipated in the ministry of the two great sign prophets of Old Testament times, Elijah and Elisha.[12] Both these prophets were agents of God's healing grace to people who were considered 'outsiders', despite the neediness of many in Israel. They did not turn their backs on Israel, any more than Jesus was doing now, but they witnessed to a God who will bring about a new day when barriers would come tumbling down. Elijah was sent, in a time of famine, to a non-Jew, a woman, a widow – a person of low status on at least three counts. Later, God led to Elisha another non-Jew, a Syrian soldier, whose leprosy further excluded him from any contact with God's covenant people. Many Jews in the time of Jesus expected Elijah to appear again before the final denouement of the kingdom of God; that Jesus invokes the same Elijah as an illustration of God's compassion for outsiders must have been galling to his audience. They themselves do not know the God of their Scriptures.

[11] Ibid., pp. 216–217.
[12] The material in 4:25–27 is largely drawn from 1 Kgs. 17:8–24 and 2 Kgs. 5:1–19, but shaped so that they stand parallel to one another.

These anecdotes are used by Jesus to underscore that his ministry to 'bring good news to the poor' embraces the unclean, Gentiles, those of little or no status in the eyes of his townspeople.

The preacher's words provoke such outrage that the congregation attempt to murder him! Since hills around Nazareth were not particularly high, they must have wanted to throw him down and stone him to death. The facts that it was the Sabbath and that they were forbidden by the Romans to exercise the death penalty reveal the intensity of their rage. Jesus seemed to have turned their world-view upside down, sabotaging the assumptions and values on which they had built their individual and collective lives. Such gospel preaching always generates opposition.

4. Contemporary challenges

a. Proclaiming Jesus and bringing release

In the previous chapter of the present book, we saw that the Servant Songs of Isaiah find their final and full embodiment in Jesus of Nazareth. Isaiah 61:1-2 shares many themes with these earlier songs, with the accent on the freedom the Servant brings. Luke places Jesus' sermon in his hometown at the beginning of his two-volume work in order to highlight its paradigmatic character. Jesus is not merely 'Joseph's son', nor does he fit the anticipated eschatological role of an Elijah or an avenging Melchizedek. He is no less than the uniquely Anointed of the Lord, empowered to inaugurate the liberating Jubilee era of the Lord. In Jesus, a new High Priest and a universal Day of Atonement has dawned. Jesus' life and death bring 'release' to all who have been excluded from God's covenant people, for whatever reason. As such, although Jesus did not lead a social uprising against the Romans, his project of inclusion and radical forgiveness was deeply revolutionary. It constituted nothing less than a restructuring of human relations, both within Israel and between Jew and Gentile, so as to reflect God's gracious reign.

More than any of the other evangelists, Luke focuses on salvation, and the attendant themes of repentance and forgiveness of sins.[13] At the end of Luke's Gospel the risen Jesus tells his disciples that

---

[13] 'The words *sotēria* and *sotērion* ("salvation") appear six times each in Luke and Acts, against no occurrences in Mark and Matthew, and only one in John. Four times salvation is mentioned in Luke's infancy narrative ... In a sense, then, Luke frames his entire body of writing with the idea of the salvation that has dawned in Christ. Among the synoptics, only Luke calls Jesus Soter ("Saviour"), once in the gospel (2:11) and twice in Acts (5:31; 13:23)' (Bosch, *Mission*), p. 105.

THE MESSAGE OF MISSION

'repentance and forgiveness of sins is to be proclaimed in his [Messiah's] name to all nations, beginning from Jerusalem' (24:47). The forgiveness he offers all sinners, Jew and Gentile, implies the restoration of true community as the rich express their repentance in showing solidarity with the poor, and tribal and national loyalties are relativized as new relationships are formed with those hitherto considered either 'nobodies' or 'outsiders'. Salvation involves the transformation of human life, and includes forgiveness of sin, healing from infirmities, the recreation of human community and release from any kind of bondage.[14] It implies both a liberation *from* (sin in all its forms) and a liberation *to* (the love of God and neighbour).

Gustavo Gutiérrez, the celebrated Peruvian theologian, reminds us that 'The entire Bible, beginning with the story of Cain and Abel, mirrors God's predilection for the weak and abused of human history.'[15] This is a truth that Christians living in the upper strata of society – like some of the late first-century readers of Luke's Gospel – are prone to forget. Wealth and power not only enslave; they deceive – and not least in our understanding and presentation of the gospel. The rich and powerful are prone to individualize and privatize the salvation Jesus brings, so Luke is concerned to spell out the implications of the coming of Jesus for the rich as well as the poor.[16] The coming of the eschatological era in Jesus implies a new world order, in which the arrogant will be scattered, the powerful humbled, the lowly lifted up, the hungry filled with good things, and the rich sent away empty (cf. Luke 1:51ff.).

Given Jesus' orientation of his ministry towards the 'nobodies' and the 'outsiders' (i.e. 'the poor') of his society, our own relation to 'the poor' of our contemporary societies, and indeed our global world, becomes not merely a question of 'social ethics' but lies at the heart of our response to the gospel itself. Repentance must include a turning away from complicity in unjust structures of exclusion and repression, and a turning in compassion towards the dispossessed, the rejected and the oppressed.

[14] Luke uses *aphesis* for both 'forgiveness' and 'release' or 'liberation': compare 24:47 with 4:18.
[15] Gustavo Gutiérrez, *A Theology of Liberation* (fifteenth anniversary edition with a new introduction by the author (Orbis, 1988), p. xxvii.
[16] Bosch observes, 'In Acts, compassion and sharing were practiced within the Christian fold where many members were poor ... Luke does not tire of reminding us of the sacrificial attitude that prevailed in the early days of the church in Jerusalem. They shared everything they had, he tells us (Acts 2:44f.; 4:32) with the result that there was no needy person among them (4:34). If rich Christians today would only practice solidarity with poor Christians – let alone the billions of poor people who are not Christians – this in itself would be a powerful missionary testimony and a modern-day fulfilment of Jesus' sermon in Nazareth' (*Mission*), p. 118.

It is through the poor that we learn that the old dichotomies of evangelical proclamation and social action are incoherent.

There is no evangelism without solidarity; there is no Christian solidarity that does not involve sharing the knowledge of the kingdom which is God's promise to the poor of the earth. There is here a double credibility test: proclamation that does not hold forth the promises of the justice of the kingdom to the poor of the earth is a caricature of the gospel; but Christian participation in the struggles for justice which does not point towards the promises of the kingdom also make a caricature of a Christian understanding of justice.[17]

b. Loving our enemies and working for peace

The first words of Jesus' public ministry are ones of forgiveness and healing, not wrath and destruction.[18]

Since forgiveness has profound political implications, we should not be surprised that the practice of forgiveness and reconciliation towards our national enemies will create new enemies of the Christian church. Peacemaking lies at the heart of Christian mission, but so often peacemakers themselves become targets of hatred and violence. But here, too, we learn from the example of Jesus. Not only did he reject, right from the outset of his ministry, the militant ideology of both oppressor and oppressed, refusing to assume the role of the Qumranic Melchizedek and declare a holy war on Israel's enemies, but when he himself became the object of collective violence he showed forgiving love both towards those crucified alongside him and the soldiers who drove the nails into his body (Luke 23:34, 42–43).

Jesus' powerful message, proclaimed in word and demonstrated in deed, goes beyond non-violent resistance to evil: it is to love our enemies, personal and national, seeking their repentance and inclusion in the covenant people of God. Among his circle of twelve disciples, Jesus counted both a tax-collector (Luke 5:27) and a Zealot (Luke 6:15; Acts 1:13). While he decisively rejected the Roman philosophy of government (Luke 22:25) his rejection did not extend to individual Romans (Luke 7:1–10). Moreover, Jesus repeatedly challenged his nation's prejudice against the Samaritans, a people discriminated against by the Jews on account of their

[17] *Mission and Evangelism: An Ecumenical Affirmation* (World Council of Churches, 1983), section 34.

[18] Bosch, *Mission*, p. 112.

religious beliefs and mixed ancestry. Luke relates the story of the ten lepers who are healed by Jesus, but of whom only one – *a Samaritan* – is commended by Jesus for his spiritual sensitivity. Luke records the parable of the good Samaritan (10:25–37), a story that would have outraged the teachers of the Law. To be invited by Jesus to learn from a *Samaritan* the kind of behaviour that pleases the God of Israel was a direct assault on their religious/national identity. In the stark words of Jürgen Moltmann:

> Everything that can be categorized as 'non-violence' in the sayings and actions of Jesus can ultimately be derived from this 'revolution in the concept of God' which he set forth: God comes not to carry out just revenge upon the evil, but to justify by grace sinners, whether they are Zealots or tax collectors, Pharisees or sinners, Jews or Samaritans, and therefore, also, whether they are Jews or Gentiles.[19]

Learning to love our enemies is, in every culture on earth, a countercultural practice. Indeed, in many contemporary contexts, people are habituated into hating their enemies and desiring vengeance – and they are often rewarded for doing so. Most of the popular films we see, whether from Hollywood, Mumbai or Taiwan, are celebrations of the hero taking vengeance on those who have harmed his family or friends. Christians, however, are called to demonstrate a counterhabituation. This must involve learning the habits and practices necessary to resist the desire for revenge, and struggling to have those desires transformed by God's Spirit into desires for love. As the American theologian Gregory Jones points out:

> That feelings of hatred and vengeance might surface and might be real is undeniable; but they need to be struggled against. For the habit of hatred and the desire for vengeance not only perpetuate the cycles of violence; they also constrict and thereby distort the vision of the hater. And they tempt us to create enemies or to foster new fantasies about our already existing enemies so that we can feel better about ourselves. Most decisively we are called to love enemies because that is what we have experienced as the enemies of God – a love that is capable of transforming enemies into friends.[20]

Christians today find themselves caught up in many situations of

---

[19] Jürgen Moltmann, *The Crucified God* (ET SCM, 1974), p. 142.
[20] L. Gregory Jones, *Embodying Forgiveness: A Theological Analysis* (Eerdmans, 1995), p. 263.

racial, class, caste or political conflict around the world. We are called, first, to ensure that the church is a locus of reconciliation, where barriers that divide men and women in the wider society are seen to be broken (or breaking) down. But, secondly, the church itself must be in the forefront of all attempts to understand and address the causes of conflict and to bring about justice and reconciliation between the warring parties.

The biblical diagnosis of human sin gives us unique insights into the nature of human conflict. Trapped in self-centredness, we tend to see others as competitors to be feared, as means to further our own ends, or as threats to our well-being. We have an innate bias towards defending and advancing our own interests. We always tend to speak of the wrongs we have suffered at the hands of others, but rarely of the wrongs we have done to others. This estrangement often turns inwards, so that we are strangers to ourselves, not understanding our motives and passions, let alone the true ends for which we exist.

Violence is covert as well as overt, collective as well as individual. Even where naked aggression and injury are absent, violence can be institutionalized in structures of discrimination and oppression. Long before intentional acts of violence happen, there is usually a history of covert violence. For instance, genocide is preceded by racial stereotyping, ridicule, misrepresentation and physical segregation. Nationalist 'histories' are written, which nurture an uncritical loyalty towards our national or ethnic group, a scapegoating of others (either foreigners or another local ethnic group) for whatever misery experienced in that society, a mythical recreation of a golden age of peace and prosperity, and a depiction of the other as either inferior human beings or not human at all. Much of this has been evident in the narratives of local history taught to children in many countries torn apart by sectarian hatred. Not only does this create a climate for violence, but it is an act of violence in itself – violence against children ('brainwashing'), and also violence against the other, the 'alien'. Christians over the centuries have disagreed over whether the use of force is ever justified, whether in defending the weak or limiting the scale of warfare. This is not the place to explore that debate. But, surely, all Christians can agree on the following:

i. We must seek creative ways of reducing the temptations to violence. Those who ignore pleas for peaceful social change will, sooner or later, have to handle violent social change. In the political sphere this means the strengthening of the mechanism of democracy, for democracy is the institutionalization of non-violence. The more democracy functions as it ought, the more likely that change can be effected by non-violent means. Creating a culture of non-violence cannot be separated from the building of a more

169

participatory style of decision-making at all levels of society. In situations of ongoing conflict Christians must resist all moves to misrepresent the other. We must be in the forefront of all attempts to draw into dialogue the perpetrators of violence, and to debunk both the romantic images of violence and the politico-historical myths that perpetuate violence on all sides. The church, with its cultural and political diversity, can also become a laboratory within which civility, reconciliation and democracy can be nurtured in the wider society. Every local church should provide a living context within which people from very different backgrounds are encouraged to share their stories, their suffering and fears, their deepest concerns in a way that contributes towards the rebuilding of trust.

Such restoration of trust is vital in situations where violence has become entrenched in a nation's life. The church must support refugees from *all* parties to the conflict, and ensure that it denounces *all* atrocities and violations of human rights. Churches are often tempted either to issue bland calls for a 'cheap peace' that ignores the demands of justice, or else to demand justice as a precondition for peace. We need to learn to practise what the South African theologian John de Gruchy has called the 'dialectic of reconciliation'; namely, understanding reconciliation as a path to achieving justice *and* as the fruit of justice.[21] The goal of all Christian approaches to justice must be both the liberation of the oppressed and the restoration of the humanity of the oppressors.

ii. We have to demonstrate the power of the gospel to free from sin and guilt and to transform human nature. If our churches are paralysed by inaction, or irrelevant action, it is usually because the gospel has not been experienced in all its fullness as a living reality by many who profess to be Christians. A church that has lost the gospel is one that mirrors the divisions in the wider society. In many situations of ethnic or tribal conflict the church has uncritically adopted the position of one party. The complicity of the church in the horrific bloodbaths of Rwanda and Burundi, the inability of many Protestants in Northern Ireland to free themselves from a sectarian mentality, or the indifference of large sections of the European churches to the pogroms against the Jews in the 1930s, have been stumbling blocks in the path of many people to hearing the gospel.

iii. We must press for the truth to be told as well as for justice to be done. Truth is as important as justice if nations are to be renewed. Peace is more than the cessation of hostilities. For forgiveness to be

[21] John W. de Gruchy, 'The Dialectic of Reconciliation: Church and the Transition to Democracy in South Africa', in Gregory Baum and Harold Welly (eds.), *The Reconciliation of Peoples – Challenges to Churches* (World Council of Churches, 1997), pp. 16–29.

meaningful, the past has to be faced with honesty and humility. For societies recovering from many years of state terror and civil conflict, some recapitulation of the history of the conflict has to be undertaken, however painful for all concerned. The demons of the past have to exorcised if new relationships are to be made possible and for those in the nation to move forward together.

So, in recent years, in countries such as South Africa, Chile, El Salvador, Haiti and Rwanda, some form of Truth and Reconciliation Commission has been set up in the aftermath of tragedy. The setting up of these commissions surely reflects the biblical conviction that repentance is the basis of genuine reconciliation. Those responsible for disappearances, torture and murder must be prosecuted. If that is not possible, because records have disappeared or witnesses have been killed or intimidated, at least they should be subject to public shaming. The victims must be allowed to tell their story, and the victimizers brought face to face with their victims.

Writing in the context of South Africa, a few years after the dismantling of apartheid, John de Gruchy urged:

> if a culture of human rights is to be nurtured and respect for the law established, then the crimes of the past must not be swept under the carpet. This is also necessary to prevent the past from repeating itself and, most important of all, to help rebuild the lives of the victims ... So remembering the past may be costly, but it may be more costly not to remember it in a way that can contribute to healing and genuine reconciliation.[22]

In the words of Walter Wink:

> In sum, a society recovering from the trauma of state violence needs as much truth as possible. Truth is medicine. Without it, a society remains infected with past evils that will inevitably break out in the future. Domination cannot exist without the Big Lie that persuades the many to offer their lives for the protection of the privileges of the few. Truthtelling not only exposes that lie, but establishes a sacred space where others will gather who will no longer tolerate the lie, as in the churches of East Germany. It is the responsibilities of religious communities to see that the truth gets told and to provide that space.[23]

Peacemaking is not a soft option for Christians.

[22] Ibid., p. 27.
[23] Walter Wink, *When the Powers Fall: Reconciliation in the Healing of Nations* (Fortress, 1998), pp. 53–54.

Matthew 28:16–20
10. The mandate Jesus gives

On my bookshelf I have a tattered, Sellotaped copy of a small paperback book, first published in England in 1961. From the date and the many squiggly notes in the margins, I judge that this was one of the first books I read as a university student. The book's title is *The Unchanging Commission: A Reappraisal of Foreign Missions and the Christian's Responsibility*, and the author is David Adeney. A few years later I became the missionary secretary of the university Christian Union, a post that David Adeney had held thirty years earlier. I did not know then that in 1971 I would become the author's co-worker, and that he would become my mentor.

In 1971 after serving as assistant minister in a church on Tyneside, my wife and I, with our four-month old son, left England and travelled to Singapore. There for the next fifteen years we worked with one, two and then three children, in an international community of Asian graduates called the Discipleship Training Centre (DTC). The purpose of DTC was spelt out as follows: 'The purpose of the Discipleship Training Centre is to glorify God by equipping Asian graduates through the discipling of the whole person within a living community under the Lordship of Jesus Christ; thus equipped, we seek to return to the church in Asia to fulfil the Great Commission.'

The great, unchanging commission referred to above is, of course, Matthew 28:16–20. With many mistakes and failures, our lives were dedicated, individually and together, to working out in practice what it means to submit to the authority of Christ, to obey his command, and experience his presence in our whole lives.

In this chapter I shall carefully review the text of this passage; then we shall look at four critical problems which arise from it. Thirdly I shall note the famous influence these verses have had on missionary thinking (in the West especially); and finally I shall propose that our understanding of these verses ought to take more account of the way in which they are tightly linked to the teaching of the whole of Matthew's Gospel.

1. The text

The last two paragraphs of Matthew are unique to his Gospel. Matthew 28:11–15 tells the story of the bribe given to the soldiers to spread the fraudulent report that the disciples stole the body of Jesus, a story which spread widely among the Jews up to the time of writing. The final, contrasting, paragraph speaks of the appearance of Jesus to his disciples and his command to them to make disciples of all nations. This paragraph is a compendium of important Matthean themes, and is in many ways a key to the understanding of his whole book.

Verse 16. This begins with the little word *But*, contrasting what really happened with the preceding story. The eleven disciples (for Judas was now missing) set out for Galilee. Matthew's story of Jesus' ministry begins and ends in Galilee: Jesus leaves Galilee to be baptized by John in the Jordan (3:13); but after John's arrest he withdraws into Galilee (4:13), and makes his home in Capernaum. Matthew sees in this a covert Messianic claim, a fulfilment of the prophecy in Isaiah 8:23 – 9:1. Jesus calls his first disciples in Galilee (Matt. 4:18) and, finally, at the end of the Gospel, he returns there. At the Last Supper Jesus predicts his crucifixion and resurrection, and announces 'after I am raised up, I will go ahead of you to Galilee' (26:32), but the assertion is submerged by Peter's protests that he will not desert Jesus. After the resurrection the angels announce to the women, 'He [Jesus] has been raised from the dead, and indeed he is going ahead of you to Galilee; there you will see him' (28:7), and the women are to tell the disciples this news. With these simple words continuity is maintained with the story Matthew has told so beautifully: the same Jesus, the same Galilee, the same relation of teacher to disciples, albeit with a much enlarged mandate; the same commanding presence. There is no reference in these comments to a specific mountain, but we do know that mountains were particularly significant in Matthew's story of Jesus: there is the mount of temptation (4:8); the mount of the famous sermon (5:1); the mount where the crowd was fed (15:29); the mount of transfiguration (17:1); and the mount of Olives discourse (24:3).[1]

---

[1] See further on this topic T. L. Donaldson, *Jesus on the Mountain: A Study in Matthean Theology* (JSOT Press, 1985).

Verse 17. In accordance with his promise, Jesus appears to his disciples. They see him, but no emphasis is laid upon this fact; the main verb of the verse is *they worshipped* and the interest of the following verses is in what Jesus *said*. Questions of curiosity about the visible characteristics of the risen Jesus remain unanswered, but it is clear that the resurrection according to Matthew is not just something which went on in the minds of the disciples. We know much about hallucinations these days, and the words *they saw him* cannot refer to a collective hallucination.

The reaction of the disciples seems wholly appropriate: *They worshipped ... but some doubted.* There is scholarly argument about precisely how to translate this phrase. Did some prostrate themselves and others doubt? Or did they all worship and doubt simultaneously? Did the disciples worship and a shadowy, larger crowd behind, doubt? Did they worship although they *had* doubted? And what is the precise meaning of the word 'doubt'? Does it mean disbelief or perplexity or hesitation or indecision? If we exercise some imaginative sympathy, the violent surprise of these reactions does not seem out of place. The walkers to Emmaus did not recognize Jesus; the fishermen did not recognize him. One does not expect to see a dead person, recently buried, appear in another part of the country. What *is* interesting is to speculate why Matthew included this reference to doubting in his story without any specific resolution of the doubt. A likely answer is that Matthew, with pastoral sensitivity, records this story so that his readers might take courage in their own struggles between worship and doubt. This touch shows that the disciples were not supermen and the resurrection was not a matter of wish-fulfilment. The Great Commission was not given to spiritual giants; it was given to an ordinary group of devoted, failure-prone learners.

Verse 18. Jesus comes towards the disciples (one presumes they shrink back), and to all Jesus' memorable words Matthew has already recorded, he adds Jesus' final authoritative commission to them in three closely connected parts:

- a statement about his authority (18b);
- a command about his mission (19, 20a);
- a promise of his presence (20b).

These fifty words (in Greek) have resounded perhaps more than any others in the international history of the Christian church and mission. Although their claim is astounding, the words are simple. Scholars have compared these words to Old Testament enthronement rituals. The parallels are not exact, but here is an enthronement and a commissioning without fanfare and panoply; and the most resounding note is the word *all*: Jesus claims *all* authority, earthly and heavenly; the disciples are commissioned to disciple *all* nations; those who turn in faith and repentance are to be baptized into the triune name, the fullness of God; converts are to be taught to obey *all* that Jesus commanded; and he promises his presence with his disciples *all* of every day until the completion of the age.

Jesus claims that God has given[2] all authority in heaven and on earth to him. In Matthew's story Jesus' authority has already been revealed (7:29); the Roman centurion (a man familiar with power hierarchies) talks with Jesus in terms of authority (8:9); in one incident Jesus argues that his power to heal a paralysed man is the vindication of his authority to forgive the man's sins (9:6); Jesus delegates his authority to his disciples when he sends them out on mission (10:1); Jesus prefaces his famous invitation to people to come to him for rest, with the claim 'All things have been handed over to me by my Father; and no one knows the Son except the Father, and no one knows the Father except the Son and anyone to whom the Son chooses to reveal him' (11:27). The altercation between Jesus and the Jewish leaders in 21:23ff. is about his authority. Finally, Jesus surrenders to powerlessness in his passion. But now, like the victorious Son of Man in Daniel 7, he has been exalted to the highest position of authority in the universe. This crucified Jew, a provincial man from Galilee, claims universal authority. The rest of the Commission basks in the floodlight of this claim. According to Isaiah 42:8, God says that he will not share or give his glory to another. But here we see Jesus raised to the highest place.

Verse 19. The word *therefore* links the command of this verse to the claim in its predecessor: the mandate to disciple all nations is only justified if the claim in verse 18 is true. The command contains four verbs, all of which are significant; the main verb is 'make disciples'; the subsidiary verbs are 'go ... baptize ... teach'.

The disciples are to *go*. Earlier they were told, 'Go nowhere among the Gentiles, and enter no town of the Samaritans ... (10:5); but now their commission is immeasurably enlarged. We shall discuss the phrase 'all nations' in more detail below.

What does the verb *make disciples* mean? The verb is uncommon in the New Testament; but the noun means learner, student or

---

[2] The construction is called a 'divine passive'; 'All authority ... has been given to me' is construed as 'God has given me ...' Jews tended to use such periphrases out of a reverent inclination to avoid overuse of the divine name.

apprentice, and was the first name for Jesus' followers.[3] To 'make disciples' means to bring people into pupillage to Jesus Christ, to enrol them in his school; it implies radical, long-term commitment. Two aspects of this disciple-making, baptism and teaching, are highlighted. Baptism in the triune name is to mark their entry into the community of disciples; and obedience to all Jesus has commanded spells out that ethical character of their discipleship. We note that it is obedience not to 'all that I will command them' but to *all that I have commanded you*; in other words, the apostolic word has primacy in the development of a disciple's life. Baptism 'in the name of' means 'passing into the possession of ... as a mark of ownership by ...' It is a sign that the baptized person is under new management.[4]

Verse 20. Finally, in verse 20, a promise is introduced with the word *Behold*. This word often draws attention to something of importance; it means more than just 'by the way' (e.g. Matt. 1:20; 4:11; 10:16; 20:18 etc.). Jesus promises to be with them in their mission as he has been God-with-them in his life, through the whole of every day[5] until the end of the age. Some writers have pointed out that Matthew has no ascension narrative; it is as if in his view the presence of Jesus has never been withdrawn, and never will be until the end of time. Other writers have pointed out that Socrates or Paul could not and did not whisper such a promise; it is in fact unique to the risen Lord Jesus. Others have reminded us that the fullness of the promise is experienced only by those who give themselves to the mission our Lord commanded; the promise was not given for us to remain in our selfish, comfort zone. John Wesley was one who knew the promise: practically his last words in great old age were 'The best of all is, God is with us ...'[6]

With these words, in typical fashion, Jesus gave a demanding challenge to those who worshipped him and a reassuring promise to those who doubted.

Four critical issues arise immediately from our consideration of this passage.

---

[3] See further Hans Kvalbein, 'The Concept of Discipleship in the New Testament', *Themelios* 13.2 (January–February 1988), pp. 48–52.

[4] 'the formula [of the divine name] does not imply utterance of the trinitarian phrase at the time of baptism. Instead, "in the name of ..." means "with fundamental reference to"' (R. H. Gundry, *Matthew: A Commentary on his Literary and Theological Art* [Eerdmans, 1982]), p. xxx.

[5] See C. F. D. Moule, *Idiom Book of New Testament Greek* (CUP, 1959), p. 34.

[6] John Telford, *The Life of John Wesley* (Hodder & Stoughton, 1886), p. 350.

2. Did Jesus foresee a Gentile mission?

The first issue concerns the Gentile mission. Some scholars claim that it is incredible that Jesus himself actually spoke these words, as they are recorded in Matthew, because the church was slow to adopt a mission to the Gentiles.[7] One might meet this objection head-on with the counter-observation that, in view of Jesus' own ministry, which was restricted to Jews, it is hard to imagine that the church ever *would* have undertaken a Gentile mission unless he had commanded it. But further, the claim lacks psychological depth: it is indeed sobering that even as late in Acts as chapter 15 the early Christians are still arguing about the Gentile mission; but are we not also familiar with the melancholy fact that we sometimes take years, decades, even centuries, to do the things we know we ought to do?

However the objection validly raises the question of Jesus' relationship with Gentiles and the likelihood that he would have commanded the mission to the Gentiles. Before the time of Jesus, relations between Jews and Gentiles were sensitive and volatile. There is evidence of friendliness and welcome to Gentiles; and in the opposite direction assimilation of Jews to Gentile ways to the point of apostasy. But there is also evidence of strong opposition to Gentile culture and ways. There was in Judaism an expectation of a massive conversion of Gentiles in the end times, when they would come flocking into Zion. But Judaism as a whole cannot be categorized as a missionary movement.

What was Jesus' own attitude to Gentiles? Some scholars affirm that he shared (or at least to some extent colluded with) popular Jewish ideas about Gentiles (e.g. that they were by definition sinners),[8] but proof that Jesus specifically refers to Gentiles with this language is lacking. The disciples are specifically commanded not to go among Gentiles and Samaritans in their first mission, but 'go rather to the lost sheep of the house of Israel' (Matt. 10:5–6). It is possible that the injunction not to throw pearls before pigs *might* refer to Gentiles (Matt. 7:6), but again proof is lacking.

But there is a considerable amount of evidence pointing in a different direction. Foreign women appear in the genealogy of Jesus; and wise men come from the east to worship him. Jesus omits the note of vengeance when he quotes Isaiah 61 in his opening speech in Nazareth (Luke 4:19; cf. Is. 61:2). Jesus' disciples are the

[7] E.g. F. Hahn, *Mission in the New Testament* (SCM, 1965): 'It is quite certain that the item of tradition at the end of Matthew's gospel does not in its present form belong to the earliest tradition,' pp. 63–64.

[8] E.g. S. McKnight, 'Gentiles', in Joel Green et al. (eds.), *Dictionary of Jesus and the Gospels* (IVP, 1992), p. 259.

salt of the earth, the light of the world. He rebukes James and John for wanting to call down fire from heaven on an unwelcoming Samaritan village (Luke 9:52–54). Jesus ministers to a number of Gentiles: the Gadarene demoniac; the Syro-Phoenician woman; the centurion of astonishing faith at Capernaum; the Samaritan woman; the Greeks who want to see him, although it appears that only in John 4 does *he* take the initiative in such contacts. Jesus foresees a future in which many Gentiles will share in his kingdom: many will come from east and west to sit at the heavenly banquet. Even now, the temple is to be a house of prayer for all peoples. The message of the kingdom is to be preached throughout the world before the end (Matt. 24:14). The story of the woman who perfumes Jesus' feet will be told throughout the world. After Jesus' death and resurrection it appears that Jesus' authority, so evident in his earlier ministry, is massively enhanced. There is nothing intrinsically improbable about his mission, now delegated to the disciples, being, correspondingly, massively enlarged.

This fits in well with the wider vision of Matthew's own Gospel. One of his earliest stories is of the prestigious oriental Magi visiting the child Jesus (2:1–12). Matthew views Jesus' early move from Nazareth to Capernaum as a fulfilment of a messianic prophecy – the light shines among the Gentiles (4:12–17). Jesus commends the faith of the Roman centurion as unlike any he has found in Israel (8:10). The faithless generation that seeks for a sign will be condemned by the rising up of the people of Nineveh and the queen of the south (12:38–42). The kingdom of God will be taken away from the wicked tenants and given to 'other tenants who will give him the produce at the harvest time' (21:41).

It would appear that David Bosch's statement is justified: Matthew's theological position is that 'a mission to Israel and one to Gentiles need not exclude but ought rather to embrace each other'.[9] John Harvey pictures the framework of Matthew's Gospel being formed by four periods of salvation-history: the period of the law and the prophets, whose mission was primarily to Israel; the period of Jesus' kingdom proclamation, whose mission was also primarily to Israel; the period of messianic travail, when mission is carried out by Jesus' disciples towards all nations; and the period of the kingdom's consummation, when mission is carried out by angels towards all nations.[10]

[9] D. Bosch, *Transforming Mission: Paradigm Shifts in Theology of Mission* (Orbis, 1991), p. 58.
[10] John D. Harvey, 'Mission in Matthew', in W. J. Larkin and Joel F. Williams (eds.), *Mission in the New Testament: An Evangelical Approach* (Orbis, 1998), ch. 7.

3. Religious arrogance

The second issue is about Christology. This passage of Matthew, with its high Christological claims, sticks in the throats of many who have a more pluralist view of religions.[11] It is assumed that the early Christians quickly and radically escalated the claims they made for the one whom they worshipped; and that Jesus, a good man, keenly aware of God and full of the Holy Spirit was 'inflated' into the unique, divine-human Son of God on whom the salvation of the human race depended. Pluralists are offended by the arrogance of those who, adhering to any humanly and historically conditioned religion, claim and insist that it is the only way for the whole human race.

One powerful tributary of this pluralist passion is a rising fear of deep-rooted religious intolerance: Israelis and Palestinians, Catholics and Protestants in Northern Ireland, Muslims and Christians in Northern Nigeria, Hindus and Muslims in India. In some places the mixing up of communities is giving rise to *greater* polarization. In such a climate, religious tolerance is one of the first priorities, and (it is asserted) exclusive claims form one of the greatest hindrances to such toleration.

We ought to feel this fear and allow it keenly to affect the way in which we go about our mission of witness and disciple-making. But as Stephen Neill said, 'we must not suppose that [the Christian] claim to universal validity is something that can be quietly removed from the Gospel without changing it into something entirely different from what it is'.[12] If God really has revealed himself in human form, and if there really has been a resurrection from the dead, then the claim to universal authority must be seen in a different light. If the pluralists are correct, the whole history of Christianity has been a story of idolatry – falsely offering to a created being what belongs only to God.

It has been common in some circles to argue that both within the New Testament and beyond it in early Christianity there was a dramatic 'escalation' of views about Jesus Christ, from the earliest view of him as a very special person, uniquely sensitive to the Spirit of God, to the full-blown belief in Jesus as the incarnate Son of God.

[11] Alan Race has helpfully defined religious pluralism as 'the belief that there is not one, but a number of spheres of saving contact between God and man. God's revealing and redeeming activity has elicited response in a number of culturally conditioned ways throughout history. Each response is partial, incomplete, unique; but they are related to each other in that they represent culturally focussed perceptions of the one ultimate divine reality' (*Christians and Religious Pluralism*, 2nd ed. [SCM, 1993]), p. 54.

[12] S. C. Neill, *Christian Faith and Other Faiths* (OUP, 1970), p. 16.

It has been suggested that, in the interests of sensitivity to those of other faiths, Christians ought to return to the earlier view of Jesus, which historical research reveals, because this allows Jesus to be compared to other outstandingly sensitive religious leaders. Professor Richard Bauckham has recently contributed to this debate by arguing that there was no escalation of Christology from 'low' to 'high' as has just been outlined. In fact, he has argued, the earliest Christians already worshipped Jesus because they recognized him as sharing God's heavenly throne. But they did not think that Jesus was *another* God. The earliest Christians (who were all Jews, trained for over a thousand years in the view that there is only one God) remained monotheistic by including Jesus within the unique identity of the God of Israel. Thus 'The earliest Christology was already the highest.'[13] There *is* indeed Christological development within and beyond the New Testament. However, it is not best described as 'escalation', but as the elaboration and flowering of what was there from the very beginning.

In our service to those of other faiths we must speak quietly, by life as well as by word. But a civilized society is not one in which there is no permission to speak in the public square of those beliefs which affect us most deeply. A civilized society is one in which courtesy, politeness, respect and hospitality are extended to the views and experiences of our fellow-citizens *and* we are free to express with enthusiasm and eagerness the good news we have discovered in Jesus Christ. It is not a society where the threat of offended sensitivities paralyses interreligious discourse, but a society where differences of belief can be expressed vigorously and debated with the rational opposition of goodwill. We cannot abandon mission if Jesus has truly risen from the dead: 'It is finally the abeyance of mission which would be the supremely damnable egoism – for this would be to keep to ourselves privately what belongs to the whole world.'[14] 'The commission to disciple all nations stands at the centre of the church's mandate and the church that forgets this, or marginalizes it, forfeits the right to the titles *catholic* and *apostolic*.'[15]

4. Baptism in the triune name

The third critical issue concerns baptism. In the book of Acts Peter urges those who hear him at Pentecost to 'Repent, and be baptized every one of you in the name of Jesus Christ so that your sins may

[13] Notes of a lecture by R. Bauckham at a conference in Oxford, 2 July 2002. He referred at the time to his recent book *God Crucified* (Eerdmans/Paternoster, 1999).
[14] K. Cragg, *The Call of the Minaret*, 3rd ed. (One World, 2000), p. 182.
[15] L. Newbigin, *International Bulletin of Missionary Research*, April 1988, p. 50.

be forgiven; and you will receive the gift of the Holy Spirit' (2:38), which large numbers accordingly did. Luke reports about the early Samaritan believers who had not yet received the Holy Spirit, that 'they had only been baptized in the name of the Lord Jesus' (8:16). After the Holy Spirit had fallen on Cornelius and his household, Peter 'commanded them to be baptized in the name of Jesus Christ' (10:48). Paul explained to some Ephesian believers how John's baptism of repentance, which they had received, pointed on to Christ. Thereupon 'they were baptized in the name of the Lord Jesus' (19:5). Late in Acts when Paul is rehearsing to the restless crowd in Jerusalem the story of his own conversion, he mentions how Ananias urged him not to delay: 'Get up, be baptized, and have your sins washed away, calling on his name' (22:16). Whose name? The name of God, or the name of the Righteous One whom he has sent.

With this evidence of Acts before us, it is proposed by some scholars that is unlikely that the order to baptize people in the name of the Father, the Son and the Holy Spirit actually goes back to Jesus himself. Because, if it *did*, why did the disciples not use this formula in their mission?

But it is likely that the word 'formula' is misleading in this context; centuries of Christian usage have focused minds on the issue of what liturgical words might have been used in a baptism service. It is far from certain that any of the words used in the New Testament in connection with baptism are meant to be interpreted in this way. It is more likely that 'baptism in the name of ...' is connected with an Old Testament phrase that implies calling upon or worshipping God; or that it is a phrase that means something like solidarity with, loyalty to, submission to.[16]

After his death and resurrection Jesus inaugurates a new phase in the advance of his kingdom. His authority (as explained above) is immeasurably enlarged; the scope of his disciples' missionary task is hugely widened; and the community into which new disciples are to be initiated by baptism is marked by the triune name; John the Baptizer had taught that his baptism of repentance pointed forward to a baptism of the Holy Spirit; and now Jesus gathers up all he has taught about the Father (a most common title of God in Matthew), about himself and about the Holy Spirit as the name (not names) of the God into whose service the disciple is enrolled once and for ever. These words, of course, strikingly distinguish from John's baptism the baptism Jesus commanded. There is also a vast

[16] See e.g. Matt. 18:20, 'For where two or three are gathered in my name, I am there among them.'

Christological claim lying behind the words, in that Jesus associates himself with the Father and the Holy Spirit.

5. All the nations

The fourth critical issue concerns the meaning of the phrase *all nations (panta ta ethnē)* in verse 19. Mission strategists, as they have surveyed the world with greater and greater attention to detail, have found ethnic groups hard to categorize, and hence they have found it hard to formulate plans to reach those who have not yet heard the good news of Jesus Christ. Some countries (e.g. Nigeria, Indonesia) contain many ethnic groups. On the other hand, some ethnic groups (e.g., as mentioned before, the Kurds found in Turkey, Iran, Iraq, Syria and Azerbaijan) straddle several countries.

It is certain that the words *all nations* in Matthew are not used with the ethnological precision some writers have suggested, to mean 'ethnolinguistic people groups', whose number is gradually becoming more precisely known. The first chapter of the fourth section ('The Strategic Perspective') of Winter and Hawthorne's famous *Perspectives on the World Christian Movement* reader is entitled 'Finishing the Task: The Unreached Peoples Challenge'.[17] This chapter distinguishes blocs of peoples, ethnolinguistic peoples, sociopeoples and unimax peoples; and it talks enthusiastically about the possibility of planting a viable indigenous, missionary church in every significant ethnic group, where 'viable' means 'not dependent on foreign support'; 'indigenous' means rooted in the local context and culture; and 'missionary church' means a church that is not just surviving, but which is itself an evangelizing church.

Neither the Old Testament nor the New Testament uses sociological and ethnological terms with great precision. In the Old Testament there is a recognizable sociological ladder from people/nation down through tribe, clan, family/household to the individual.[18] Matthew starts his Gospel by referring to Abraham, and it is almost certain that God's promise to Abraham in Genesis 12:1–3 and following underlies his report of the Great Commission at the end of his Gospel. In Genesis 12 the Lord commands Abraham to leave his father's *house*; God promises that Abraham will become a great *nation*, and that in him all the *clans* of the earth will be blessed. Later, in Genesis 18:18, the Lord muses that Abraham will become a great *nation* and all the *nations* of the world will be blessed in him.

[17] R. D. Winter and Bruce Koch, 'Finishing the Task: The Unreached Peoples Challenge', in idem, *Perspectives on the World Christian Movement* (William Carey Library, 1999), pp. 509–524.

[18] See e.g. the procedure adopted in Josh. 7 in searching out the sin of Achan.

In Psalm 22:27-28 the psalmist pictures the widest possible worshipping multitude, and the phrase 'families of the nations' is parallel to 'ends of the earth', and all are united in the worship of the Lord. It is possible to list a large number of Old Testament passages which are either exhortations that God's name should be praised among the nations, promises that one day all nations will worship the true God, prayers that this will come to pass, or plans of the psalmist to play his part in making God's greatness known internationally.[19]

In the Greek translation of the Old Testament (the Septuagint) *ethnos* appears about a thousand times (mostly in the plural) and in the overwhelming majority of cases it stands for non-Jewish peoples.[20]

Ethnos occurs in the New Testament 162 times (43 times in Acts and 54 times in Paul's letters – he was above all the apostle to the Gentiles). Sometimes this word refers to the Jewish people; and in about a hundred instances it is used in the polar pairs Jew/nations or Christian/nations. But usually, especially in the phrase *panta ta ethnē* and almost always in Matthew, it refers to the non-Jewish peoples.[21] The New Testament inherits the Old Testament vision of the widest possible multitude being drawn into the praise of the living God, but it also uses a variety of sociological and ethnological terms: people, nation, Gentiles, crowd, city, language. It would appear that *ethnos*, the word Matthew uses, is the most capacious term to define a group of people linked by a common history, culture or community allegiance.

In intertestamental times the word *ethnos* had a somewhat derogatory ring about it: it referred to those who were *not* the people of God. But here in Matthew our Lord's words are inclusive. The blessing promised to and through Abraham is to come true in undreamed of ways. All are to be invited to become disciples of the risen Lord. The kingdom promised by him is not territorial and the commission is not a territorial commission. But the disciple-making activity of the church is to prepare for that great day of God in the future when there will be 'a great multitude that no one could count, from every nation, from all tribes and peoples and languages, standing before the throne and before the Lamb, robed in white, with palm branches in their hands [worshipping God]' (Rev. 7:9).

---

[19] J. Piper, *Let the Nations be Glad! The Supremacy of God in Missions* (IVP, 1993), pp. 184–187.

[20] C. Brown, *The New International Dictionary of New Testament Theology*, vol. 2 (Paternoster, 1986), p. 790.

[21] Stephen Hre Kio, 'Understanding and Translating "Nations" in Matthew 28:19', *Bible Translator* 41.2 (April 1990), pp. 230–238.

6. A classic world-mission text

This passage of Matthew has had a pre-eminent place in the history of the church in mission.

The Reformers, in general, limited this great commission to the time of the apostles. A French Protestant settlement under Admiral Coligny in Brazil in 1555 had made a brief, unsuccessful attempt to evangelize the natives. King Gustavus had attempted to evangelize the Lapps in his country. In the same century a Belgian divinity professor, Adrianus Saravia, who became a political refugee in England, wrote a treatise (in Latin) in 1590 (five years before the first Dutch commercial venture to the East Indies) on the different degrees of Christian priesthood. He argued that the missionary mandate of Matthew 28 was still binding on the church, especially its bishops; but his argument was submerged in his defence of episcopacy, and came to nothing.

Justinian von Welz, the son of a seventeenth-century Austrian nobleman forced to leave his country for Germany on account of his Lutheran faith, wrote four tracts in the 1660s passionately appealing for Protestants to join a gospel-preaching brotherhood ('A society of the love of Jesus') to follow this command of Christ. Practising what he preached, he went to Surinam, where he died.[22]

In the eighteenth century Isaac Watts wrote a hymn on Psalm 72, entitled 'Christ's kingdom among the Gentiles', which included the following verses:

> Jesus shall reign where'er the sun
> doth his successive journeys run;
> his kingdom stretch from shore to shore
> till moons shall wax and wane no more.

> Behold the Islands with their Kings,
> and Europe her best tribute brings;
> from North to South the Princes meet
> to pay their homage at his feet.

> There Persia glorious to behold,
> there India stands in Eastern Gold;
> and barbarous nations at his word
> submit and bow and own their Lord.

[22] H.-W. Gensichen, 'Welz, Justinian von', in G. H. Anderson (ed.), *Biographical Dictionary of Christian Missions* (Simon & Schuster/Macmillan, 1998), p. 722.

Philip Doddridge was minister in Northampton from 1729 until his death in 1751. He made proposals for the deepening of the spiritual life of churches and rules for the formation of a missionary society in 1741, but these came to nothing.[23] John Newton (1725– 1807), the ex-slave trader who became the minister at Olney and later in London, preached fifty sermons in 1784–85 at St Mary Woolnoth on texts from Handel's *Messiah*, which was then enjoying a spectacularly successful rerun at Westminster Abbey. But nowhere in all these sermons does Newton show any inclination to consider what practical steps needed to be taken to extend the Messiah's kingdom.

Thus English-speaking Protestants look to William Carey (1761– 1834) as the 'founder of modern missions'. Section 1 of his famous *Enquiry* is entitled 'An Enquiry Whether the Commission Given by our Lord to his Disciples Be not Still Binding on us'.[24] Carey, of course, concluded that it *was* still binding: 'Where a command exists nothing can be necessary to render it binding but a removal of those obstacles which render obedience impossible, and these are removed already.'

In July 1794 Dr Ryland of Bristol received a letter from William Carey, which he shared with Mr David Bogue, a minister in Gosport. The news was so moving that a prayer meeting was formed in Whitefield's Tabernacle in Bristol and David Bogue wrote an article for the *Evangelical Magazine* for September 1794, with the curious title (considering its content), 'To the Evangelical Dissenters who Practise Infant Baptism'. Part of this article reads:

We are commanded 'to love our neighbour as ourselves'; and Christ has taught us that *every* man is our neighbour. But do we display this love while we allow gross darkness to cover the Pagan and Mahometan nations, and are at no pains to send to them the glad tidings of salvation through the sufferings and death of the Son of God? Perhaps we have not considered our duty resulting from that command which was directed from the supreme authority to every follower of the Lamb: *Go ye into all the world and preach the Gospel to every creature.*[25]

A couple of months later, in November 1794, a careful review of a book by Melville Horne entitled *Letters on Missions: Addressed to the Protestant Ministers of the British Churches* appeared, written

[23] See G. F. Nuttall (ed.), *Philip Doddridge 1702–1751: His Contribution to English Religion* (Independent, 1951), ch. 4, 'Doddridge and the Missionary Enterprise'.
[24] See n. 28 in chapter 5 of this book.
[25] R. Lovett, *The History of the LMS 1795–1895* (Henry Frowde, 1899), p. 7.

by Dr Thomas Haweis, chaplain to Lady Huntingdon. Melville Horne had been an Anglican chaplain in Sierra Leone for a very short time before being forced home by ill health. His book also specifically mentions the great commission as a motive for missions.[26] Many readers of Bogue's article and Haweis's review met in London on 4 November 1794 to discuss the possibility of founding a new missionary society. The sermon preached at the society's opening noted, 'From that time there appeared a gradual increase of cordial friends to the perishing heathen, though many respectable characters whose early patronage of this cause was desired yielded to cautious hesitation, and some were perhaps disposed to attach presumption to the undertaking.'

A survey of nineteenth-century missionary meetings would probably reveal countless appeals to the Great Commission as a motive for missionary obedience.

The evangelical missionary leader John R. Mott issued a famous small book that went through at least four editions in 1900; it was entitled *The Evangelisation of the World in This Generation*. In chapter 1 Mott defines what is meant by this phrase; and in chapter 2 he explains the obligation to evangelize. In both these chapters reference is made to the Great Commission, in its different versions.

Right up to the present time, for example in John Stott's *The Contemporary Christian*, published in 1992, the Great Commission is still a classic text for world mission. In his chapter 'Our God is a missionary God' Stott argues that

This great commission to the nations has never been rescinded; it is still binding on the people of God. It was issued by the risen Christ who was able to claim that 'all authority in heaven and on earth' had been conferred on him. A link between the 'all authority' he claimed and the 'all nations' he commissioned his followers to disciple is clearly intended. The universal mission of the church springs from the universal authority of Jesus.[27]

7. Doing mission in Christ's way

The last command of Jesus is not to be fulfilled in any way we think best. Jesus' disciples are to fulfil their mission by following in the steps of their Master. It is instructive to notice how closely this passage in Matthew 28 is laminated into and forms the climax of the whole Gospel. In particular, three themes come to a climax in

[26] Ibid., p. 11.
[27] J. R. W. Stott, *The Contemporary Christian* (IVP, 1992), p. 329.

Matthew 28:16–20. They are (1) mission under the authority of Jesus, (2) mission in the steps of Jesus, and (3) mission with the presence of Jesus. We shall look at these in turn.

8. Mission under the authority of Jesus

The notion of the fulfilment of the Old Testament is very strong in the early chapters of Matthew. Matthew is full of Old Testament citations and allusions, but these are especially prominent in the infancy narratives: Jesus is the Messiah (the anointed One, the Christ); he is attested by the angel to Joseph as Son of David and as Emmanuel (God with us); he is the son of Abraham, through whom the whole world will be blessed. The wise men look for the King of the Jews to worship; John the baptizer announces the coming of the Lord; God himself attests Jesus as his dear Son at his baptism; and he is immediately attacked in this capacity by the devil.

The most important titles Matthew uses for Jesus are Messiah (Christ), Son of David, Lord, Son of man, and Son of God. But of course the importance of Jesus in Matthew is not just revealed by a few titles. He is the new Moses, the new Israel; greater than Solomon, greater than Jonah; greater than the temple and the priesthood. He is the servant predicted by Isaiah; he is God's wisdom personified; he is a teacher of matchless authority, whose mighty acts, forgiveness of sins and supernatural knowledge suggest God himself at work. He demands total allegiance and declares that a person's ultimate destiny depends upon him.

Jesus' authority is displayed in his regal expression 'I say unto you . . .'; he heals the sick, delivers the demonized, raises the dead, calms storms, feeds thousands. His authority is questioned by religious leaders, acknowledged by crowds, submitted to by disciples and finally universalized by his resurrection and vindication. Christian mission can never be understood apart from its authorization in the authority of Jesus; and the Jesus upon whose authority universal mission is based is the Jesus of Matthew's careful presentation, uniquely powerful in word and deed.

9. Mission in the steps of Jesus

As we think of the unfolding of our missionary obedience, we should observe the parallelism with which Matthew depicts the mission of Jesus and his disciples.

In Matthew 4:17ff. Jesus begins his preaching, teaching, healing ministry to Israel. His famous sermon (chs. 5 – 7) calls his disciples to live a life of kingdom-revealing, law-fulfilling, justice-righteousness.

Of all the Gospels, Matthew is the most elaborate in setting forth the ethical requirements of the kingdom. Ten mighty acts follow (chs. 8 – 9), representative of a wider ministry of compassion. In chapter 10 Jesus sends his disciples out on a mission like his, but warns them about rejection and persecutions (10:16–39). In the next section of the Gospel (chs. 11 – 16) the theme of rejection intensifies: John the baptizer questions, cities are unrepentant, religious leaders are solidly opposed – even his family do not understand him. He still heals, feeds the crowds (who are ambivalent), but he teaches the disciples more about the kingdom (ch. 13) and draws from them the confession that he is the Messiah. After 16:21 Matthew's story focuses more and more on the passion: the geographical indicators lead towards Jerusalem and Jesus' predictions of his suffering are repeated. Earlier Jesus *taught* his disciples, but now he will *show* them his passion. The disciples stumble towards a greater understanding of who Jesus is and Jesus teaches them more about life in the kingdom (ch. 18). Controversy with Jewish leaders increases, Jesus enters Jerusalem and drives traders out of the temple, launches the parable of the wicked tenants against the leaders, avoids their traps, and finally charges them with hypocrisy in a blistering series of seven woes in chapter 23. This is the context for the fifth major discourse in Matthew regarding the need for faithfulness in suffering, steadfast endurance and preaching the gospel everywhere (chs. 24 – 25). Finally, Jesus is betrayed, tried and crucified, but recognized by Roman soldiers as the Son of God.

In this long journey to the cross Jesus is tempted by the devil, hindered by Peter, struggles with his own horror in the garden of Gethsemane, and experiences mockery and contempt. In his teaching of his disciples he urges on them the qualities of self-denial, childlike humility, forgiveness and servanthood, which he himself displays.

The more closely we study the Gospel the more parallels we see between the ministry of Jesus and that of his disciples. He itinerates in Galilee and so do they; he preaches, teaches and heals and so do they; they share his authority; those who receive him receive them; the disciples will share the judgment throne with him. He is persecuted and so will they be; he is delivered up, scourged, appears before king and governor, is killed but vindicated – and so will they be. Yes, disciples must walk like Jesus in the way of the cross.

Disciples too are to fulfil their mission with Jesus-like behaviour. In the Gospels he exemplifies love for God and neighbour and so should they; he shows law-fulfilling justice in his life; he submits to the will of God; he prays, 'Not my will but thine be done,' and so should they. He is meek; he is a servant; he shows compassion; he is vigilant – the list of parallels could go on and on. And we who seek to obey his last command to go, make disciples, baptize and teach, need to walk in the path he walked. It is an exaggeration to see the five major discourses in Matthew as a new law for Christians; but it is suggested that Matthew's carefully structured presentation of narrative and discourse is designed to present Jesus as a model in word and deed. It is particularly significant to note that Jesus commits to his disciples the task of teaching the baptized so that they will both know and obey all that he, Jesus, has commanded them. This is a much wider, deeper and longer task than has filled the sights of some of those who think that a mission blitz can carry the gospel through the world or complete the task within a specific (usually short) time. It includes bringing people to the point of putting their trust in Jesus Christ; but it goes on to encompass bringing them to mature, integrated, witnessing discipleship; it includes the development of their personal holiness of character; their enfolding into the church; and their personal and corporate commitment to revealing the kingdom, fulfilling the law and embodying in their own lives and in society the righteousness of the kingdom.

10. Mission with the presence of Jesus

From first to last Matthew is the Gospel of 'God with us'. In times of revival and mass movements, church growth and great receptivity, and in lifetimes of removing stones, in times of suffering, rejection and martyrdom, the sense of the presence of Jesus has been a reason for rejoicing and a solace.

Matthew uses the word 'Father' for God 44 times, far more than any other Gospel writer. Jesus is presented as Son of God in Matthew, at his baptism, temptation, transfiguration and in the centurion's confession. He talks frequently of 'My [heavenly] Father'. But Jesus also designates God as 'your Father', referring to the disciples; and it is the sense that they have an all-seeing, all-knowing faithful Father that enables disciples to sail steadily through seas of trouble.

Wherever two or three disciples are gathered in his name, Jesus declares that he is in their midst; when he goes through his agony in the garden, they are to watch with him; when he comes to the heavenly banquet, his disciples will drink the cup with him. Everywhere, always, till the end of the age Jesus will be present with his disciples as they seek to follow him.

Jesus has never left his church; the last paragraph of Matthew's story is vibrant with authority, urgency and benediction. Matthew's first readers and every successive generation of disciples finish their reading of his story with a worldwide mission based on Jesus' worldwide authority, to be conducted in a Jesus-like manner with the promise of his worldwide and history-long presence.

John 12:20-26; 13:34-35
11. The way Jesus commands

Narayan Vaman Tilak (1862–1919) of Maharashtra in India was one of the acknowledged leaders of the 'romantic revival' in Marathi literature at the end of the nineteenth century. Many of his poems express his longing for India to come to Christ, and for the church to become truly Indian and so to offer India's rich cultural heritage to Christ:

> When shall all these longings be sufficed
> That stir my spirit night and day?
> When shall I see my country lay
> Her homage at the feet of Christ?
>
> Yea, how behold that blissful day
> When all her prophets' mystic lore
> And all her ancient wisdom's store
> Shall own His consummating sway?
>
> Of all I have, O Saviour sweet,
> All gifts, all skill, all thoughts of mine,
> A living garland I entwine,
> And offer at Thy lotus feet.[1]

'What are you looking for?' (1:38) are the opening words of Jesus in the Fourth Gospel. Throughout the narrative men and women from different religious traditions are searching for something, and their search culminates in an encounter with Jesus. In chapter 3 Jesus is approached by Nicodemus, a representative of the *Jewish*

---

[1] Translated N. McNicol; cited in R. H. S. Boyd, *An Introduction to Indian Christian Theology*, rev. ed. (ISPCK, 1975), pp. 116–117.

leadership. In chapter 4 he meets a woman of the *Samaritans*. And in chapter 12 some *Greeks* approach Philip and express a desire *to see Jesus* (v. 21). All these encounters are the occasion for some memorable sayings on the part of Jesus, sayings that have a significance far wider than their immediate setting.

We have seen (in chapter 4 of the present book) that the theme of 'sentness' is prominent in the Fourth Gospel. Jesus has a strong conviction of having been sent by the Father for a particular purpose. He sees himself as fulfilling the hope of Israel for God's rule, a rule that includes the 'gathering in' of the nations as he reveals the face of the invisible God to a humanity that is searching for its true goal. Thus, as the good shepherd (a metaphor of kingship), Jesus tells the Jewish leaders that he has to gather the 'other sheep that do not belong to this fold' (10:16). He has to die for the Jewish nation, but also 'to gather into one the dispersed children of God' (11:52). And now, as soon as he hears of the request of the Greeks at the Passover in Jerusalem, he sees that the *hour* has arrived for him to be *glorified* (12:23), a glorification he connects with being crucified and so drawing *all people* to himself (12:32–33).

Thus the gathering of the nations into the redeemed people of God is always associated with the death of Jesus. *Very truly, I say to you, unless a grain of wheat falls into the earth and dies, it remains just a single grain; but if it dies, it bears much fruit* (12:24). On the other side of the cross will emerge a new humanity, a multinational people of God comprising both Jew and Gentile united under his gracious rule (10:16; 17:20).

1. Freedom and suffering

Throughout the Gospel narrative Jesus appears as the freest of human beings. He cares little what others think of him; he is not a slave to social convention or the expectations of family or peers. What matters is to do 'the will of him who sent me' (5:30). This is his meat and drink (4:34). Even his imminent death is a fate he can avoid: 'No one takes it [my life] from me, but I lay it down on my own accord' (10:18). While he gives himself for others, including his enemies, *they* do not determine how he should serve them. It is this single-minded obedience to the One he calls 'Father' that is the essence of his freedom. As such, it profoundly challenges our secular notions of freedom.

If God in Christ is free for humankind, if God has chosen to be God only in a relation of self-giving love to us, then we can no longer think of freedom as a substance or as something individualistic. It is not a quality, an object at hand that we possess. Freedom is a relationship between persons. Freedom is something that happens to me through the 'other' and which I receive for the 'other'. To be free means 'being-free-for-the-other', because I receive my being from God and through others.

It follows that the surest way to lose my freedom is to cling to my life as if it were my own possession rather than a gift entrusted to me by God for others. *Those who love their life lose it, and those who hate their life in this world will keep it for eternal life* (12:25). 'Loving and hating' is a Hebrew way of placing emphasis: in order to love God and do his will in the world, our natural human instincts for self-preservation and security must be overridden.

Out of his desire for his creatures God in Christ chooses to suffer, and because he chooses to suffer he is not overcome by suffering; it has no power to overwhelm him because he has made the alien thing his own. The British theologian Paul Fiddes observes:

> When someone accepts as his own the suffering that is inflicted upon him, the person who inflicts it loses all power over him; the torturer or oppressor loses the ability to dominate him in any ultimate sense. When the sufferer has lost his fear of suffering as something strange to his being, he has the strength to resist and rebel against the tyrant, even if only mentally.[2]

Fiddes continues:

> He fulfils his own being *through* suffering, since he can only become more truly himself through suffering with the world, but the suffering itself is not the fulfilment of his purpose. What actually fulfils God is satisfaction of his desire. The God who has a future suffers to bring many sons and daughters to glory, and in this he is glorified.[3]

The mystery of the God who freely suffers in Christ, bearing the shame, sin and guilt of the world, is a notion that runs counter to all the religious teachings of humankind. It is deeply offensive especially to the Muslim mind which sees it as compromising the transcendence of God. Yet it is the life, death and resurrection of Jesus that provoked a radical rethinking of what the transcendence of God actually means:

[2] Paul Fiddes, *The Creative Suffering of God* (Clarendon, 1992), p. 107.
[3] Ibid., pp. 108–109.

The transcendence of a suffering God can only be understood as a transcendent suffering, not a transcendence beyond suffering. Only the thought of God as Trinity can make sense of transcendent suffering ... He can include all suffering in himself as he includes all human relationships, yet he is other than the world in his unique suffering, taking our suffering into himself out of the depths of the more profound and terrible suffering which remains his own.[4]

2. Suffering and mission

How, then, does the church witness to this triune God? Jesus' primary call to his disciples is to be where he is: *Whoever serves me must follow me, and where I am, there will my servant be also* (12:26). And where is Jesus? He is about to die – outside the walls of Jerusalem, in utter ignominy and abandonment! So where is the disciple-community called to be? In the words of Dietrich Bonhoeffer, writing from a prison cell in 1944 because of his opposition to the Nazi regime, 'To be a Christian does not mean to be religious in a particular way, to cultivate some particular form of asceticism (as a sinner, a penitent or a saint), but to be a man. *It is not some religious act which makes a Christian what he is, but participation in the suffering of God in the life of the world.*'[5]

In another paper written in prison Bonhoeffer noted that it is

infinitely easier to suffer in obedience to a human command than to accept suffering as free, responsible men. It is infinitely easier to suffer with others than to suffer alone. It is infinitely easier to suffer as public heroes than to suffer apart and in ignominy. It is infinitely easier to suffer physical death than to endure spiritual suffering. Christ suffered as a free man alone, apart and in ignominy, in body and in spirit, and since that day many Christians have suffered with him.[6]

Christians, of course, suffer for a variety of reasons. We share in sickness, disease, accident, natural disasters and wars which are part and parcel of the human lot in a not-yet-renewed-creation. We are not immune to this common human suffering. We also suffer sometimes for our foolishness – as when we incur the wrath of communities for our culturally insensitive and brash methods of

---

[4] Ibid., p. 143.
[5] Dietrich Bonhoeffer, *Letters and Papers from Prison* (ET SCM, 1953), letter of 18 July 1944, p. 123 (my emphasis).
[6] Ibid., 'Of Suffering', p. 145.

evangelization. We also suffer because of historical circumstances and prejudice. For instance, whenever the US goes to war against a Muslim state, Christian churches in the Middle East and other populous Muslim-majority states such as Indonesia and Pakistan become the targets of mob violence. Ancient Christian communities in the Middle East (many predating the rise of Islam) are still tainted with the brush of Western colonialism.

But the suffering that Jesus invites his disciples to is a suffering like his that is *freely chosen*. Also, unlike self-denial in Advaita Hinduism or Theravada Buddhism, Christian self-denial is ethical, not metaphysical. Christians deny themselves in order that they may give themselves fully to God for his purposes in the world. If Christians say 'No' to their own lives, it is so that they may affirm the lives of others. When Christians choose to risk violence or sickness (and incur their families' ridicule) by serving God in the decaying inner cities of Western nations or in the shanty towns or barrios of developing-world megacities, they are falling into the earth and dying like grains of wheat.

Let your imagination roam to the North African city of Carthage in AD 251. A great epidemic, probably of measles, has struck the city. Christians have just been recovering from the torrid persecution suffered under the emperor Decius. Their leaders have been killed or imprisoned, their homes burned down, their businesses looted by mobs. In this situation of great danger, when wealthy pagans were fleeing Carthage because of the epidemic, Bishop Cyprian preaches to his congregation from Matthew 5:43-48, urging them not to protect their own lives, nor even to be concerned about the survival of the church, but to love their enemies who have recently been persecuting them. This was an opportunity to show the love of Jesus by staying in the city and nursing sick pagans and Christians alike. A recent study has argued plausibly that not only did the minority Christian community, which did not flee but stayed to provide nursing, have a higher survival rate than their pagan neighbours, but that the pagans who had been cared for through the crisis by Christians were likely to be open to a faith that, unlike their own, had demonstrably worked.[7]

Here is a more recent example (from personal correspondence), one among many we could quote. Antoine, a young graduate working with the International Fellowship of Evangelical Students in Rwanda, lost most of his family and friends in the terrible massacres of Tutsis in 1994. When he himself was herded into a

---

[7] R. Stark, 'Epidemics, Networks, and the Rise of Christianity', *Semeia* 56 (1992), pp. 159-175.

refugee camp, friends abroad invited him to spend some time in Europe following theological studies. Antoine refused the invitation, and wrote to his friends, 'How can I share my people's joy [when sanity and stability is restored] if I do not share with them their pain?' He chose to remain and work among the refugees, confronting the sin of his own tribe, and as a result of that witness some have come to faith in Christ.

At the heart of Jesus' ministry lay a vigorous challenge to the powers of evil, whether in the disease that afflicts the body, the demons that torment the mind, the guilt and indignities that crush the person, or the idolatry and hypocrisy that destroy community. Yet it was a challenge that he made in utter vulnerability. It led to the agony in Gethsemane and the God-forsakenness of Golgotha. The cross itself was his supreme parable, expressing the paradox of his mission. In what seemed total defeat, the victory of God was accomplished. The weakness of God spells the conquest of evil. 'Now is the ruler of this world driven out' (12:31).

As he voluntarily embraced the shame and humiliation of the cross, Jesus demonstrated God's loving solidarity with all who suffer brutalization at the hands of others. Of course he died in solidarity with *all* sinners, the executioners and bystanders as much as the victims. But we must not forget that he died a victim of a political system and on a political charge. His loving solidarity with all made him a victim with some at the hands of others. It is as one of the victims that his forgiveness extends to those who uphold the system. But the latter can only receive that forgiveness when they are willing to turn around ('repent') from their complicity in God-denying structures. Those who follow Jesus are called to identify with those 'at the bottom' of our social and political systems, to embrace a suffering that may not be directly our own. This would involve learning to see the world from their perspective, thus rejecting the comfortable perspectives of those who benefit from the present world order.

The way of Jesus, then, is the way he calls his church to go. It is neither a withdrawal from the world into a religious sanctuary, nor an engagement with the world on the world's own terms. It is nothing less than an unflinching yet vulnerable challenge to the powers that control the present world order, but in the name of the reign of God present in the crucified and risen Jesus. To the extent that the church participates in the suffering of Jesus it becomes the bearer of the risen life of Jesus for the sake of the world.

This sort of thinking is far removed from the ideology of 'success' and the methodologies of church growth that abound in evangelical circles today. Christian mission is not a 'success story' in the way the world reckons 'success'. It has often been noted that the outstanding examples of vibrant Christian witness in this century have been in places where success in worldly terms has been denied the church. For instance, in China, where the church emerged from the horrors of the cultural revolution and the waves of repression, greatly renewed and strengthened; or in Eastern Europe, where the courage and holiness of Christians kept hope in God alive, despite attempts by powerful governments to stamp it out; or in Latin America, where countless believers have been imprisoned and killed for resisting tyranny, and where the church continues to minister out of poverty and weakness.

Ever since the church's first great conflict with the power of imperial Rome, the victory of the gospel has been won not by the efficiency of its mission strategists, the effectiveness of its fund-raisers or even the cleverness of its preachers. But by the blood of its martyrs.

3. Mission and transformation

Unless a grain of wheat falls into the earth and dies, it remains just a single grain; but if it dies, it bears much fruit (12:25). The grain falls into the earth and is buried. It embraces obscurity. Nothing seems to be happening for many months. But when it eventually emerges, yielding a harvest of wheat (or rice, or whatever), it has itself been changed beyond recognition.

The church engages in mission not only in order that the world may be transformed, but that she too may be transformed more into the truth and purity of her Lord. The church does not claim to possess all truth and righteousness, but rather to point the world to the truly righteous one who *is* the truth; namely, Jesus Christ. And in that process of directing the world to Jesus Christ, the church is herself drawn into a deeper understanding of, and obedience to, the same Jesus. In the Fourth Gospel, even as the Holy Spirit bears witness to the truth of Jesus before the world, he also draws the church more deeply into that truth (16:13).

We see this process beginning in the book of Acts. Consider, for instance, Peter's encounter with the Roman centurion Cornelius (Acts 10:1 – 11:18). Here we are introduced to a stupendous sight, unimaginable in the ancient world, of a Jewish peasant under the same roof as a Roman military officer. What has brought about this astonishing new phenomenon is a set of events that we could call a 'double conversion'. Cornelius, upright and God-fearing though he is, still needs to hear the message of the gospel from the lips of Peter (not even from those of an angel!) in order that he might receive the

197

forgiveness of sin and the gift of the Holy Spirit. Peter, witnessing the same Holy Spirit at work in a Gentile's life, comes to a recognition of his own cultural prejudice under the deepening impact of the gospel on his thinking. Cornelius has come to a saving knowledge of Christ. Peter has come to a deeper discipleship, a more profound conversion of his life and cultural heritage towards Christ.

For the Christian, dialogue is a fundamental aspect of bearing witness to the truth of Christ. Where there is a genuine longing for the other to come to 'the light of the knowledge of the glory of God in the face of Jesus Christ' (2 Cor. 4:6), there will always be a posture of *humble listening*. For it is the desire to communicate that motivates us also to listen well. Listening to people involves taking their beliefs, fears and aspirations with utmost seriousness, even being prepared to be disturbed and challenged by them ourselves. All witness, and thus all true dialogue, is a risky undertaking. *Whoever serves me must follow me, and where I am, there will my servant be also* (12:26). It is not the missionary who carries Jesus to others; on the contrary, it is the crucified and risen Jesus who leads us in our witness into places where we fear to venture.

The birth of the ecumenical movement in the last century is an example of how those at the cutting edge of Christian witness to non-Christian peoples helped the church to recover biblical teachings that she had neglected for centuries. Several Christian missionaries and national Christian leaders in India had long been involved in challenging the inequities of the caste system and challenging the prevalence of caste consciousness in some Indian churches. But the more articulate Indian Christians were unhappy over the inconsistency between the missionaries' insistence that caste-related discrimination be renounced by the church while they themselves prohibited intercommunion with Christians of other denominations. They also noted the glaring colour and class distinctions many missionaries continued to practise.

Thus, in the words of the Indian lay leader Dhanjibhai Fakirbhai (1895–1967):

> Another thing which greatly surprised me was that if any high caste person accepted the Christian Faith the Indian Christians and the missionaries would tell him that he must entirely give up caste discrimination – and they made him do it! Yet nobody told the missionaries to give up their colour discrimination. Everyone assumed that the missionaries belonged to a different caste, and so there was no need for them to have relations of intermarriage with Indian Christians. It seems that there was very little

difference between our caste-discrimination and this kind of colour discrimination.[8]

These were factors in the movement for church union, in which South India gave the lead. If Christianity was really concerned with the overcoming of divisions between peoples, then surely the denominational differences among Christians, particularly at the Lord's Table, nullified the gospel and needed to be overcome if the church was to have a credible witness in a fragmented society. Sadly, it seems that, despite the diligent efforts of the more far-seeing Christian leaders, caste divisions and caste discrimination continue to paralyse the witness of many churches in the Indian subcontinent at the same time that denominational barriers have been eroded.

Christian witness, then, must include the confession of corporate sin. We may have to say with the psalmist, in whatever social and political situation we find ourselves, 'we and our ancestors have sinned' (Ps. 106:6). In the South African context of apartheid, Charles Villa-Vicencio reminds us that 'the mention of the Christian God within the South African constitution has probably done more to alienate black people from the church than any secular or atheist state philosophy could ever have accomplished'.[9]

The conversion of the church obviously does not mean that we react to the church's complicity in sin and error by rejecting all that we have received in our Christian tradition. What it does mean is that we resist the temptation to preserve our past uncritically as though the church were a museum, rather than allowing our past to contribute to our witness today. Our conversion is towards more faithful witness, to more creative and prophetic translations of the gospel into whatever context we inhabit.

Our trinitarian faith enables us to be open to what God is doing in history today. If we neglect to pay attention to what the Holy Spirit may be doing, whether in (post)modernity or in the transformations experienced in traditional religious traditions and communities, we may be guilty of idolatry. The Roman Catholic encyclical *Redemptoris Missio* notes:

the universal activity of the Spirit is not to be separated from his particular activity within the Body of Christ, which is the Church. Indeed, it is always the Spirit who is at work, both when he gives life to the Church and impels her to proclaim Christ, and

[8] Cited in R. H. S. Boyd, *Manilal Parekh, 1885–1907; Dhanjibhai Fakirbhai, 1895–1967; A Selection* (Christian Literature Society, 1974), p. 41.
[9] Charles Villa-Vicencio, *A Theology of Reconstruction: Nation-Building and Human Rights* (CUP, 1992), p. 265.

THE MESSAGE OF MISSION

when he implants and develops his gifts in all individuals and peoples, guiding the Church to discover these gifts, to foster them and receive them through dialogue.[10]

We can (and often do) misread the 'signs of the times' and so may end up following Antichrist rather than the living Christ. Hence the need for spiritual discernment. The Taiwanese theologian Choan-Seng Song, for instance, writing in 1973, hailed as 'salvation history' the efforts of the Chinese Communist Party under Mao Zedong to 'transform man and his society', and announced triumphantly that the new China was 'destined' to represent a 'future classless society in which the dictatorship of the proletariat will prevail completely'.[11] It is not only with hindsight that we see how naive this reading of Chinese history was, but many Chinese Christians caught up in the turmoil within China could have advised Song differently. More seriously, such readings neglect the tragic dimension of sin that the gospel story discloses. The Antichrist is the satanic parody of the Christ, mimicking the liberation he brings, and present in all those visions of progress that deny the need for atonement and forgiveness.

Similarly, the 1989 San Antonio meeting of the Commission on World Mission and Evangelism of the World Council of Churches, stated confidently, without any qualification, that 'The rising up of the people against injustice is the creative power of God for the people and for the whole world ... The acts of the people become God's mission for justice through creative power.'[12] This is where listening to one another in the wider body of Christ can correct our blind spots and keep us from surrendering the gospel to the latest political or cultural fashion. As *Redemptoris Missio* cautions us:

It is true that the inchoate reality of the Kingdom can also be found beyond the confines of the Church among people everywhere, to the extent that they live 'Gospel values' and are open to the working of the Spirit who breathes when and where he wills (cf. John 3:8). But it must immediately be added that this temporal dimension of the Kingdom remains incomplete unless

[10] Encyclical Letter *Redemptoris Missio* (7 December 1990), section 29. Available at the Vatican website <http://www.vatican.va/holy_father/john_paul_ii/encyclicals/documents/>.
[11] C. S. Song, 'New China and Salvation History – a Methodological Inquiry', in S. J. Samartha (ed.), *Living Faiths and Ultimate Goals* (World Council of Churches, 1974), pp. 80, 84.
[12] *The San Antonio Report*, ed. F. R. Wilson (World Council of Churches, 1990), section II.6.

it is related to the Kingdom of Christ in the Church and straining toward eschatological fullness.[13]

4. Mission and unity

All proposals for building human community presuppose some understanding of the human condition and have as their unifying centre some programme or person. The form such community takes (whether, say, in the Nazi Party, a scientific institution, or a multinational corporation) will depend on the nature of that unifying centre. The new human community that God creates is through the suffering, death and resurrection of Jesus. ' "And I, when I am lifted up from the earth, will draw all people to myself." He said this to indicate the kind of death he was to die' (John 12:32-33).

In chapter 13 of the Fourth Gospel, Jesus enacts a parable of his impending death. In the upper room, after the final supper with his disciples, he takes a towel and basin of water and goes around the group washing each one's feet. This was the menial work of a household slave. Simon Peter, whose sense of propriety is deeply injured, objects vehemently. He is ready to wash his Master's feet, but he cannot accept his Master washing *his* feet. Jesus replies that unless Peter allows his feet to be washed, 'you have no share with me' (13:8). The Christian life begins with the receiving, not the giving, of service. We can love only because we ourselves have been loved. We can lead others in the new community only when we ourselves have learned to be led.

After he has washed their feet, Jesus invites them to reflect on what they have experienced: 'You call me Teacher and Lord – and you are right, for that is what I am. So, if I, your Lord and Teacher, have washed your feet, you also ought to wash one another's feet' (13:12-14). He has set them an example (v. 15) and given them a new commandment: *Love one another. Just as I have loved you, you also should love one another. By this everyone will know that you are my disciples, if you have love for one another* (13:34-35). Later he prays to the Father for the disciples in the journey through the world, 'that they may be one, as we are one' (17:11). He also asks the Father that all who believe in him through their word will be united so that 'the world may believe that you have sent me' (17:21). He repeats this request: 'I in them and you in me, that they may become completely one, so that the world may know that you have sent me and have loved them even as you have loved me' (17:23).

The atoning work of Christ has broken down all human barriers,

[13] *Redemptoris Missio*, section 20.

so that one new humanity is born out of the old fragmented, alienated race (cf. Eph. 2:14–18; Gal. 3:28; John 10:16 etc.). Accepting Christ as Lord, therefore, involves commitment to a new global community through which all our prior loyalties are redefined. A Christian's primary identity is now derived from the body of Christ, and no longer from biological family, ethnic group, denominational affiliation or nation states. This inevitably leads to conflict, since these other human associations no longer have absolute priority over our lives.

The famous Barmen Declaration of 1934, produced by some Christian leaders in Germany to counter the propaganda and subversion of the church by the Nazis, reminds us that

> All the churches of Jesus Christ, scattered in diverse cultures, have been redeemed for God by the blood of the Lamb to form one multicultural community of faith. The 'blood' that binds them as brothers and sisters is more precious than the 'blood', the language, the customs, political allegiances, or economic interests that may separate them. We reject the false doctrine, as though a church should place allegiance to the culture it inhabits and the nation to which it belongs above the commitment to brothers and sisters from other cultures and nations, servants of the one Jesus Christ, their common Lord, and members of God's new community.[14]

Clearly for Jesus, the most powerful apologetic for the gospel of the incarnation is the deepening visible unity of his disciple-community across the world. It is this that will convince sceptics that not only is Jesus the supreme locus of divine revelation but that Christians have been caught up into the eternal love of the Father for his unique Son. The church that is called to heal the social life of nations must itself manifest godly social life to the world. As the Second Vatican Council document *Lumen Gentium* (light of the nations) puts it, 'By her relationship with Christ, the Church is a kind of sacrament or sign of intimate union with God, and of the unity of all mankind. She is also an instrument for the achievement of such union and unity.'[15]

---

[14] *The Barmen Declaration of 1934*, cited in M. Volf, *Exclusion and Embrace: A Theological Exploration of Identity, Otherness, and Reconciliation* (Abingdon, 1996), p. 54.

[15] Second Vatican Ecumenical Council, Dogmatic Constitution on the Church *Lumen Gentium*, 1.1. Available at the Vatican website <http://www.vatican.va/archive/hist_councils/ii_vatican_council/documents/> or in print in A. Flannery, *Vatican II: Conciliar and Post-conciliar Documents* (Fowler Wright, 1981), ch. 29 and later editions.

As indicated in the previous section, this has, perhaps, been the biggest 'blind spot' of evangelical Christians and the Western missionary movement in recent times. We have failed to see that the church is central to the good news of Christ we are called to proclaim. We have inherited individualistic understandings of salvation, and hence of the gospel. In our obsession to see the nations 'won for Christ' we have failed to ask ourselves the prior question 'To which Christ are we trying to win the nations'? Some missiological 'think tanks' based in the US have exported their techniques of 'church growth' to other parts of the world. Working with a somewhat naive anthropology, they classify humanity into various 'unreached people groups' and propose that the aim of mission is to plant an 'indigenous' church within each such 'people group'. In keeping with our technology-driven modern culture, this is a quantifiable goal that, in the most optimistic projections, can be reached within the present generation.

Thus, Ralph Winter and Bruce Koch claim that 'We are in the final era of missions. For the first time in history it is possible to see the end of the tunnel, when there will be a church movement within the language and social structure of every people group on earth, powerful face to face evangelism taking over in all peoples.' They continue:

> We need only a small percentage of dedicated believers to be mobilized and equipped ... Notice how more do-able the mission task seems when we focus on the size of the potential mission force and on penetrating people groups. Instead of talking of evangelizing 2 billion individuals, we can talk of beginning in approximately 3000 ethnolinguistic peoples and then finishing in maybe as few as 10,000 unimax peoples. Within a very short time all of the 3000 'least evangelized' ethnolinguistic groups will be targeted and engaged by some mission-sending structure in the world.[16]

The advantage of such people-group thinking is that it alerts us to the existence and special needs of communities we might other-wise overlook in mission. However, apart from language and perhaps ethnicity, the application of the concept to other human groups is problematic. The boundaries between people, and their self-identifying markers, are porous and constantly shifting. (Even definitions of ethnicity are usually political acts, and what constitutes

[16] R. D. Winter and Bruce A. Koch, 'Finishing the Task: The Unreached Peoples Challenge', in idem, *Perspectives on the World Christian Movement* (William Carey Library, 1999), pp. 523–524.

a 'cultural heritage' for one generation is understood differently by the next.) But, more importantly, the moment we make 'planting churches within people groups' the aim of Christian mission, even in heterogeneous geographical areas, we inevitably distort the gospel so that it no longer confronts the idolatries of politics and culture. It no longer challenges converts to identify with the 'outsider' and even the 'enemy'. For Jesus, as we have seen, the latter is not an optional 'higher teaching' for a special group within the church, but fundamental to Christian discipleship.

The late David Bosch, writing in the context of a racially divided South Africa and the Afrikaner-speaking churches' justification of apartheid on dubious sociological grounds, summed up the missiological challenge:

> Paul could never cease to marvel at this new thing that had caught him unawares, as something totally unexpected: the Church is one, indivisible, and it transcends all differences. The sociologically impossible ... is theologically possible ... All this most certainly does not mean that culture is not to play any role in the Church and that cultural differences should not be accommodated ... However, cultural diversity should in no way militate against the unity of the Church. Such diversity in fact should *serve* the unity. It thus belongs to the *well-being* of the Church, whereas the unity is part of its *being*. To play the one off against the other is to miss the entire point. Unity and socio-cultural diversity belong to different *orders*. Unity can be *confessed*. Not so diversity. To elevate cultural diversity to the level of an article of faith is to give culture a positive theological weight which easily makes it into a revelation principle.[17]

If we take visible unity seriously, as the gospel demands that we must, then some Christian churches, mission agencies and parachurch organizations may need to withdraw from a locality if they are stumbling blocks to true Christian witness. This will require great humility and courage, but it is one contemporary test of our commitment to live by the gospel. Those agencies and organizations that remain, face no less severe a challenge; namely, to work towards missionary partnerships that involve the radical sharing of human and financial resources, the willingness to learn from each other and to confront each other lovingly in face-to-face dialogue around the Word of God.

[17] David Bosch, 'Church Unity Amidst Cultural Diversity', *Missionalia* (April 1982), reprinted in *Evangelical Review of Theology* 8.2 (October 1984), pp. 252–253.

The unity that Jesus pleaded for is clearly a far cry from the ecumenism understood today as a vague notion of uniting 'all people of faith'. In the context of Jesus' prayer for unity, he assumes that the basis of their unity is acceptance of his word as 'truth' and faith in him as the one whom the Father has sent into the world (cf. 17:6-8, 17, 18) and who knows the Father in a way the world does not (17:25, 26). This is an *evangelical ecumenism*, evangelical because it arises from a common allegiance to his word as truth, which is to be obeyed and proclaimed to the world. Even as unity is essential for mission, so it is mission that fosters unity.

In many cities around the world there are signs that this is beginning to happen, as pastors from local churches gather together to pray for their cities. Sometimes this leads to fresh reflection on the gospel and missionary practice in the light of both Scripture and personal experience. The communication of the gospel is not primarily the work of visiting evangelists; rather, it is the work of local Christian communities who patiently articulate to others what Christ is doing so obviously in their own collective life. Christians who come from outside the local situation must first seek out local believers and identify with them. Where there is a local church, incarnational missionaries put themselves and their special skills at the disposal of the church, and they are accountable primarily to its leaders and not to a home church or mission agency.

Missionary concern for other parts of the world is only authentic where a church is first faithful to Christ in its own national situation. However:

> Every local congregation needs the awareness of its catholicity which comes from its participation in the mission of the church of Jesus Christ in other parts of the world. Through its witnessing stance in its own situation, its prayers of intercession for churches in other parts of the world, and its sharing of persons and resources, it participates fully in the world mission of the Christian church.[18]

As a report of a study group comprising Roman Catholics and Protestants expressed it two decades ago:

> Often it is socially and politically more difficult to witness together since the powers of this world promote division. In such situations common witness is particularly precious and

---

[18] *Mission and Evangelism: An Ecumenical Affirmation* (World Council of Churches, 1983), section 37.

Christ-like. Witness that dares to be common is a powerful sign of unity coming directly and visibly from Christ and a glimpse of his kingdom.[19]

5. Conclusion

In our technology-obsessed age it is salutary to remember that Jesus never taught his disciples any techniques or methodologies of mission. But he did leave with them two abiding missionary principles, both of which are sadly absent from most modern discussions of global evangelization. They are both found in the Fourth Gospel as part of the teaching of Jesus in the last week prior to the crucifixion, and they are intimately related to each other.

The first is the principle of *dying*. What is true of the biological order is also true in the spiritual realm: there is no life without death (12:24). The disciple-community of Jesus, walking in the footsteps of their Master, must be prepared to be buried in a world of cruelty, poverty, bigotry, violence, hopelessness – the same world which crucified their Master. The church that seeks security, prestige and worldly power is no longer the church of the crucified Jesus. The power of the gospel can only be demonstrated in vulnerability and humility, as the gospel is lived out in the public squares of the world. The founder of the Iona Community in Scotland wrote:

> I simply argue that the Cross be raised again at the centre of the market place as well as on the steeple of the church. I am recovering the claim that Jesus was not crucified in a Cathedral between two candles, but on a Cross between two thieves; on the town garbage heap; on a crossroads so cosmopolitan that they had to write his title in Hebrew and Latin and in Greek; at the kind of place where cynics talk smut, and thieves curse, and soldiers gamble. Because that is where he died and that is what He died about. And that is where churchmen should be and what churchmen should be about.[20]

The second great principle of missionary fruitfulness is *loving*. The church is part of the gospel, and so it follows that authentic witness can only be ecumenical witness. The visible love of disciples for one another is what convinces a sceptical world that the Father

---

[19] *Common Witness: A Study Document of the Joint Working Group of the Roman Catholic Church and the World Council of Churches* (World Council of Churches, 1982), section 64.

[20] George Macleod, *Only One Way Left*; quoted in Donald E. Messer, *Contemporary Images of Christian Ministry* (Abingdon, 1989), p. 170.

has sent the Son into the world (17:22–23) to bring about a new creation. When we have learned to die to our own plans and projects, including our plans for world evangelization, then we can truly love one another and move forward into every dimension of life under the leading of the triune God of mission.

Acts 2:1–47
12. The Spirit of mission

1. Acts 2 in the modern age

The story of the twentieth-century Pentecostal movement begins with the experience of Mrs Agnes Ozman ('one who had a sweet, loving experience and all the carnality taken out of her heart') at the Parham Bible School in Topeka, Kansas, as early as 1901. A report written a few years later, speaks of the students laying aside commentaries, studying the Bible and praying night and day to God. Finally, after three months the Holy Ghost came in power and Mrs Ozman spoke in an unknown tongue. The report continues, 'This made all the Bible school hungry, and three nights afterward, twelve students received the Holy Ghost and prophesied, and cloven tongues could be seen upon their heads. They then had an experience that measured up with the second chapter of Acts ...'[1]

In October 1905 a 35-year-old black preacher with the Saints (later the Church of God Reformation movement), William J. Seymour, heard about the gift of tongues from a friend. In December he was allowed to enrol at Rev. Charles Parham's Bible School, although he had to sit outside the door because Parham practised strict segregation. Seymour heard Parham's teaching, but did not have the experience. In January 1906 Seymour travelled to Los Angeles, preached in a black holiness mission, was locked out by a Mrs Hutchins and forced to move into the home of a Mr and Mrs Edward Lee. They continued in prayer through February and March. On 9 April Seymour preached on Acts 2:4, a person named Edward Lee burst into tongues and then the entire small company was engulfed in tongues and joy. The first woman to speak in

[1] Fred Corum (ed.), *Like as of Fire: A Reprint of Old Azusa Street Papers*, privately published 1981; *Apostolic Faith* 1.1 (September 1906), p. 1, col. 2.

tongues was Jennie Evans Moore (later Seymour's wife) who lived across the street. 'She does not know how to play the piano but under inspiration of the moment she plays and sings in her lovely voice six professed foreign languages with interpretation for each: French, Spanish, Latin, Greek, Hebrew and Hindustani.'[2]

Since those days in Los Angeles a hundred years ago Pentecostal and charismatic Christianity has expanded numerically and spread around the world, until, in the twenty-first century, it probably amounts to about a quarter of the global Christian community.[3]

This is just one story of many that links experiences of the church in history with the story of Pentecost told in Acts 2, to which we now turn.

2. The day of Pentecost

Acts 2 is a wonderful story of the springtime of the church. In spring, new life surges everywhere: trees that have stood bare all winter suddenly dress themselves, shoots burst from the ground, colours are fresh and vibrant. And so it is in this story. One might have expected that the disappearance of Jesus from the disciples' sight might have triggered a wave of uncertainty, confusion and hesitancy. But this was not the case.

Bishop Lesslie Newbigin was invited to bring a greeting to Trinity College, Bristol, shortly before his death. Without notes (for he was nearly blind) he stood up at the end of lunch, recited Luke 24:50–52 from memory, smiled and said, 'Mission begins with an explosion of joy!' His whole face shone as he said it, leaving a profound impression on all who heard him.

We may look at the story of Acts 2 under the headings 'What happened?', 'How was Pentecost interpreted?' and 'What was the result?'

3. What happened? (Acts 2:1–13)

In the first four verses of the chapter we are told about the coming of the Holy Spirit, and are informed concisely of the place, the time, the noise, the sight, the experience and the result. The apostles are all together in a house in Jerusalem; we don't know exactly where this

---

[2] Douglas J. Nelson, 'For Such a Time as This: The Story of Bishop William J. Seymour and the Azusa Street Revival' (PhD diss., University of Birmingham, 1981), p. 57.

[3] David B. Barrett, George T. Kurian and Todd M. Johnson, *World Christian Encyclopaedia: A Comparative Survey of Churches and Religions in the Modern World*, 2nd ed., vol. 1 (OUP, 2001), p. 20, table 1-6a.

THE MESSAGE OF MISSION

is, but it is not far from where crowds can gather. The feast of
Pentecost was in May/June and was a harvest festival celebrating the
completion of the barley harvest (Deut. 16:9) and the gathering of
the firstfruits (Exod. 23:16; Rom. 8:23). By New Testament times it
was also celebrated as the anniversary of the giving of the law at
Mount Sinai, seven weeks after the Exodus (Jubilees 1:1; 6:17). The
noise is described as like the sound of the blowing of a violent wind,
and the sound evidently fills the whole house; it is not a private
experience. What is seen, and has been represented in hundreds of
paintings and icons, is something like tongues of flame, one resting
on each of them. It is hard to visualize, and Luke spends no further
time explaining it. We are told that they are all filled with the Holy
Spirit and begin to speak in other tongues, explained a little later
with a different word as 'native languages'. It would appear
incorrect to describe this phenomenon, therefore, as ecstatic utterance.[4] A multisensory experience is here described with considerable restraint: there is wind and fire, there is hearing, seeing and
speaking; but above all there is the pouring out, the coming down,
the filling, of the Spirit.

Remarkable results quickly follow. The Pentecostal noise[5] is
evidently heard by a large number of people, who quickly converge
on the spot. We are told that they are God-fearing Jews (i.e. not
necessarily Hebrew children of Hebrew parents), staying in Jerusalem, perhaps temporarily for the feasts, but gathered from all over
the biblical world of the Mediterranean and Western Asia.[6] If we
find this miraculous gift of foreign languages hard to understand
and believe, we are in good company, because Luke also indicates
that the crowd is bewildered (v. 6), amazed and astonished (v. 7),
amazed and perplexed (v. 12) – in other words completely
astounded! They recognize their own dialects or native languages,
although the apostles are Galileans; and they recognize that the
apostles are speaking about God's mighty works. As often happens
in similar events, some are curious, asking, 'What does this
mean?' while others are contemptuous: 'They are filled with sweet
wine!'

[4] 'Tongues' are mentioned in two other places in Acts. In 10:46 it is mentioned in
connection with 'extolling God'. In 19:6 it is mentioned in connection with
prophesying. It does not seem as if either of these references implies 'foreign
languages' as in Acts 2.
[5] Understood by F. F. Bruce as the sound of the apostles praising God, rather than
as the sound of the violent wind. See *The Book of Acts* (Marshall, Morgan & Scott,
1977), p. 59.
[6] No completely convincing explanation is available of why Luke mentions the
particular nations he does, nor of the order he follows, nor of the puzzling 'Judea' in
the middle of the list.

Many early Pentecostals believed that the world would shortly end, and thus that the miraculous gift of speaking foreign languages would be given to missionaries in order to spread the gospel quickly before the end.[7] The fact that this belief was incorrect does not justify the dismissal of all reports of xenolalia, or the speaking of foreign languages by those who have not learnt them.

Reflection on this story within the canon of Scripture as a whole makes it inevitable that we are tempted to elaborate on the symbolism of the wind and the fire; and also perhaps to interpret the events of Pentecost as a *reversal* of the confusing of the world's languages in the story of the Tower of Babel. Luke himself does not give any specific prompts in these directions – except one, and that is the *inclusivity* of the Pentecost story, punctuated as it is by the words *all, entire, every, each* (see vv. 1, 2, 3, 4, 5, 6, 7, 8, 12).

4. How was Pentecost interpreted? (Acts 2:14-36)

Peter's life may have been changed in certain radical respects by the events of Jesus' death and resurrection, but one thing that hasn't changed is his quickness of speech. Thus we find him rising immediately to the questions and comments of the crowds. His sermon, which has been reliably summarized by Luke,[8] is characterized by friendly appeal,[9] frank speaking and appeal to three significant passages of the Old Testament. The whole message centres on the Pentecostal events being the fulfilment of Old Testament promises in Jesus, and that these two things together (the fulfilment of the Old Testament and the pouring out of the Spirit) attest Jesus of Nazareth to be, in truth, God's Lord and Messiah.

He begins on a semi-humorous note by remarking that the apostles can hardly be drunk at nine o'clock in the morning! No, the gift of the Spirit and the preaching this inspires are a sign that the 'days' or the 'great day of the Lord' prophesied by Joel centuries before has now arrived: the Spirit has now been poured out; the portents foreseen by Joel are now occurring; the prophetic

---

[7] Allan Anderson has collected examples of early, overheated expectations in this regard in his paper 'Signs and Blunders: Pentecostal Mission Issues at "Home and Abroad" in the Twentieth Century', available at <http://www.martynmission.cam.ac.uk/CSigns.htm>.

[8] For a brief resumé of the debate, coming down on the side of Luke's reliability in recording the different messages in Acts, see J. R. W. Stott, *The Message of Acts* (IVP, 1990), pp. 69–72.

[9] *Men of Judea* (v. 14); *Men, Israelites* (v. 21, fn.); *Men, brothers* (v. 29, fn.), receiving a responsive *Men, brothers* in v. 37, fn.

preaching implied by *prophesy ... visions ... dream ...* is taking place; and this blessing is for all sorts of people.[10]

Joel's prophecy envisages a plague of locusts from the north as instruments of God's judgment. When the people repent, God has pity on his land and people and afterwards brings in a new era when the spirit of prophecy is no longer restricted to a specific band of 'prophets' but is spread widely throughout the community. Hence Joel calls upon his people to repent and call upon the Lord.

The New Testament shows an intense interest in this passage in Joel, first of all applying its imagery to the return of Christ (e.g. Mark 13:34), but also, according to Peter's preaching here, teaching that these 'last days' of which the prophet speaks have begun to be fulfilled in the life of Jesus of Nazareth. Around the time of Jesus' death there were unusual signs, such as darkness and earthquakes; and now there is another unusual sign in the pouring out of the Holy Spirit. So it is not surprising that Peter passes immediately from this introduction to focus on Jesus himself.

Peter draws attention to five aspects of Jesus' life: first, his remarkable and widely attested works and wonders, which marked him out as a man sent from God; secondly, his cruel death by crucifixion. Here Peter deftly combines a quiet accusation, 'you did it', with the accompanying phrases which recognize that it was the Romans ('men outside the law', v. 23) who were responsible for the verdict and, more amazingly, that what happened was somehow according to the will of God. Thirdly, God raised Jesus up (*of that all of us are witnesses* Peter adds in v. 32); and here Peter refers to his second Old Testament passage, Psalm 16:8–11. In its place this psalm appears to refer to David's hope to live in God's presence for ever, even after death. But Peter points out that everyone knows that David is dead, and thus his psalm must be a prophecy referring to someone else. The obvious candidate is one of David's descendants, because God promised that one of David's descendants would sit upon his throne. Who could this descendant be? Peter has the explanation: David was speaking of the Messiah (Christ); and the Messiah is this Jesus of whom he, Peter, has been speaking. Fourthly, Peter refers to the ascension and exaltation of Jesus (not just into the sky but) to the right hand, the executive hand, of God. And fifthly, Peter comes to current events: the pouring out of the promised Holy Spirit, which is where his sermon started. The ascension is the final proof of Jesus' exalted status, says Peter,

---

[10] It seems clear that by *all flesh* in v. 17 Peter had in mind 'all kinds of Jews', because later in 10:45 surprise is expressed that this blessing is for Gentiles also. But within Luke's scheme of things we may well hear the resonance 'all sorts of people' behind the phrase.

quoting another psalm (Ps. 110), because it was not David who ascended, but he himself speaks of God, the Lord, speaking to a person whom he, David, calls *my Lord* – apparently a descendant who is after him, yet greater than him.

So, Peter concludes triumphantly, may all his Jewish hearers be quite convinced that this Jesus is both Lord and Messiah. It is an astonishing claim, for 'Lord' was a word traditionally reserved for God. The detailed theological working out of this claim is done by later New Testament writers, but Luke has accurately presented this earliest of Christian sermons; and the danger Peter's Jewish hearers are in is that they may be among those (a *crooked generation*, v. 40) who have made themselves Jesus' enemies (v. 35).

5. What was the result?

The effects of the Pentecostal outpouring of the Holy Spirit and of Peter's preaching are recorded in two phases.

The first is the immediate effect (vv. 37–41): consciences are stabbed awake; repentance, baptism and receiving the Holy Spirit follows (apparently without any signs in this case); and about three thousand people are added to the group of disciples.

The longer-term effects are described in verses 42–47: these encompass public and private worship, including teaching, fellowship, prayers and sharing food; signs and wonders done by the apostles; great and single-minded generosity in the sharing of possessions *as any had need*; much joy in God and favour with the public; and significant numbers of people being added to the fellowship on a daily basis. These halcyon days[11] were not to continue long, as Luke himself faithfully records, but the picture of the church which they give has nourished the hearts of Christians ever since.

6. The Spirit of mission

Max Turner in his profoundly helpful Grove booklet summarizes the manifold witness of the New Testament writers to the activities of the Holy Spirit as follows:

> For the NT writers ... baptism in the Holy Spirit [Turner prefers the term 'charismatic Spirit-encounter'] was probably a very plastic symbol encompassing all activities of the risen Lord

[11] Max Turner speaks of 'an almost paradisal community of harmony, unity, joyful worship and service that radically embodies the good news Jesus preached' (*Baptism in the Holy Spirit*, Grove Renewal Series R2 [Grove, 2000]), p. 15.

through the Spirit, from 'new birth' and 'washing with the Spirit' to deeper sanctification through the Spirit (expressed in the 'fruit of the Spirit') and empowerings of the Spirit for acts of service (both to edify the church and to evangelize the world), all the way to the final overwhelming cleansing of God's people in resurrection effected by the Spirit.[12]

Turner believes that different sections of the church have borne witness to different parts of this teaching (one might add, 'at different times and in different ways') and his summary proposes a larger synthesis that might unite them.

After nearly 900 pages of reflection on Paul's teaching about the Holy Spirit, Gordon Fee concludes, 'Both Paul's explicit words and his allusions to the work of the Spirit everywhere presuppose the Spirit as an empowering, experienced reality in the life of the church and the believer.'[13]

It is perhaps common for Christians to interpret Jesus' words in Acts 1:8 ('you will be my witnesses') as a command, an obligation, a duty. But the construction uses a future tense and should be interpreted as a promise, a prediction of what will be the case. We do not find in Acts many exhortations to obedience to the Lord's final command, as is common in many churches today. Rather, Luke's narrative portrays mission as the overflow of joy and energy, given by the Holy Spirit: what Jesus predicts actually comes to pass when his followers are filled with his Holy Presence.

The Pentecost story is set centrally in Luke's large two-volume work in the New Testament. He has shown the Spirit at work in the life of Jesus in his Gospel; and in Acts he shows the continuation of that work in the life of Jesus in his church. There are 56 references to the Holy Spirit in Acts; the references cluster especially in the Pentecost story; the story of Stephen in Acts 6 and 7; the story of Philip in Samaria in Acts 8; and in the story of Cornelius in Acts 10 and 11.

Many aspects of the Christian life are described in Acts in association with the Holy Spirit; it is he who transforms lives and empowers mission. Luke uses his terminology fluently and fluidly and without taxonomic precision. He refers frequently to 'filling with the Spirit' but also uses the terms 'pour out', 'come down', 'come on'. It is instructive to study the references in Acts to prayer, fasting, the laying on of hands, tongues and prophecy, and healing and deliverance. It is perhaps surprising to note that tongues is only

[12] Ibid., p. 20.
[13] Gordon D. Fee, *God's Empowering Presence: The Holy Spirit in the Letters of Paul* (Hendrickson, 1994), p. 897.

referred to once in connection with the laying on of hands (19:6).[14] There is more connection of the Holy Spirit with prophecy in Acts than with tongues. A careful study of the healings and deliverances recorded in Acts shows that they took place with or without prayer, with or without the laying on of hands, and with or without reference to the name of Jesus. One striking feature of Acts is the way in which the Spirit *speaks* – to Stephen (6:10); to Philip (8:29); to Peter (10:19); to church leaders gathered in worship and fasting (13:2); to Paul and Timothy (16:6); to the disciples in Tyre (21:4) and to Agabus at Caesarea (21:11).

Through all these stories there is a sense of immediacy of contact with the risen Jesus through the dynamic experience of the Holy Spirit. Gordon Fee notes how the church has often lost this sense of the Spirit's presence and guidance: the Spirit has been marginalized in the academy and domesticated in the church; and Fee pleads for a 'recapturing of the Pauline perspective of Christian life as essentially the life of the Spirit, dynamically experienced and eschatologically oriented – but *fully integrated into the life of the church*'.[15]

The picture comes to mind of a boat stuck in the mud in a tidal creek. When the tide is out, however hard one may struggle it is almost impossible to shift the boat. But when the tide comes in, the boat lifts quietly off the mud and may be moved with the lightest touch of a finger. Again and again revival has been experienced in the church as a tidal lifting of the church's whole life, deepening the lives of Christians and empowering them for joyful witness.

7. Mission in love and unity

This chapter began with reference to William Joseph Seymour and his Pentecostal experience in April 1906. Seymour and others believed that this experience was part of God's prophesied sign for the end of the age. On 17 April the San Francisco earthquake made 300,000 homeless and left 10,000 dead. By May huge crowds of every race, nationality and class were attending the Azusa Street mission. Seven to eight hundred people would squeeze inside the mission house, while four to five hundred more would stand on the pavement outside.

In September Seymour started to publish *The Apostolic Faith* and the circulation quickly climbed from 5,000 to 50,000. A. A. Boddy, an English clergyman from Sunderland, described the movement as surpassing the Welsh revival. A. G. Garr went to India and China;

[14] Pentecostals often *suggest* that tongues is implied in 8:15–17 because Simon could evidently *see* that the Samaritans had received the Holy Spirit.
[15] Fee, *Empowering Presence*, pp. 899–903.

Welsh revival influence had already reached the Assam hills and thence to Pandita Ramabai's community by 1905. 'This Pentecostal movement is too large to be confined in any denomination or sect,' wrote Seymour. 'It works outside, drawing all together in one bond of love, one church, one body of Christ ... God makes no difference in nationality, Ethiopians, Chinese, Indians, Mexicans and other nationalities worship together.'[16] Again and again Seymour referred to this uniting feature of Pentecostal power; he called it the Azusa standard or the Jesus standard or the Bible standard: 'the complete wholeness of the body of Christ across every division of humanity, required by the cross and signified by the outpouring of the Spirit in glossolalia'.[17]

It seems that Seymour was a meek man and not at all a rabble-rouser. William Durham called him 'simple-hearted as a little child, and at the same time so filled with God that you feel the love and power every time you get near him'.[18] D. J. Nelson interviewed the 99-year-old Elder C. C. Carhee, who remembered Seymour's face as the face of an angel.[19]

It is sad to report that the unity didn't last. Charles Parham arrived in Los Angeles in October 1906 and was shocked by 'white people imitating unintelligent, crude negroisms of the Southland and laying it on the Holy Ghost'. He called this 'animalism' and a split ensued.[20] Seymour's marriage in 1908 was controversial for reasons not fully understood. The mission secretary departed to Portland with all-important mailing lists and the circulation of *The Apostolic Faith* began to decline. In 1911 William Durham split the movement again with a new teaching that promised complete sanctification at conversion. Later Durham's own movement split again over Jesus-name baptism.

Restorationist movements continue to split the church with claims that they – and perhaps they alone – are reverting to or restoring the (one and only?) New Testament pattern for the church. Nelson's assessment of the Azusa Street movement is that the inclusiveness was more important than the glossolalia; but whites accepted the glossolalia and rejected both Seymour and the Christian interracial equality. 'It is likely', he wrote despondently, 'the loss of glossolalic and healing power is related to declining love and loss of unity.'[21]

[16] *Apostolic Faith* 1.1 (September 1906), p. 1, col. 3.
[17] Nelson, 'For Such a Time', p. 205.
[18] *Apostolic Faith* 1.6 (February–March 1907), p. 4, col. 3.
[19] Nelson, 'For Such a Time', p. 77, n. 64.
[20] Ibid., p. 208.
[21] Ibid., p. 207.

The fissiparousness of this movement and its successors is perhaps the reason why Gordon Fee pleads for a fresh understanding of the life of the Spirit in our time to be *fully integrated into the life of the church*. Richard Lovelace has drawn attention to the delta-like effect of renewal movements in the church, as like the main channel of a river that splits into many smaller streams. He calls this the 'law of inverse cohesion among the orthodox'.[22] In another image, as he reflects on the ways in which revivals go wrong, he quotes Jonathan Edwards's observation that 'in spring when the birds sing, frogs and toads also croak'.[23] The book of Acts does not gloss over disagreements which arose in the early church; indeed, halfway through the book, in chapter 15, the evidence is there that the church is still divided over the issue of whether Gentiles have to become Jews in order to become Christians. There is no way for us to rewrite or rewind the story of the church and pretend that we are the first generation again. But the example of the joyful unity of the earliest group of Christians in Acts 2 continues to be an inspiration to all those who long to see fresh outpourings of the Spirit today.

8. Mission and the forgiveness of sins

Peter urges his hearers to repent so that their sins may be forgiven. God has exalted Jesus to his right hand 'that he might give repentance to Israel and forgiveness of sins' (Acts 5:31). Peter repeats this theme in his sermon in the house of Cornelius (10:43). Luke has noted that this was also the theme of Jesus, at the beginning and the end of his ministry (Luke 3:3; 24:47). He also notes that this was part of Paul's own understanding of his vocation: 'to open their [the Gentiles'] eyes so that they may turn from darkness to light and from the power of Satan to God, so that they may receive forgiveness of sins ... ' (Acts 26:18); and so we find the theme in Paul's famous sermon at Antioch (Acts 13:38). Forgiveness of sins, the cleansing of a guilty conscience has huge transformative power in people's lives: it brings a new liberty and joy to their hearts, and it empowers them to forgive where they themselves have been wronged.

Here we are at the very heart of the good news of the gospel. In a world where diabolical things happen and are done to people, the power of forgiveness to change people's lives is well attested; so also, unfortunately, exists the power to cripple lives when bitterness is cherished and there is a refusal to forgive. Many stories of

[22] R. Lovelace, *Dynamics of Spiritual Life* (IVP, 1979), p. 321.
[23] Ibid., p. 251.

forgiveness emerged during the hearings of the Truth and Reconciliation Commission in South Africa.[24] In 1994 hundreds of thousands of people were killed in ethnic violence in Rwanda. A Bible Society video shows one pastor mention that out of 67 members of his family, only 3 survived. In another section of the video the reporter visits a church where 5,000 terrified people who fled there for sanctuary were brutally murdered, including the parents of the woman showing the reporter around.[25] 'If there is no forgiveness, there is no second chance,' says one of the reconciliation workers interviewed. 'Human beings need a second chance.'

Corrie ten Boom was a Dutch woman interned during the war at Ravensbruck concentration camp where her sister died. She tells in her autobiography of a moment after the war when she met and recognized one of the guards from the camp, and was confronted suddenly with unprecedented intensity with the challenge to forgive. Later she wrote, 'Forgiveness is the key that unlocks the door of resentment and the handcuffs of hate. It is a power that breaks the chains of bitterness and the shackles of selfishness. He who cannot forgive others, breaks the bridge over which he himself must pass.'[26]

9. Mission and the sharing of resources

Acts 2:44, 45 pictures the early Christians sharing their possessions, and selling and distributing the proceeds to the needy. There is no indication that this was compulsory, or a policy: in Acts 5 where Ananias and Sapphira fall under God's judgment, it is not because they withhold property, but because they have lied to the Holy Spirit.

Leonard Verduin's book *The Reformers and their Stepchildren* is a study of Anabaptist movements, and each chapter is titled with a word that reflects an insult cast against these so-called 'stepchildren'. Chapter 7's title is 'Kommunisten!' The issue of community of goods was a point of tension between the Reformers and the Anabaptists. Article 36 of the Belgic Confession of 1561 notes community of goods as one article in their detestation.[27] It is mixed up there with rejecting higher powers and magistrates, subverting

[24] See <http://www.doj.gov.za/trc/>. A particularly moving story of a woman who forgave the policemen who murdered her husband and son was published in the June 1999 newsletter of the Mennonite Church Peace and Justice Committee.

[25] Bible Society video *Deeper Than the Wound*.

[26] See <http://www.eauk.org/contentmanager/content/face-values/fv/html/forgiveness/quotes.htm>.

[27] L. Verduin, *The Reformers and their Stepchildren* (Paternoster, 1964), p. 221.

justice and confounding that decency and order which God has established. Luther got into trouble for arguing that begging should be ended in Christendom; in contradicting him Jerome Enser argued that this would bring the meritorious practice of almsgiving to an end.[28] It is clear that radical experiments in social order were viewed as subversive. Sometimes, to make the charge more scandalous, it was alleged that these radical Christians shared their wives also. This may have arisen in connection with rumours about Christian love feasts, or because some Restitutionists refused the sacrament of matrimony, or because when husbands were away preaching for long periods (as was often the case) other members of the fellowship cared for the women left at home.[29]

Careful study reveals what these Christians did and didn't mean by 'community of goods'. When Zwingli accused Balthasar Hubmaier of community of goods in 1526, two years before he was burned in March 1528, Hubmaier replied carefully:

I have always and at all places spoken about community of goods as follows: that a man must at all times be concerned for his fellow man, in order that the hungry may be fed, the thirsty given to drink, the naked clothed. For we are verily not lords over our own possessions, only administrators and dispensers. There is, believe me, no one who advocates taking another man's goods and making it common ... ![30]

Menno Simons, after whom the Mennonites are named, repudiated the charge that he and his fellow-Christians practised forced community of goods. He replied somewhat triumphantly that although his people had a lot of poor among them because of persecutions and confiscations, none had been left to beg. 'This mercy, this love, this community of goods we do teach ... If this is not Christian practice then we might as well abandon the whole Gospel of our Lord Jesus Christ, his holy sacraments and the Christian name.'[31]

For some communities, for example the Hutterites to this day, the community of goods is still the rule, a practice which originated in the desperation of an impoverished community fleeing from persecution. But even this is a voluntary submission to a law of community, not an imposition. It seems that it was the compulsory requisitioning of people's property during the siege of Münster in

28 Ibid., p. 239.
29 Ibid., p. 226–227.
30 Ibid., p. 231.
31 Ibid., p. 234.

1525, and the events surrounding that whole tragedy, which fostered general fears about radical Christianity. Verduin is of the opinion that until modern times the picture of Anabaptism has been painted on the canvas of Münster.

It is natural for the generosity of Christians within their own communities to overflow into 'works of mercy', a theme taken up already in several chapters of this book. In 1968 the Evangelical Alliance in the UK started a relief fund, 'TEAR Fund' as it was known. Thirty years later the budget of Tearfund is over £25 million annually – a barometer of a gigantic shift in the perception of evangelical Christians about their Christian responsibility in and to a needy world. The twenty-fifth anniversary history of Tearfund by Timothy Chester was entitled *Awakening to a World of Need: The Recovery of Evangelical Social Concern.*[32] This book tells the story of rising Christian social concern in the UK, since the 1960s, especially influenced by the Lausanne movement and the initiative and perseverance of developed-world Christian leaders in the direction of integral, holistic evangelism. As the world becomes smaller the church's obligations increase, for Christians know not only about the needs down the street or in their town or society; they also know from every visit to the supermarket or department store that they are connected to and part of a global distribution system, from which they benefit, but at what cost to others in the chain? Jubilee 2000, Traidcraft, Fair Trade are just a few of the movements trying to address the issues, so that Christians can adjust their lifestyles accordingly.

10. Mission and translation

The crowds from many countries on Pentecost day were astounded because they heard the apostles speaking in their own languages about God's wonderful deeds of power (Acts 2:11). Since that time Christians have never stopped trying to continue this work of communicating the good news to all peoples in their own languages.

On the website of the Summer Institute of Linguistics one can read the *Linguistic Creed*, which includes the following sentences:[33]

We believe that language is one of God's most important gifts to man, and of all human characteristics, language is the most distinctly human and the most basic. Without language, culture and civilization would be impossible.

[32] T. Chester, *Awakening to a World of Need* (IVP, 1993).
[33] See <www.sil.org>.

As the most uniquely human characteristic a person has, a person's language is associated with his self-image. Interest in and appreciation of a person's language is tantamount to interest in and appreciation of the person himself.
All languages are worthy of preservation in written form by means of grammars, dictionaries, and written texts. This should be done as part of the heritage of the human race.
Every language group deserves to see its language in print and to have some literature written in it.
Minority language groups within a larger nation deserve the opportunity of learning to speak, read, and write the national language.

Bible translations into the main languages of the ancient world were made very early in the history of Christianity. The Latin Bible reigned for many centuries in Europe, but around the time of the Reformation there was a renewed flurry of Bible translations into European languages especially. In the eighteenth and nineteenth centuries many new Bible translations were made by missionaries, some of whom became world experts in languages.

Today the work of Bible translation is continuing, although it is hard to count exactly what has been done and what remains to be done. David Barrett counts up to 13,500 languages, which he arranges in nearly 300 pages of detailed tables with codes indicating their proximity or distance from other languages.[34] Another catalogue of world languages and Bible translations is Ethnologue, which speaks of 6,800 languages in 231 countries.[35] Wycliffe International has 1,500 translation projects in 70 countries in progress, and they have recently reformulated their organizational goal towards providing Bible translation for every community that needs one by 2025. On their website they mention that 380 million people in over 3,000 language groups still wait for the good news in their own language.[36] A Bible Society press release in 1999 reported that at least a part of the Bible is now available in 2,212 of the world's 6,500 languages.

There is a Forum of Bible Agencies,[37] and in the year 2000 there were 137 societies in more than 200 countries working on Bible

[34] Barrett, Kurian and Johnson, *World Christian Encyclopaedia*, vol. 2, part 9, 'Linguametrics'. Barrett is heavily dependent on David Dalby, *The Linguasphere: Register of the World's Languages and Speech Communities* (Linguasphere, 2000).
[35] See <www.ethnologue.com>.
[36] See <www.wycliffe.net>.
[37] See <www.scripturesources.com>.

translation projects and the whole delivery chain (translating, checking, revising, printing, publishing, importing, distributing), which will bring such translations into the hands of those who need them at an affordable price.

It is hard perhaps for those whose shelves are stuffed with books, including many versions of the Bible and books about the Bible, and who are daily overwhelmed by the media barrage of newspapers, magazines, radio and TV, to transport themselves to a world where a Bible may be the only printed possession of its owner. 'We never imagined it possible to have the Bible in our own language,' said a Myanmar elder. 'But when the Falam Bible was made available we discovered the wonderful richness of reading God's Word in our own language. It was so good we could not stop. We now realize that the Bible freed us from the "slavery" and domination of other ethnic groups. We have come to realize that we are special, one of the races our God created. How can we ever thank God and you enough?'

'Is Christianity also for the Iraqw [sic] people?' asked an old woman in Tanzania, when she heard the New Testament being read in her own language. 'I thought it was only for those who spoke Swahili.'

There was nearly a riot when the Edo Bible was launched in Nigeria, but it was announced that copies would not be on sale until a later date. One man offered to leave his motorbike as security to ensure he received a copy. 'It means so much to me,' he said. 'Other language Bibles have been speaking to me in languages which require an intepreter, but this one is in my mother tongue.'

When the Ngbaka Bible was published in the Democratic Republic of Congo, Pastor Weka Musuku was overjoyed: 'I have often wondered whether I have understood the full meaning of a Bible passage [in French],' he said. 'Now we have the Bible in Ngbaka, God speaks clearly and directly to our hearts, and we understand his message for our lives today.'

When Daniel Mndeke received his own copy of the New Testament in the kiSagalla language in 1995, he was delighted: 'Now I have food for my spirit. And I will be able to tell others that this is the way to heaven and life for ever.'[38]

Professor Lamin Sanneh has written a pioneering work in which he considers the missionary impact on culture in the light of missionary translating work.[39] His thesis is that Christianity was characterized from the beginning by translateability with two

---

[38] Stories from Bible Society's *Bible A Month Club*.
[39] Lamin Sanneh, *Translating the Message: The Missionary Impact on Culture* (Orbis, 1990).

historical effects: the relativization of its Jewish roots and the destigmatization of Gentile culture. However imperialistic and highhanded Western missionaries may have been in their attitudes and behaviour, missionary adoption of the vernacular 'was tantamount to adopting indigenous cultural criteria for the message, a piece of radical indigenization far greater than the standard portrayal of mission as Western cultural imperialism'.[40] In some cases missionaries were responsible for initial dictionaries and grammars of languages, for the first teaching of literacy, and for the preservation of precolonial stories and histories. Sanneh says, 'We have to recognize the immense contribution to the revitalization of Africa that this represents.'[41] Translatability recognizes that all languages are capable of bearing the good news to those who speak those languages: 'all languages and cultures are, in principle, equal in expressing the word of God'.[42] It didn't even matter *that much* if the translation was good or bad; the fact that it was possible meant that the foreigner was subverting his foreignness, marginalizing himself and, intentionally or unintentionally, empowering those who heard the message in their own language to make up their own minds about the meaning and the implications.

Learning another language is an arduous task, and translating the Bible is even harder, with no end in sight because languages flow endlessly like rivers. But the joy of seeing people able to read their own language, or listen to it (if they are still illiterate) is one of the most memorable works of cross-cultural service.

11. Conclusion

Luke's story of Pentecost is richly suggestive in many ways, not all of which have been touched on here. The story repays repeated return visits for personal inspiration and for its picture of the church's life.

We have noted in particular the fundamental need for the church to live continually in the experience and power of the Spirit: an initial Pentecostal endowment is not enough; neither is a 'second' or subsequent blessing – we need to 'live in the Spirit'.

Acts 2 is also utterly compelling in its vision of the church living in love and generosity, spreading the good news to all who will hear it, in their own languages, and growing upwards, downwards, outwards and in numbers.

[40] Ibid., p. 3.
[41] Ibid., p. 166.
[42] Ibid., p. 208.

The ancient hymn 'Veni Creator' invokes God's empowering presence for the task (my emphasis):

> Come Holy Spirit ever one
> With God the Father and the Son:
> Come swiftly, Fount of grace, and pour
> Into our hearts your boundless store.
>
> With all our strength, with heart and tongue,
> By word and deed your praise be sung:
> *And love light up our mortal frame*
> *Till others catch the living flame.*
>
> O Father, that we ask be done
> Through Jesus Christ, your only Son,
> Who with the Spirit, reigns above,
> Three persons in one God of love.
>   Amen.

Acts 19:8–41
13. A model of mission

It seems to have been the apostle Paul's missionary policy to focus on the strategic cities of the Roman Empire. What drew him to the cities was probably that they contained the Jewish synagogues, the influential leaders and a cosmopolitan atmosphere. And, like all great cities today, they attracted local and foreign visitors who could be the carriers of the gospel to their own native lands. On his third missionary journey Paul travelled from Antioch to the regions of Galatia and Phrygia (18:23), and returned by an inland route to the city of Ephesus where he had left his fellow-workers Priscilla and Aquila and where he himself had enjoyed a short period of ministry in the Jewish synagogue (18:18–21).

Ephesus was the principal city of the Roman province of Asia, situated at the mouth of the river Cayster on an important trade route inland. It was a free city with its own assembly, and boasted a magnificent temple of the goddess Artemis, one of the wonders of the ancient world. Under the patronage of the goddess, religious 'mystery cults' and occult practices of all kinds flourished. The city was famous for its 'Ephesian writings' (*grammata*), which were papyri containing written charms and magical incantations, often rolled up into small cylinders or lockets and worn as talismans around the neck. Ephesus was a point of convergence for various cultural and religious movements, and the Jewish community in Ephesus was the largest in the area, having been there since the third century BC.

The New Testament scholar Ben Witherington III notes:

It is here in Ephesus that [Paul] has the longest stable period of ministry without trial or expulsion, here that he most fully carries out his commission to be a witness to all persons, both Jew and Gentile (see 22:15). Viewing this material retrospectively on the

225

basis of the content of the Miletus speech in 20:18–35 reinforces the notion that here Luke is intending to present a lasting model of what a universalistic Christian mission ought to look like. The crucial nature of this material is also shown later when it is Jews from Asia who incite the riot in Jerusalem, and they do so because they believed Paul brought an Ephesian Gentile Christian into the temple (21:27–29, see 24:19).[1]

1. The power of persuasion

Paul begins by returning to the synagogue where he taught about a year before (18:19–21). The subject of his preaching is described as *the kingdom of God* (v. 8; cf. Acts 8:12; 20:25). It is unlikely that this means that Paul is preaching a different message from that in 17:31; 18:5; and other places where he is concerned with Jesus as the Messiah. The message is about Jesus *and* the kingdom (28:31), and all commentators agree that Luke employs the different terms simply for literary variation. To the Jewish mind, it was inconceivable that one could talk about the Messiah without reference to the reign of God over all that opposes his reign; and for Paul and the early church, it was Jesus who had ushered in God's reign through his unique life, death and resurrection.

It is worthwhile dwelling briefly on this point. In some circles within the older Christian denominations today there is a tendency to reduce Christian mission to spreading the *values* of the kingdom of God in society, and to downplay the public proclamation of the King who inaugurates and embodies that kingdom. So, for instance, the Indian theologian and ecumenical leader, Stanley Samartha, has argued that claims concerning the Lordship of Jesus over all of life must be confined to the liturgical life and worship of the Christian community, whose sole calling it is to 'contribute to the pool of values' which will undergird and nurture the secular, pluralist character of the Indian state.[2]

But how can values such as 'justice' and 'unity' be affirmed apart from challenging some beliefs about the true nature of things? For example, isn't the miserable condition of outcastes (Dalits) in India itself an expression of a *just* cosmic order – according to Brahmanical Hinduism? Also, isn't it unjust, given the individualist understanding of human beings in liberal Western states, to interfere with what many would claim is their 'right' to unlimited consumption?

[1] Ben Witherington III, *The Acts of the Apostles: A Socio-Rhetorical Commentary* (Eerdmans/Paternoster, 1998), pp. 572–573.
[2] S. J. Samartha, *One Christ – Many Religions: Towards a Revised Christology* (South Asia Theological Research Institute, 1992), p. 53.

All values derive from a conception of the world and the place of human beings within that world. Christian values are grounded in a vision of things given in the historic story which finds its climax in Jesus Christ. The latter calls into question other visions of how things are. To call the church to contribute values prised out of that story, but without proclaiming the story that makes sense of those values, is to call the church to deny its identity and the most important thing it has been entrusted with for the sake of the world.

Observe, moreover, the intellectual passion with which Paul presented the gospel to his contemporaries. In the synagogue he *spoke out boldly, and argued persuasively* (v. 8). When the message was resisted and maligned, he hired a *scholē*, a public auditorium or lecture hall, and *argued daily* (v. 9) with whoever was willing to engage him in discussion. The Western (Bezan) text adds the detail that Paul did this *from eleven o'clock in the morning to four in the afternoon* (NRSV footnote). In the Graeco-Roman world the business day or the period of public affairs began at dawn and ended at 11am. The wealthier classes would then retire for a meal and an afternoon siesta. It is likely that Paul rented the hall used by a local teacher or orator called Tyrannus, during the period when Tyrannus himself went away for his siesta. Since the English word 'tyrant' is derived from the Greek *tyrannos*, most commentators cannot resist the urge to speculate that this was the name his students gave him!

Both in the religious atmosphere of the Jewish synagogue and in the secular lecture theatre of Tyrannus, Paul combined argument (*dialegomai*) with persuasion (*peithō*). These words recur in Luke's presentation of Paul's ministry in both Corinth and Ephesus (Acts 18:4, 13; 19:8, 9, 26). 'This vocabulary', observes John Stott, 'shows that Paul's presentation of the gospel was serious, well-reasoned and persuasive. Because he believed the gospel to be true, he was not afraid to engage the minds of his hearers. He did not simply proclaim his message in a "take it or leave it" fashion; instead, he marshalled arguments to support and demonstrate his case. He was seeking to convince in order to convert, and in fact, as Luke makes plain, many were "persuaded".'[3]

There is, of course, an unattractive form of apologetics that is more concerned to win arguments than to win genuine converts to Jesus Christ. Sadly, it is possible to be more enamoured by our arguments for the existence of God than by God himself. Another reason Christian apologetics is shunned in many Christian circles today is because it is often perceived as a narrowly rationalist

[3] John R. W. Stott, *The Message of Acts* (IVP, 1990), pp. 312-313.

enterprise, with those who are good debaters often showing little humility in the face of mystery, and scant respect for the cultural context in which they debate. Paul, however, is depicted in the narrative of Acts as always 'contextualizing' his approach and message. Thus he argues from the Jewish Scriptures when proclaiming the gospel to Jews in the synagogues, from God's general revelation in creation when pleading with idolatrous pagans, and from Greek philosophers when addressing cultured Greeks in the Areopagus at Athens (e.g. Acts 14:15ff.; 17:22ff.).

Temple Gairdner (1873–1928) was an Anglican missionary who worked in Cairo for thirty-one years. He was a gifted linguist and understood Islam well enough to be able to debate publicly in Arabic with religious scholars from Cairo's famous al-Azhar university. In her biography of Gairdner, Constance Padwick noted Gairdner's distress that the kind of Christian apologetics Muslims had been accustomed to was dry, scholastic disputation.

Gairdner believed (for was he not nightly battered with anti-Christian arguments?) that there must needs be an apologetic literature, unafraid of controversial points. Silence, he felt, was tantamount to denial of the truth he knew and lived. But the literature must be humanized and written for fellow-men, not only for the defeat of arguers. Moreover, to Gairdner, stories, history, drama, music, poetry, pictures, all that could bear the impress of the Spirit of Christ, was a reasonable part of the Christian apologetic to the whole man.[4]

In Gairdner's own words, 'We need the *song* note in our message to the Muslims ... not the dry cracked note of disputation, but the song of joyous witness, tender invitation.'[5]

What another great missionary to the Muslim word, Kenneth Cragg, asserts below is also applicable to other religious and secular cultures:

If Christ is what Christ is, he must be uttered. If Islam is what Islam is, that 'must' is irresistible. Wherever there is misconception, witness must penetrate; wherever there is the obscuring of the beauty of the Cross, it must be unveiled; wherever persons have missed God in Christ, he must be brought to them again ... In such a situation as Islam presents, the Church has no option but to present Christ.[6]

---

[4] Constance Padwick, *Temple Gairdner of Cairo* (SPCK, 1929), p. 149.
[5] Ibid., p. 158.
[6] Kenneth Cragg, *The Call of the Minaret* (OUP, 1956), pp. 304–305.

Luke also records that Paul conducted his Ephesian 'school' for two years, and that as a result of this ministry the residents of the Roman province of Asia were evangelized (v. 10).[7] This could have happened in two ways. First, people from the countryside who flocked to the city on market days or for the numerous religious festivals would have dropped in to listen to this strange new philosopher whom everyone was talking about. Those who received the gospel would have carried it back with them to their farms and towns. John Stott comments that 'This is a fine strategy for the great university and capital cities of the world. If the gospel is reasonably, systematically and thoroughly unfolded in the city centre, visitors will hear it, embrace it and take it back with them to their homes.'[8]

Secondly, Paul would also have been training his co-workers and sending them out, from time to time, to the nearby towns in the Lycus valley. We know that the churches in Colosse and Laodicea, for instance, were founded by Paul's travelling companions and not directly by the apostle himself. Ephesus was Paul's base of operations: if we add the two years in the lecture hall to the three months in the synagogue plus the *some time longer* (of v. 22), we arrive at the 'three years' Acts 20:31 says was the length of Paul's tenure in Ephesus.

2. Power encounters 1: miracle and magic

Paul's persuasive preaching was accompanied by remarkable healings and exorcisms. *God did extraordinary miracles through Paul, so that when the handkerchiefs or aprons that had touched his skin were brought to the sick, their diseases left them and the evil spirits came out of them* (vv. 11–12). There are three important matters that Luke's account raises.

First, although Paul himself refers to the signs, wonders and mighty works which accompanied his ministry (2 Cor. 12:12; Rom. 15:19; cf. Gal. 3:5; see also Heb. 2:4), Luke recognizes that what happened at Ephesus was not typical, even for apostolic 'miracles'. Not content to describe these events as mere 'miracles', *dynameis*, demonstrations of divine power, he adds the adjective *tychousas*, which is variously translated 'special' (AV), 'singular' (NEB), 'remarkable' (JB) and 'extraordinary' (RSV, NRSV, NIV). The unusual character of Paul's powers was seen in the fact that even pieces of clothing which had touched his body were taken to the sick and exercised a healing influence on them.

[7] Luke's *daily* (v. 9), like his *all* (v. 10), is probably rhetorical hyperbole (cf. v. 17).
[8] Stott, *Acts*, p. 314.

Secondly, Luke does not say Paul traded in healing handkerchiefs and the like, or that he initiated such practices. These incidents cannot be used to justify the practice of some Pentecostal evangelists who offer to send handkerchiefs which they have blessed to the sick and the handicapped with the promise that they will be instantly cured. The word translated 'handkerchiefs' is the word customarily used for the sweat-rags used by manual labourers. Paul supported himself, as he had done earlier in Corinth, by labouring at his leather-making trade during the mornings or nights (Acts 20:34). People would come to watch this philosopher-healer at his work and take away the sweat-rags and aprons he disposed of. When they discovered the beneficial influence of these rags, they probably came back for more.

Thirdly, although this seems to support the widespread pagan belief in *mana*, or sympathetic influence – the conveying of the power of healing through the medium of a piece of clothing (or even the shadow) of a healer – Luke makes emphatically clear that it is God who causes these miracles to happen. They are best understood as an act of divine *accommodation* so characteristic of God's way of dealing with us in our ignorance and sin. Just as Jesus condescended to the timorous faith of a woman with a haemorrhage (Luke 8:43ff.), so in Ephesus we find that God condescends to making his power known through the channels to which people are accustomed. But, we must pay close attention to the flow of the narrative which concludes with the repudiation of magical practices and books, and a public acknowledgment of the supremacy of Jesus.

A 'vigorous little anecdote'[9] follows (vv. 13–16), which provides some comic relief in Luke's otherwise sober narrative. The sons of a Jewish 'high priest' Sceva,[10] attempt to rival Paul's powers by invoking the name of Jesus over a demon-possessed man. The demon, rather than Paul, challenges their right to use that name. The man turns violent and beats them up. Those who try to strip the man of the demon end up being stripped of their clothes, and flee in shame.

The story tells us much about the environment of early Christianity. Jewish exorcists were held in high regard in the Hellenistic world, and wandering Jewish exorcists were not an uncommon sight, especially in an area where the practice of magic was prevalent

[9] I. Howard Marshall, *The Acts of the Apostles: An Introduction and Commentary* (IVP, 1980), p. 310.
[10] Marshall (p. 311) suggests that Sceva was either a member of a high-priestly family or someone who took the title to impress a gullible public, like some modern quacks do with the title 'doctor' or 'professor'.

and was seen as the chief means of warding off evil spirits and demons. The syncretism that characterized much religion in the region had affected Judaism in Roman Asia, with the result that both Jews and then Christians dabbled in the magical arts while still practising their faiths. 'Exorcisms were in some respects the Jewish counterpart and answer to the felt need for magical help.'[11]

Clinton Arnold observes that 'in religion one prays and requests from the gods; in magic one commands and therefore expects guaranteed results'.[12] He states further:

The overriding characteristic of the practice of magic throughout the Hellenistic world was the cognizance of a spirit world exercising influence over virtually every aspect of life. The goal of the magician was to discern the helpful spirits from the harmful ones and learn the distinct operations and the relative strengths and authority of the spirits. Through this knowledge, means could be constructed (with spoken or written formulas, amulets, etc.) for the manipulation of the spirits in the interests of the individual person.[13]

Magical exorcism is rooted in an animistic world-view which turns over most of life to the realm of spirits. There is no concept of a sovereign God, or of a fallen natural order in which evil and illness occur without direct intervention by malicious spirits. It is the world-view of large numbers of people today, not only in the villages and cities of the developing world, but also among otherwise 'sophisticated' men and women in Western nations. All misfortune is caused by an offended spirit, or by a human curse, or a wrong planetary configuration. The naming of evil spiritual forces, the appeal to benevolent powers, the concoction of magical portions, and the observance of taboos are all essential aspects of animistic techniques to ensure health and protection in an unpredictable world. As the anthropologist Paul Hiebert points out:

[In animism] most things that happen are brought about ... by spirits, ancestors, ghosts, magic, witchcraft and the stars. It is a world in which God is distant and in which humans are at the mercy of good and evil powers and must defend themselves by means of prayers and chants, charms, medicines and incantations.

[11] Witherington III, *Acts*, p. 573.
[12] C. E. Arnold, *Ephesians: Power and Magic* (CUP, 1989), p. 19.
[13] Ibid., p. 18.

Power, not truth, is the central human concern in this world-view.[14]

Magic has a long history, usually traced back to ancient Egypt and Babylon. In Europe it enjoyed immense popularity in the Middle Ages with the codification of the Jewish mystical tradition of Kabbalah and the translation into Latin of ancient Greek writings like the *Hermetica*. The 'occult sciences' of astrology and alchemy flourished alongside the rise of modern science. The continuing fascination with magic is shown by the phenomenal popularity of J. K. Rowling's Harry Potter novels, no less than the more sinister growth of witchcraft and satanic societies. The repressive secularity of modern societies has always generated bizarre quests for transcendence. From W. B. Yeats to Carlos Castaneda, Led Zeppelin to Marilyn Manson, a kind of domesticated occultism has also become the folk religion of the bored, affluent classes.

The Jewish exorcists in Ephesus who try to use Jesus' name as a magical technique come to grief. The residents of Ephesus, both Jews and Greeks, are *awestruck; and the name of the Lord Jesus was praised* (v. 17). This is not to be taken as a mass conversion, but rather as an act of self-preservation in the face of a new and powerful deity, and general respect towards the missionaries and their message (cf. Acts 3:10; 4:21). Moreover, the recent believers *confessed and disclosed their practices* (v. 18). Since the power of spells lies in their secrecy, to divulge them was to render them powerless. A public burning of magical books followed (v. 19), presumably by the wealthier Christians (since a drachma, or 'silver coin', represented a day's wage). Although the burning of writings considered dangerous or subversive was practised by Roman authorities from time to time, the difference in Luke's account is that this was a purely voluntary act by the owners themselves.

The Christian faith is thus presented in this narrative as an alternative to the 'popular religion' of the empire, the religion of magic and mysteries, astrology and the fates. Ben Witherington III notes:

> Christianity is also being portrayed in Acts 19 as a religion which one cannot manipulate for one's own ends, or dabble in without harm. In other words, Christianity is being portrayed as the real source of human and world transformation and redemption, in

[14] Paul Hiebert, 'Healing and the Kingdom', in James Coggins and Paul Hiebert (eds.), *Wonders and the World* (Kindred, 1989), p. 117. See also David Burnett, *Unearthly Powers: A Christian Perspective on Primal and Folk Religion* (MARC, 1988).

contradistinction to both popular panaceas (such as magic) and to 'official' saviours such as the emperor. If Christianity is true and the Christian faith really changes lives, then the emperor has no divine clothes.[15]

However it usually takes some time for pagan ways of thinking to be purged from those who may have had a genuine Christian experience. Paul's correspondence with the church in Corinth shows that Christians there took some time to be persuaded that sexual immorality and participation in idol feasts were incompatible with their new faith (1 Cor. 6:9–11). Similarly, the demonstration of the futility of magical techniques to master evil spirits led many of Paul's Ephesian converts to realize that the occult practices to which they were still attached were both useless and sinful.

Cross-cultural missions rarely lend themselves to strategic planning, because missions – like everything else in the Christian life – are a rich interplay between the divine and the human. The miraculous and timely interventions of God in the story of the advance of the gospel are often ignored in mission studies and the writing of church history textbooks. But it is impossible to write an accurate account of the conversion of indigenous tribes in Europe, Africa or Asia without a recognition of the crucial role that dreams, visions, signs, exorcisms and miraculous healings have played in 'opening up' an animist people to the power of the gospel. American Pentecostal church historian Gary McGee observes that for native peoples, whose world-views parallel those of apostolic and post-apostolic eras, 'paranormal phenomena have indeed played a vital role in the growth of Christianity, although whether in every local context and to what extent must still be determined'.[16]

One example from nineteenth-century Africa that McGee gives is that of the Methodist minister W. J. Davis, called the 'Missionary Elijah' for reasons that will become obvious from the story below. In a Bantu-speaking part of South Africa during the late 1840s, a severe drought caused the soil to dry up, and cattle began to die. Fears of famine led the tribal chief to employ the services of professional rainmakers. When they were unsuccessful, they blamed their failure on the presence of missionaries. Realizing the danger to his family, Davis knew that he had to act quickly. Riding on his horse to the chief's village, he announced, 'Come to chapel next sabbath, and we will pray to God, who made the heavens and the earth, to give us rain, and we will see who is the true God, and who

[15] Witherington III, *Acts*, p. 578.
[16] Gary B. McGee, 'Miracles and Mission Revisited', *International Bulletin of Missionary Research* (October 2001), p. 154.

233

are his true servants, and your best friends.' After the chief accepted his offer, Davis and his fellow-believers spent the next day in fasting and prayer. On Sunday, and without a cloud in the sky, the chief and his retinue entered the church. Then as Davis and the congregation knelt in prayer, 'big rain drops began to patter on the zinc roof of the chapel ... The whole region was so saturated with water that the river nearly became so swollen that the chief and his mother could not cross it that night, and hence had to remain at the mission-station till the next day.'[17] The chief and his family were impressed but remained unconverted. But antipathy towards the gospel dissolved in the face of this power encounter, and it paved the way for a future indigenous Bantu church.

3. Power encounters 2: conversion and self-interest

Luke's story moves from the world of 'extraordinary miracles' to the prosaic, but no less providential, world of social upheaval. Here God advances the cause of the gospel not by directly intervening to rescue his servants from deadly peril, but through the wise intervention of human authorities who do not acknowledge the name of Jesus.

Paul believes that he has finished his work in this region, and his plan is to travel westwards to the very heart of the empire in Rome. He is under divine compulsion (*in the Spirit ... I must also see Rome*, v. 21). It is not as a tourist that he desires to visit the Eternal City, but as an ambassador of the gospel. But he must go by way of Jerusalem, presumably to deliver the financial offering of the Gentile churches for their brethren in Judea. So he sends his co-workers to complete the collection in Macedonia while he lingers in Asia Minor until their return.[18]

It is interesting that Luke describes the Christian movement as 'The Way', particularly in the Jerusalem sections of his narrative and here in Ephesus. Both at the heart of Jewish culture and in the Hellenistic culture of Roman Asia the disciples of Jesus form a socially cohesive movement, without the conventional religious paraphernalia of temples, priests and ritual sacrifices. This is a transcultural movement of people who follow Jesus as the Way from God and back to God, and it is not locked into any geographical, linguistic or ecclesiastical centre. It is a new way of

---

[17] William Taylor, *Christian Adventures in South Africa* (Phillips & Hunt, 1880), pp. 275–276, cited in McGee, 'Miracles', p. 152.

[18] His remark in v. 21 should be compared to what he wrote on a later occasion when he was in Corinth, and indeed vv. 21–22 should be read in conjunction with Rom. 15:23–25.

living that challenges the ways of life taken for granted in the ancient world.

That this is how the movement was perceived is illustrated by the incident that follows. Ephesus was not only the magic capital of the empire, but was the *temple-keeper of the great Artemis* (v. 35), who was worshipped at shrines from Syria to Spain. This was one of the most powerful pagan cults in the Mediterranean world. Indeed, several scholars believe that some of the magical words or phrases meant to ward off demons or curses were engraved on the crown, girdle and feet of statues of Artemis sold all over the empire. The Greek goddess Artemis was a virgin huntress; but in Ephesus she had somehow become identified with an Asian fertility goddess. Ephesian Artemis, even before Paul's day, had taken on many attributes of the Greek Artemis while retaining some of her local traits as the Anatolian 'Great Mother'. The city guarded with immense pride both her grotesque many-breasted image and the magnificent temple which housed it. Being four times the size of the Parthenon in Athens, and adorned by many beautiful paintings and sculptures, it was regarded as one of the seven wonders of the world.

We are introduced to a silversmith, Demetrius, whom the text tells us made *silver shrines of Artemis* (v. 24). A bronze matrix of Artemis in her temple, dating to the second or first century BC, is on display in the Metropolitan Museum of Art in New York. This was the mould into which the silver would be poured to make the miniature shrines described in this verse. These were not simply religious souvenirs for the tourist trade (as in modern Ephesus), but they would be used as amulets, in family worship in the home, and as votive offerings dedicated to the goddess when one visited the temple. We are told that the making of these shrines brought *no little business* (v. 24b) to artisans such as Demetrius.

The conversion of some of the people of Ephesus and the neighbouring towns to the Way, which resulted in their renunciation of magic and temple worship, led to a loss of revenue for artisans like Demetrius and those working in related trades. By exaggerating the threat the missionaries posed, Demetrius is able to whip up his federation of employers to a religious frenzy. An argument from economic self-interest alone was unlikely to prove very attractive; but when cloaked as a defence of cultural identity and as zeal for the honour of the goddess herself, his demagogy wins them over. They begin their religious chanting (v. 28), and a crowd quickly gathers. A protest march through the city follows, and two of Paul's travelling companions are dragged along by the mob (v. 29). The city is in uproar.

The site for a public meeting of any size in many Greek cities was the open-air theatre: the one in Ephesus has been excavated and estimated to have been capable of holding 25,000 persons. It is there that the mob headed, apparently to persuade the city officials to take action against the missionaries. Anyone who has had the experience of being swept along in political or religious protests today will understand Luke's somewhat cynical observation that *some were shouting one thing, some another ... and most of them did not know why they had come together* (v. 32). The *assembly* (v. 32) that normally took place in the theatre would have been an official meeting of the citizen body of the town. But here the assembly is nothing but an unruly crowd.

As Paul ventures to address the crowd, he is dissuaded from doing so by *some officials of the province of Asia, who were friendly to him* (v. 31). These 'Asiarchs', as they were known, were the leading men of the province, members of the wealthiest local families. They were presidents or ex-presidents of the provincial councils of Asia Minor, and one of their main tasks was to promote the imperial cult, the worship of the emperor and the goddess Roma, and so secure allegiance to Rome. Since Paul was a Roman citizen, and known publicly as an orator, he would have been known to the Asiarchs. Ben Witherington suggests that 'The friendship language here could mean that Paul had one or more of the Asiarchs as a patron or at least as an advocate in Ephesus (could this be how he obtained the hall of Tyrannus?).'[19] Any riot in the city was actually to their advantage, as they had no stake in the Artemis cult and preferred stronger Roman control of the city and its cultic activities. That is perhaps why they were not so eager for Paul to try to 'cool things down'.

But a new figure now appears on the scene, the *town clerk* (v. 35), who proves to be a master at crowd control. This person was a city official charged with keeping records, and the scribe of official assemblies of the citizen body. He was not appointed by Rome but came from within the local assembly itself. In order to appreciate his argument one needs to bear in mind that this was a free assembly, and subject to careful scrutiny by the Roman officials, especially the proconsul of the province. Any irregularities might give the Romans an excuse to take away the city's freedoms, including the right to their popular assembly, in the name of 'peace and order'.

For the clerk the long-standing reputation of the city and the divine accreditation of the cult of Artemis were undeniable facts (vv. 35, 36). There was, therefore, no need for such agitation. No

[19] Witherington III, *Acts*, p. 595.

grounds had been offered for a charge against the missionaries. There was no properly formulated accusation for them to answer. They were *neither temple-robbers nor blasphemers of our goddess* (v. 37). There was, in other words, nothing of public concern at issue. If, however, there was something of private concern between the silversmiths and the missionaries, then there were properly constituted channels for dealing with such a matter (v. 38).

The town clerk has adroitly turned the tables on the crowd. If there was an unlawful assembly the city could be charged with rioting, acting seditiously, creating factions in the empire. The terminology the clerk uses at the end of his speech is precisely legal. If questioned, the Ephesians could give no legal justification for this irregular meeting of the assembly, and so would be suspected of, and as verse 40 puts it, perhaps be charged with, subversive activity.

Even as one man's speech began the riot, it took another's to quell it. Having silenced the crowd, having argued them out of any vigilante actions, and having in fact accused them of potentially bringing down the law on their own heads, the town clerk dismissed the assembly, and we hear no more about it. Paul is free to begin his final journey to Jerusalem and beyond Jerusalem, to Rome.

From a historical perspective, Luke's narrative functions as a political apologetic for his times. Those who oppose the Way do so because their own vested interests, usually economic and political, are threatened. Right-thinking officials, concerned with upholding the rule of law, have nothing to fear from Christians. Perhaps the latter should be given the same legal recognition and status given to Jews and Judaism within the empire. Ironically, though they followed a leader who had been crucified by the Roman power as an enemy of the state, the first Christians saw in Roman law the hand of divine providence. Their challenge to the system of Roman power was not overt (they would quickly have been suppressed, in any case) but subtle, in the changed relationships they practised in their common life and in their dealings with outsiders.

4. Conversion and opposition

Throughout history, whether East or West, the Christian gospel has been a powerful ideological force for social transformation. We have seen in earlier chapters that whether we consider the renewal of native languages and cultures, the emancipation of women and slaves, the protection and care of newborn babies, the rise of modern experimental science, the affirmation of the dignity of even the most destitute and degraded of human beings, the church has

237

stood out – despite its many betrayals of the gospel – as a movement deeply subversive of the status quo. (Even socialism and liberal democracy can only be understood properly against their Christian roots.) Not surprisingly, wherever conversion to Christ has threatened the vested economic, status or political interests of power blocs in society, the missionaries and local converts have been bitterly opposed.

Consider the Indian subcontinent, by way of illustration. The concern of men like William Carey (1761–1834), the cobbler from Northampton who made India his home, to educate Indians in the vernacular languages of India was opposed both by the Orientalists who championed the classical languages of Sanskrit, Persian and Arabic for Indian learning, and the Anglicists who wanted to transform India through an English education. Carey's printing of Matthew's Gospel was the first prose literature in Bengali. By compiling Bengali grammars, translating the Indian classics from Sanskrit into Bengali – so that ordinary men and women, and not just the pundits or scholars, could read them – Carey and his fellow Serampore missionaries paved the way for the mid-nineteenth-century 'Bengal Renaissance'. Carey's breadth of vision was rooted in the global reach of the gospel. He provided schools for women and Dalits, an asylum for lepers, persuaded the British officials to outlaw such social evils as infanticide and widow-burning, pioneered forestry projects in Bengal and became one of the founding members of the Agricultural and Horticultural Society of India. Little wonder that Rabindranath Tagore called Carey the 'Father of Modern Bengal'.[20]

The impact of Christians, whether indigenous or missionaries from Western lands, on Indian society cannot be assessed by numbers alone. The radical and unprecedented social and religious changes witnessed in nineteenth-century India were quite out of proportion to the number of converts made or churches established. The ideal of disinterested service which missionaries and indigenous Christians provided was unique. It is easy to understand charity for the sake of achieving religious merit or as an inducement to religious conversion. But that charity and social betterment should have no other motive than love itself – this was an alien notion. Hence the suspicion with which any Christian initiatives in social welfare and social action are viewed even today by intelligent Hindus and Buddhists in Asia. As Richard Young, a historian of nineteenth-century missions in South Asia, notes:

[20] See the essays in the bicentennial volume *Carey's Obligation and India's Renaissance*, ed. J. T. K. Daniel and R. E. Hedlund (Serampore College Press, 1993).

historically it can be argued that until Protestant Christianity
arrived in South Asia the organizational infrastructure for expressing disinterested benevolence was almost entirely lacking ... it
might be said that the wheel of social change in South Asia has a
Christian hub and a Buddhist-Hindu rim.[21]

This is a history largely suppressed in secular and Hindu/
Buddhist histories of the Indian subcontinent. The missionary
movement is routinely dismissed as an adjunct of the colonial
powers. Indigenous Christians are vilified by militant Hindu and
Buddhist organizations as agents of Western neocolonialism. Tribal
Christians in many parts of India are subjected to severe coercion
from Hindu organizations, often with overt political support, to
'reconvert' to Hinduism. These tribal peoples have never been
Hindus, but have followed their own primal religions. Until the
advent of Christian missionaries, native or foreign, they were
illiterate and thus easily exploited by ruthless caste Hindus with
the connivance of the local police. (Tribal peoples inhabit rich forest
areas, and their timber and other natural resources have traditionally
been bought at grossly undervalued prices.) Once converted, the
tribal groups learn to read and write; they are encouraged to stand
up for their civil rights and to resist their exploitation. Hence the
persecution they suffer today, a persecution which (like the rabble-
rousing of Democritus of Acts 19) is disguised in the self-righteous
rhetoric of 'protecting our traditional cultures'.

5. Conclusion

Acts 19 wonderfully brings together, in the ministry of Paul in
Ephesus, what is usually wrenched far apart in the modern seminary
and church; namely, the use of rational persuasion in the communication of the gospel, the role of 'signs and wonders' in bringing
people to faith, and the political and economic consequences of
Christian conversion.

In his farewell address to the Ephesian church elders at Miletus,
Paul reminds them how he 'testified to both Jews and Greeks about
repentance towards God and faith towards our Lord Jesus' (20:21),
and that he 'did not shrink from declaring to you the whole purpose
of God' (20:27). Such a comprehensive ministry springs from a
comprehensive grasp of the gospel. In the letter to that same church,
he writes of the 'one new humanity' that God has created through

[21] R. Young, 'Ripple or Wave? Protestant Missions and the "Protestantization" of
Religion in Nineteenth-Century Sri Lanka', unpublished paper delivered in
Colombo, Sri Lanka, 8 February 1992.

the cross of Christ (Eph. 2:15), and how his mission throughout the Gentile world is 'to make everyone see what is the plan of the mystery hidden for ages in God who created all things; so that through the church the wisdom of God in its rich variety might now be made known to the rulers and authorities in the heavenly places' (Eph. 3:9–10).

We are the result of that Gentile mission, continued down the centuries by faithful men and women and entrusted to us in our own generation. Wherever the 'one new humanity' is glimpsed through the church, the 'wisdom of God' is proclaimed to the powers of this age. Desmond Tutu, when he was Dean of Johannesburg, wrote:

> As I have knelt in the Dean's stall at the superb 9.30 high mass, with incense, bells and everything, watching a multiracial crowd file up to the altar rails to be communicated, the one bread and one cup given by a mixed team of clergy and lay ministers with a multiracial choir, servers and sidesmen – all this in apartheid-mad South Africa – then tears of joy sometimes streamed down my cheeks, tears of joy that it could be indeed that Jesus Christ had broken down the wall of partition, that here was the first fruits of the eschatological community right in front of my eyes.[22]

---

[22] Desmond Tutu, *Hope and Suffering* (Fount, 1983), pp. 134–135.

Part 4
Doxology

Psalm 104
14. The consummation of creation's song

The final part of this book is entitled 'Doxology', for mission begins and ends with praise. Lesslie Newbigin's inspiring sentence, based on the last verses of Luke, 'Mission begins with an explosion of joy,' has already been quoted. And, just as mission begins with joy, so it will end in joy. Peter, in his sermon to the astonished crowds in Solomon's Portico, in Acts 3, speaks of times of refreshing coming from the presence of the Lord, and of the time of universal restoration of all things, long ago announced by the prophets (vv. 20–21). Paul speaks in the widest possible terms of the reconciling work of Christ when he says that through Jesus Christ 'God was pleased to reconcile to himself all things, whether on earth or in heaven, by making peace through the blood of his cross' (Col. 1:20).[1] The next chapter of this book focuses on the vision in Revelation of God's creation transformed, the realization of true human community, the consummation of human work and culture, the reclamation of wealth and aesthetics and the transcendence of religion when Christ will be all in all. This chapter focuses on an Old Testament vision of the song of creation, and asks the question 'What place is there in our theology of mission for our stewardship of creation?'

In 1990 the Anglican Consultative Council defined mission as including proclaiming the good news of the kingdom; teaching, baptizing and nurturing new believers; responding to human need

---

[1] J. Moltmann sees this verse as summarizing the full extent of Christ's work in space and time: 'his messianic intensity pervades the spaces of creation to their depths; his messianic extensity pervades the times of creation to their furthest origins' (*The Way of Jesus Christ* [SCM, 1990]), p. 304.

by loving service; and seeking to transform the unjust structures of society. It then added a fifth mark of mission: striving to safeguard the integrity of creation and to sustain and renew the life of the earth. The Council justified this addition by noting that it 'acknowledges the concern and apologetic relevance of Creation care for the Church's ministry and evangelism'.[2] This addition seems to make creation care a derivative and secondary concern, important for its buttressing value to more important concerns of ministry and evangelism. Two years later an influential symposium entitled *Missionary Earthkeeping* was published.[3] The editors were a professor of environmental science and the Director of the Royal Botanic Gardens, Kew. The title of the book indicates a developing consciousness of the importance and priority of earth-keeping in the overall missionary responsibility of the church. Andrew Kirk is quite clear that concern for the created world must have a place in our theology of mission: 'I believe the Church at large has to endorse the finding of the San Antonio Conference of the WCC's Commission on World Mission and Evangelism that "mission in Christ's way must extend to God's creation. Because the earth is the Lord's, the responsibility of the church towards the earth is a crucial part of the church's mission." '[4]

1. A song to David

> Glorious the sun in mid career;
> Glorious th' assembled fires appear;
> Glorious the comet's train:
> Glorious the trumpet and alarm;
> Glorious th' almighty stretch'd-out arm;
> Glorious th' enraptur'd main:
>
> Glorious the northern lights a-stream;
> Glorious the song, when God's the theme;
> Glorious the thunder's roar:
> Glorious hosanna from the den;
> Glorious the catholic amen;
> Glorious the martyr's gore:

---

[2] Anglican Consultative Council, *Mission in a Broken World*, 1990, p. 14.

[3] Calvin DeWitt and Ghillean Prance, *Missionary Earthkeeping* (Macon University Press, 1992).

[4] A. Kirk, *What Is Mission? Theological Explorations* (Darton, Longman & Todd, 1999), p. 167. The reference is to F. Wilson (ed.), *The San Antonio Report: Your Will Be Done, Mission in Christ's Way* (World Council of Churches, 1990), p. 54.

Glorious – more glorious is the crown
Of Him that brought salvation down
By meekness, call'd thy Son;
Thou that stupendous truth believ'd,
And now the matchless deed's achiev'd,
Determin'd, dar'd, and done.

These verses are the culmination of a long and astonishing poem,
A Song to David, first written (much of it scratched with a key on the
walls of the apartment in which he was confined) in 1763 by the
eighteenth-century English poet Christopher Smart. Born in 1722
and educated in Cambridge, he made an early living by writing
copy and songs for London theatres. He lived a dissolute life and was
arrested for debt in 1747. Later he apparently suffered from some
sort of religious mania and his friend Dr Johnson wrote, 'My poor
friend Smart showed the disturbance of his mind by falling upon his
knees and saying his prayers in the street, or in any other unusual
place.' However, Johnson was opposed to Smart's being locked up
in a madhouse, which he was from 1756 to 1763: 'His infirmities
were not noxious to society. He insisted on people praying with him;
and I'd as lief pray with Kit Smart as anyone else ... '[5]
   A recent sympathetic writer about Smart speaks of 'his dedication
to a poetry of absolute praise'.[6] Professor Richard Bauckham writes
enthusiastically of Smart's attentive observation of the natural
world (and particularly of his cat, Jeoffry), and of his wonder
and adoration that arise continually to the Creator God from and
through these observations. Smart helps us to praise God *through*
our acute attentiveness to the world he has made: 'it is attention to
the quiddity of (each created thing) that continually assists our
praise of the God who gives them themselves and surpasses them
and us'.[7] What is also striking about Smart's poem is that the summit
of all the wonders he has so minutely surveyed in many stanzas,
'more glorious' than any of them, is the salvation that has been
brought down to us through Jesus Christ, David's and God's son.
   Smart wrote his poem in praise of David and his matchless
psalms. Psalm 104 is a giant song of creation praise, which may
help us to think through our responsibility for and to the wonderful
world the Creator has given us.

   [5] James Sutherland (ed.), *The Oxford Book of Literary Anecdotes* (Futura, 1977),
no. 139.
   [6] E. Hirsch, *How to Read a Poem* (Duke University Center for Documentary
Studies, 1999), p. 77.
   [7] Richard Bauckham, 'Joining Creation's Praise of God', *Ecotheology* 7.1 (July
2002), pp. 45–59.

245

2. How manifold are your works!

Structurally, the psalm is bracketed by calls to bless the Lord in verses 1 and 35; in this respect it is linked to the psalm that precedes it, which has as its theme gratitude for God's saving mercy. 'Together the two psalms praise God as Saviour and Creator, Father and Sustainer, "merciful and mighty". In the galaxy of the psalter these are twin stars of the first magnitude.'[8] There is a broad correspondence in this psalm with the creation sequence of Genesis 1, but it is not followed rigidly, and the themes overflow, like a waterfall, from pool to pool. O LORD in verse 24 parallels O LORD my God in verse 1, but it seems almost like a pause for breath amid the cascading richness of the song. There are also striking resemblances between this psalm and an Egyptian 'Hymn to the Sun' from the time of Akhenaton in the fourteenth century BC.[9] But amid the resemblances there is a most striking difference: in the Egyptian hymn the sun is worshipped as the Creator; but in our psalm the sun is but one of the Lord's many creations, and, far from being supreme, is 'demoted' to verse 19.

Verses 1–4 speak of light, heavens, rain, clouds, wind, fire and flame. These awesome natural and meteorological phenomena are but the Lord's garment, tent, chambers, chariot. Verses 5–9 speak of the dry land and the ocean deep, the $t^e h\hat{o}m$. The $t^e h\hat{o}m$ is the primeval chaos, the waters of the flood, the opposite end of the universe from heaven above, deeper than the deepest sea, the fearsome valley at the bottom of the world (Gen. 1:2; 7:11; 49:25; Job 28:14). But here the Creator has ordered the dry land and the ocean deep, laying out the $t^e h\hat{o}m$ like a blanket over the world. One is reminded of the famous TV series aptly entitled *The Blue Planet*. The shoreless sea has given way to a shaped pattern of land and sea. These first nine verses of the psalm set out panoramically the huge, beautifully ordered environment, the sky, the land and the sea, which is our natural world. But in this psalm, as in the Bible generally, the work of creation is not deistically conceived, as if God just started the world off and left it to run by itself. The following verses describe, in present tenses, God's continual creative and preserving work in adapting all sorts of living creatures to their respective environments. He is the Creator *and* Sustainer. This psalm is, one might say, an early ecological survey, summarizing

---

[8] F. D. Kidner, *Psalms 73–150* (IVP, 1975), p. 364.
[9] The text of the Egyptian hymn may be found in J. B. Pritchard (ed.), *Ancient Near Eastern Texts Relating to the Old Testament* (Princeton University Press, 1950), pp. 370–371.

with poetic beauty the mutual relationships between many organisms and their environment.

Verses 10–13 focus on the provision of water, without which plants die, animals die and finally humans die. Fortunate readers who live in a temperate climate where there is always enough rain are likely to forget that the Bible was written on the edge of a huge desert, long before modern irrigation schemes. The former rains, which soften the ground, and the latter rains, which fatten the growing grain, are indispensable to life. They are a miracle as every dweller in Palestine knew. The vision of these verses is not selfishly narrow; the psalmist is not just concerned with the domestic animals essential for farming. Wild animals, untamed donkeys, birds of the air, the whole earth are the beneficiary of God's generous provision of rain.

Verses 14–18 concentrate on food and shelter. Also, unlike the creation stories of Genesis, which place human beings at the pinnacle of all that God created, this song places human beings in the middle of a zoo of creatures, cattle, birds and storks, goats and rock badgers, not forgetting the trees, especially the wonderful cedars of Lebanon.[10] God has provided trees for the birds, and mountains and rocks for the creatures that live there. He has also provided food, wine, oil and bread for human beings. There is a stress on the generosity of this provision – not just water, but wine, abundant rain, and oil to make faces shine!

Verses 19–23 recognize the rhythm and pattern of life, moon and sun,[11] dark and light, day and night. Amid all the unpredictabilities of life and of human behaviour, the regularity of day and night is a testimony to the faithfulness of the Creator. Candles, gas and electricity have transformed this rhythmical behaviour of man and animals with results that are not all good. But still the lives of a large proportion of the world's population, and their work and toil from sunrise to evening are structured on this diurnal pattern; and we all, for survival, need the alternation of activity and rest which these verses describe. We may also note that verse 21 recognizes predation: when the young lions roar for their prey, seeking their food *from God*, they do not get it by sitting and waiting for it to be delivered. It is implied that in our modern world, where some animals prey on others, this is, in some senses at least, 'from God'. The messianic kingdom in which the wolf will live with the lamb,

---

[10] It is possible that *trees of the LORD* means 'huge trees', with the divine name used as a sort of superlative. Alternatively there may be a theological purpose – the trees are not just there for plundering: they have an Owner.

[11] A contrast with the Egyptian Hymn to the Sun is that the moon is mentioned first in v. 19!

and the calf, lion and fatling will lie down together (Is. 11:6–7), will involve new dietary arrangements.

In verse 24 the psalmist bursts out in praise of the marvellous, manifold and intricate wisdom by which the Lord has set all this wonderful creation in order. In particular, his attention returns to the huge sea, usually regarded as so threatening and dangerous by Jewish landlubbers, which the psalmist sees instead as a huge menagerie of creatures, and as a playing field for the sea monster Leviathan! The NRSV speaks of Leviathan sporting in the ocean. The Talmud speaks of Leviathan whom the Lord had formed 'to play *with you!*'

As his song climaxes in verses 27–30 the psalmist looks to God's face, his hand and, above all, his breath or Spirit.[12] We creatures do our work, we gather up what we can, we work in season and out of season, but we are all totally dependent on the Creator's breath of life. As any visitor to a mortuary or a chapel of rest knows, all of the person you knew and loved is present before you, *except* for one thing – the breath of life which makes the difference between a person and a corpse.

Finally the psalmist reviews his commitments in verses 31–35. He invokes the enduring majesty of God as a blessing; he commits himself to lifelong praise; he asks that his meditations on this (and other) themes may be pleasing to God; and, shooting a glance at the wicked, who increase the world's sorrows, he asks in effect that 'God's kingdom may come, as in heaven, so on earth' and finishes with a hallelujah.

3. The integrity of creation

At the United Nations Conference on Environment and Development in Rio de Janeiro in June 1982 scientists and senior policy-makers from 179 countries adapted what was called 'Agenda 21'[13] and also the 27 principles of the Rio Declaration on Environment and Development.[14] The mission mandate of the World Council of Churches since the Vancouver assembly in 1983 has included prioritizing 'justice, peace and the integrity of creation'. The Rio conference was followed up in 1992 by the United Nations Framework Convention on Climate Change, which was an attempt to recognize the problem of global climate change and to make

---

[12] The Hebrew word *rûaḥ* can be translated 'breath' or 'spirit'.

[13] See the text of this Agenda at <http://www.un.org/esa/sustdev/agenda21text. htm>.

[14] See <http://www.un.org/documents/ga/conf151/aconf15126-1annex1.htm>. A beginner's guide to these issues is to be found at <http://unfccc.int/resource/beginner. pdf>.

proposals that would help to stabilize at acceptable levels the concentration of greenhouse gases in the atmosphere. The lion's share of action in these matters was to be taken by the rich countries which consume the major part of the world's resources and are responsible for the largest emissions of toxic gases. This convention took effect on 21 March 1994; but additions and amendments have been added since, and these have been summarized in the 28 articles of the Kyoto Protocol in 1997.[15] A lasting source of international frustration in the past decade has been the refusal of the USA to agree to the articles of the Kyoto proposals. There have also been many other conferences and commissions on topics related to the Rio summit and Agenda 21 since 1992.[16]

At the time of writing (August 2002), 50,000 people, including more than 20,000 delegates, have gathered in Johannesburg for the World Summit on Sustainable Development.[17] 'Sustainable development' is a phrase used to include economic growth, social development and environmental protection.[18] The five themes of the summit are water, energy, health, agriculture and biodiversity.

In preparation for this unprecedently huge conference in South Africa an avalanche of numbers and statistics has been prepared. There are some encouragements but also many great problems to address:

- In 1950 the population of the world was 2.5 billion; by 2025 this is projected to have risen to 8.5 billion. The huge bulk of this growth is taking place in the developing world.
- AIDS in sub-Saharan Africa is reducing life-expectancy by 15 years to 47.
- The number of hungry people is slowly declining from 950 million in 1970 to 800 million in 2002, but this number is still unacceptably enormous. The official statistics use the term 'hunger', but of course there is no such 'thing' as hunger, only hungry people.
- Income inequality is greatest in Latin America and sub-Saharan Africa and between these continents and the developed countries.

[15] A 'protocol' is an international agreement that stands on its own, but is linked to an existing treaty.
[16] See <http://www.earthsummit2002.org/es/documents/default.htm>.
[17] See <http://www.johannesburgsummit.org>.
[18] 'Sustainable development is development that meets the needs of the present without compromising the ability of future generations to meet their own needs.' See <http://www.doc.mmu.ac.uk/aric/eae/Sustainability/Older/Brundtland_Report. html>.

- Food production and consumption have been increasing in all areas, from an average of 2,100 to 2,700 calories per person per day in 1970, to 3,000 to 3,400 calories per person per day in 1999. But the potential to expand crop production is limited and agricultural expansion threatens other ecosystems.
- Water use has increased sixfold over the past century (twice as much as population growth). The vast majority of water is used for agriculture. Freshwater sources are being degraded in various ways, by excessive withdrawals, by pollution and by invasive species. It is projected that by 2025 half the world will face water shortages.
- Forests have continued to decline by 2.4% per annum, which equates to an area of approximately 90,000 sq km. These forests are almost all tropical forests, in Latin America and Africa.
- Energy consumption is growing continually. Fossil fuel and carbon dioxide emissions continue to grow, especially in North America and Asia. People in developed countries use ten times as much fossil fuel as those in developing countries.
- Climate change is a reality. It is estimated that the global average surface temperature has gone up 0.6 degrees centigrade since 1900. Sea levels are rising 1 cm per decade. The amount of Arctic sea ice has declined by 40% since 1960. It seems that droughts in Asia and Africa are increasing. Insurance companies (whom we may assume to be hypersensitive to increasing liabilities) paid out $2 billion annually in payment for flood and storm damage in the 1980s. This figure has increased to $30 billion annually in the 1990s.
- In developed countries most deaths have been from incommunicable diseases, but in developing countries most deaths continue to be from communicable, especially diarrhoeal and respiratory, diseases, some of which are easy to cure if resources are available.[19]

Since the late 1970s in the UK there has been a huge shift of evangelical Christian money from traditional evangelistic and church-planting missionary agencies towards Christian relief and development agencies, of which Tearfund is the largest. As the TV has brought into our homes the reality of suffering and devastation around the world, Christian consciences have been moved and troubled and Christian understanding of the depth and extent of human need has been greatly increased. In the last ten years there has been increasing theological reflection by evangelicals on the

[19] All these data are taken from websites associated with the Johannesburg summit.

topic of earth-keeping, produced by and producing changes of missionary practice and priorities. One indication of this was the issuing in 1994 of *An Evangelical Declaration on the Care of Creation*, and the publication in 2000 of what was called a theological commentary on this declaration, focusing concern and action, edited by R. J. Berry, and entitled *The Care of Creation*.[20]

It is impossible in this short chapter to review the range of concerns raised by the Johannesburg conference and reflected on in Professor Berry's book. Neither can one passage, from the Old or New Testament, provide a theological framework for an adequate consideration of these topics. But it is possible for Psalm 104 to remind us, as we bring our book to a close, of some important themes of the church's 'integral mission'.[21]

4. Wonder and worship

Psalm 104 and other similar passages are suffused with a sense of amazement at the wonders of the natural world, meaning not just the sensational and spectacular sights but also the dependable orderliness of nature and the provision of the Creator for all sorts of creatures. Pondering and wondering at these things brings wisdom.

> Wisdom is generated and sustained by wonder. To wonder is to be intrigued, engaged, to behold and to be beholden to something. It is to be held in contemplation, to be provoked into thought. To wonder is to seek *to come to terms* with the unfamiliar. It is, then, the birth place of language, the natal point of speech ... This is the posture of waiting, of attentiveness. This is the time of wakefulness and gathered silence.[22]

Peter Harris, the International Director of the A. Rocha Trust has written, with some desperation, about the need for this whole issue to be framed not just in terms of 'What shall we do about the environment?' but much more widely in terms of 'What sort of a God do we believe in?' He insists that God cares for the whole creation and not just its human component, and suggests that Psalm

---

[20] R. J. Berry (ed.), *The Care of Creation: Focusing Concern and Action* (IVP, 2000).

[21] Professor C. Ringma sets out his reasons for preferring this phrase to the phrase 'holistic mission' in 'Holistic Ministry and Mission: A Call for Reconceptualization', *Crux* 38.2 (June 2002), pp. 20–34.

[22] Robert Forrest, 'Worship, Wonder and Study', unpublished article on philosophy as the love of wisdom (no pagination).

104 (rather than just a few proof texts), 'written about creation after the fall, might [give] a more adequate testimony to God's love for all creation as we know it'.[23]

It is not difficult to find examples of early European scientists who had this sense of wonder. Thomas Kepler, for example, who discovered the laws of planetary motion, spoke of 'thinking God's thoughts after him' as he examined the night sky. But in more recent times this sense of wonder and awe has given way to a much more exploitative and managerial approach to nature. One may even see this trend of thought in the way the vocabulary in use to discuss these topics has changed – from talking about 'creation' (which implies a Creator) to talking about 'environment' which cloaks the issue of agency. How different is the language of Psalm 104, which is a delighted dialogue between 'You', the Creator, and 'I', the psalmist.

George Herbert wrote a poem in which he spoke of the role of human beings in relation to creation:

> Of all the creatures both in sea and land
> Only to Man thou hast made known thy ways,
> And put the pen alone into his hand,
> And made him Secretary of thy praise.[24]

Later in the poem Herbert speaks of man as the world's 'high priest'. Richard Bauckham has objected to 'this arrogant assertion that only through human mediation can the rest of creation be itself in relation to God' and asserts that there is no trace of such a view in the Scriptures.[25] In Psalm 104, as elsewhere in the Old Testament, the song of praise which rises to God from all created things, does not have to be channelled through a human mediator. The seas roar, the forests clap their hands, eagles fly, mice squeak, geese honk, pigs grunt and flowers bloom, perhaps their whole life long, unseen by any human eye – and this chorus of praise ascends to God, unmediated by any human interference. Herbert is right in supposing that 'man' is the 'secretary' of such praise, if he refers to writing about it; chimpanzees do not write out their songs. But the praise which arises to God from all created things, animate and inanimate, does not *need* the interposition of human beings to present or amplify it.

It is here that missionary earth-keeping begins and ends. The first obligation of every living thing is towards the Creator; worship and

[23] Peter Harris, 'A New Look at Old Passages', in Berry, *Care of Creation*, p. 135.
[24] 'Providence', available in various editions of his poems.
[25] R. J. Bauckham, 'Joining Creation's Praise of God', *Ecotheology* 7.1 (July 2002), p. 50.

prayer come before work. And the story of creation finishes, not with the creation of human beings, but with the sabbath, which is declared holy, and on which human beings are to rest from their work and remember their Creator. Jürgen Moltmann has noted the ecological wisdom of this sabbath provision, and has proposed the addition of an annual 'Earth Day' to the great festival days of the church. He suggests it might be in Europe on 27 April, the anniversary of the catastrophic explosions at Chernobyl.[26]

5. Working and waiting

Psalm 104:20–22 pictures the wild animals coming out in the evening and seeking their food from God until the sunrise (v. 22) when they withdraw and go back to their dens, while verse 23 pictures people going out to work in the morning and returning in the evening. Human working is here presented in the context of 'animal working'. An ecological balance is implied, which has traditionally been explained with the use of the concept of the human 'stewardship' of creation. Because of the use of the words 'rule' and 'have dominion' in the Genesis account, some writers (e.g. Lynn White, Jr) have written scathingly of the Judaeo-Christian world-view being responsible for the current environmental crisis in the world.[27] More recently, writers have noticed that because White and others did not pay attention to the *other* verbs used in the Genesis account, particularly the verbs 'serve' and 'keep', their accusations have been unbalanced. Human beings, including Christians, must take a lot of criticism for their irresponsible exploitation of the natural world, but the biblical teaching is more fairly summarized as human beings have been given responsibility for 'stewarding' the earth and its resources, keeping it safe and tending it like a shepherd.[28] In seventeenth-century England this view was developed as an alternative to the Baconian view of the domination and manipulation of nature by technological mastery. But there are still many Christians who are not at all interested in, or who may actually be quite vigorously opposed to, the environmental concerns touched on above. It is noticeable that this opposition comes

[26] J. Moltmann, 'God's Covenant and our Responsibility', in Berry, *Care of Creation*, p. 113.

[27] E.g. Lynn White, Jr, 'The Historic Roots of our Ecological Crisis', *Science* 155 (1967), pp. 1203–1207; I. L. McHarg, *Design with Nature* (Natural History, 1969).

[28] See e.g. E. Whitney, 'Lynn White, Ecotheology and History', *Environmental Ethics* 15 (1993), pp. 151–169; D. J. Hall, *Imaging God: Dominion as Stewardship* (Eerdmans, 1986); J. Cohen, *'Be Fertile and Increase, Fill the Earth and Master it':* *The Ancient and Medieval Career of a Biblical Text* (Cornell University Press, 1989).

largely from people in the richer countries, where they have the means and the leisure to develop their opposition. Many pastors and teachers from poorer countries, however much they emphasize preaching the gospel, making converts, planting churches and developing disciples, are also unavoidably engaged in developing clinics for the sick, trying to get clean water, introducing education, especially female literacy, agricultural projects and many other such concerns.

There will still be some who are wondering, 'Is Earth-keeping *really* part of the *missionary* responsibility of the church qua church?' They have been used to understanding 'missionary' in a more restricted sense in terms of evangelism, disciple-making, church-planting and the like. It is obvious that people with limited time and resources do not have time to get involved with many aspects of care for the environment, like those listed above. But each person has the opportunity to get involved in *some* aspect, to specialize in one area, to be interested in and active on one issue. They will only do so if they perceive it as a priority. I have a friend who was a full-time minister in two churches in the extremely multicultural town of Southall on the outskirts of London. Since then, without losing his evangelistic concerns, he has become involved in a conservation project on a huge area of wasteland next to the town. He has found that this engagement with the environment of *all* those who live in Southall has given him greatly increased contacts with all sorts of people, young and old, from many of the different communities in the town. His engagement with the environment has enlarged his missionary engagement with the people he lives among.

An Ethiopian pastor's tree-planting project to improve the hot, dusty, degraded environment of a useless piece of land given him by the government, gave him unforeseen opportunities to talk with his Muslim friends about why Christians should do such caring things for the wider community when they themselves will not get much immediate benefit. The issue here is not about what ancillary activities might make our 'evangelism' more effective, however that is computed; the issue is how creation care and people care converge as we, for theological reasons, become involved in the whole lives of our communities. Mother Teresa was criticized at times for pulling dying people out of the gutter without attending to the structural issues in Indian society which caused such suffering in the first place. Her priority, with her limited time and strength, was direct care for the dying. Dame Cicely Saunders, with similar compassion, was able to found a hospice movement. The question each of us needs to answer is 'What is the significance of our whole lives and work as an expression of the love of God for the communities of which we are a part?'

Some are anxious that radical evangelicals today are making the same mistake or mistakes about those who became 'social gospellers' one hundred years ago.[29] Dr Brian Stanley has noted, however, that evangelical involvement in politics and social action in the nineteenth century (especially in the UK) was at least as important as liberal theology in the rise of the social gospel movement. He has observed that 'evangelical involvement in politics progressively extended as the categories of what was integral to the gospel broadened'. He has also noted how F. B. Meyer campaigned strongly for the Liberal Party in 1906, although later he began to withdraw from such overt political involvement because of the spiritual cost of that politicization.[30]

On the other hand, as social beings, we do not have the option of 'neutrality'. Either our everyday activities (whether working, shopping, playing etc.) are serving to preserve the economic, cultural, social and political structures within which we live, or we are shaping them in a direction that approximates the values embedded in the gospel of Christ. Moreover, it has often (sadly) been the case that evangelicals who are outspoken campaigners against social evils tend to be marginalized by conservative churches, and so inevitably drift towards the more 'radical' end of the theological spectrum.

The phrase 'kingdom of God' has come to be used very widely in the discussion of social ethics, sometimes in a very loose way, which was criticized by R. T. France in a careful article on biblical interpretation.[31] It is over twenty-five years since J. R. W. Stott insisted, in a conversation with R. Sider, that 'the kingdom of God in the New Testament is a fundamentally *Christological* concept, and ... may be said to exist only where Jesus Christ is consciously acknowledged as Lord'.[32] This discussion is continuing, but it is unclear how this concept is helpful in developing a social policy for a mixed community. Probably it would be more helpful to talk of 'reforming' rather than 'redeeming' society; or (with Karl Barth)[33]

[29] See Melvin Tinker, 'Reversal or Betrayal? Evangelicals and Socio-political Involvement in the Twentieth Century', in idem, *Evangelical Concerns: Rediscovering the Christian Mind on Issues Facing the Church Today* (Mentor, 2001), pp. 139–166.

[30] B. Stanley, 'Evangelical Social and Political Ethics: An Historical Perspective', *Evangelical Quarterly* 62.1 (January 1990), pp. 19–36.

[31] R. T. France, 'The Church and the Kingdom of God', in D. A. Carson (ed.), *Biblical Interpretation and the Church – Text and Context* (Paternoster, 1984), pp. 30–44.

[32] R. J. Sider (with a response by J. R. W. Stott), *Evangelism, Salvation and Social Justice*, Grove Booklet on Ethics 16 (Grove, 1977), p. 23.

[33] K. Barth, *Church Dogmatics*, III/4 (T. & T. Clark, 1978), pp. 565–594.

to picture God's activity in the world as two concentric circles: the inner circle is the 'kingdom of God', centred on and inaugurated by Jesus Christ; the outer circle is the realm of God's providential rule over all things.

According to Psalm 104 we have many wonderful reasons for praising God in the magnificent world in which he has placed us and all creatures, even though we now recognize, as never before, the degradations which our lovely planet has suffered and is suffering. The responsibility and mission of the Christian, individually and corporately, in this environment, is to show through our creation care our love for the Creator. We do this in our work of stewardship, by all appropriate means, with the advice of scientists, and steering our way as best we can through the unavoidable arguments between the different co-inhabitants of our earthly home. At the same time we wait for 'a new heavens and a new earth' in which righteousness dwells. Under the influence of a pessimistic premillennial eschatology that envisaged the world falling more and more into ruin, some Christians have neglected creation care, picturing their evangelistic responsibility as if they were pulling people from a burning building. This narrow concept of mission needs to be replaced by one which holds in fruitful and energizing balance the understanding of God as Creator as well as Redeemer, who calls us to care for all that he has made as well as seeking to save the lost.

6. Witness to the Word made flesh

Professor Oliver O'Donovan, in his response to the *Evangelical Declaration on the Care of Creation*, noted the somewhat bleak tone of the declaration, picked up on the use of the word 'evangelical', and asked, 'What is the Good News in which it calls us to put our trust?'[34] We need to lift our eyes constantly beyond our environment, wonderful and degraded as it is, to the God who made and holds it in his judgment and care. The psalmist was aware of the fragility of man's position in nature: when he lay in bed at night he might hear the lion's roar and ponder the fact that though he might be the ruler of the day, perhaps the lion, or other animals were ruling by night, when it would be dangerous for him to be out and about.

Is there anything more that we should add to the contemplation of creation and Creator to fill out our understanding of what our individual and corporate responsibilities are as those who have experienced the love of God? This would be an appropriate place to

[34] O. O'Donovan, 'Where Were you ...?' in Berry, *Care of Creation*, p. 92.

notice that Psalm 104 is sandwiched between two other lengthy psalms which have complementary themes to the creation theme of Psalm 104. Psalm 105 is a review of Israel's history, of the covenant the Lord made with Abraham, Isaac and Jacob, and of the early deliverers Joseph and Moses, who were responsible for two of the most significant acts of salvation in Old Testament times. This psalm reminds us that the Creator of Psalm 104 is also the Lord of history, of time as well as space. This promise-remembering of a faithful Deliverer is a reason for joyful celebration with singing, as is creation (v. 43). The reason for the recital is given in verse 45; namely, that Israel 'might keep his statutes / and observe his laws'. Readers of this psalm who also read the rest of the Old Testament will be only too aware how Israel failed in this privilege and responsibility.

Psalm 103, which is the other side of this poetic 'triptych', is a personal celebration of the Lord as Redeemer. This psalm celebrates in personal terms the forgiving love of God, casting our sins to the edge of the universe, lifting us up from the Pit, promising his steadfast love for ever and ever.

Taken together these psalms prompt the question 'Is there a yet clearer place where we see the creating and redeeming love of God more sharply focused, at a particular time and place and spreading out from there through all time and space?' Christians answer that there *is* such a place and it is in Jesus Christ our Lord, the Word made flesh, without whom nothing was made that was made, who is the light and life of humanity, in whom, for whom and through whom all things exist, and in whom one day all creation will be brought to consummation. A powerful Old Testament word expressing this anticipation is the word 'shalom', of which 'peace' is an inadequate translation. Shalom expresses the highest joy of living before God, of living in one's particular physical surroundings, in living in harmony with one's neighbours and oneself. Shalom also describes the kingdom of the Messiah in which there also will be unprecedented harmony between humans and animals and within the animal kingdom. This shalom is for those on whom God's favour rests. And Jesus Christ is the One who came and preached, by life and word and deed, shalom to those who were far off and to those who were near; he is called the Prince of Peace. Those who receive peace from the Prince of Peace are commissioned to be agents and bearers of that shalom throughout the world. Thus, says Nicholas Wolterstorff, 'Shalom is both God's cause in the world and our human calling.'[35]

---

[35] N. Wolterstorff, *Until Justice and Peace Embrace* (Eerdmans, 1983), p. 72.

7. Corporate and personal change

These are not matters for occasional token gestures, although sometimes token gestures are the beginning stages of more fundamental life and world-view changes. Below is an example of an environment policy that one church in Northern Ireland has developed in connection with many of the issues mentioned in this chapter:

The Rector and the Select Vestry of St Molua's recognize that concern for all components of the environment is a fundamental responsibility of all Christian people as stewards of God's creation. The following policy was therefore adopted by the Select Vestry at its meeting on 13th December 1999.

- We are dedicated to carrying out all of our functions and activities in a way which minimizes negative impact on the environment.
- We are committed to ensuring that all activities undertaken on parish premises or on behalf of the parish will comply with legislation.
- It is an objective of the parish to cooperate with statutory, voluntary and community bodies in an attempt to reduce negative impact on the environment. In keeping with this policy we will:
  - Monitor and improve energy use
  - Set targets for reduced waste generation
  - Promote recycling within the parish
  - Minimize the risk of land, water and air pollution
  - Include environmental considerations in the decisions of the Select Vestry
  - Inform and update all staff, parishioners and contractors on policy
  - Generally apply sustainability objectives in all aspects and activities
  - Attempt to make ongoing improvements to this policy.[36]

All sorts of personal changes are possible, more than can be catalogued here. We need to become better informed. We need to pray more – including probably more time and more depth. We are travelling more than ever and we have the opportunity to travel with more insight. We need to make connections between different parts of *our* own lives, and also between our lives and the lives of

---

[36] Taken from the website of St Molua's Church of Ireland church in East Belfast, <http://www.molua.org.uk/>.

other people, whom we may never have seen, but whom our lifestyle affects. We need to consume less. We are participating in the mission of God in and to his world: we need more and more for our whole lives to be shaped by that image and precedent.

8. The God who set the stars in space

It will be appropriate for this chapter to conclude with a song, as the Bible and this book both conclude with reference to the songs of the book of Revelation. For as we worship we are reminded about, and challenged and energized by, the God of love who created and commissions us to be his agents in his world.

> The God who set the stars in space
>   and gave the planets birth
> created for our dwelling place
>   a green and fruitful earth;
> a world with wealth and beauty crowned
>   of sky and sea and land,
> where life should flourish and abound
>   beneath its Maker's hand.
>
> A world of order and delight
>   God gave for us to tend,
> to hold as precious in his sight,
>   to nurture and defend;
> but yet on ocean, earth and air
>   the marks of sin are seen,
> with all that God created fair
>   polluted and unclean.
>
> O God, by whose redeeming grace
>   the lost may be restored,
> who stooped to save our fallen race
>   in Christ, creation's Lord,
> through him whose cross is life and peace
>   to cleanse a heart defiled
> may human greed and conflict cease
>   and all be reconciled.
>
> Renew the wastes of earth again,
>   redeem, restore, repair;
> with us, your children, still maintain
>   your covenant of care.

May we, who move from dust to dust
    and on your grace depend,
No longer, Lord, betray our trust
    but prove creation's friend.

Our God, who set the stars in space
    and gave the planets birth,
look down from heaven, your dwelling place,
    and heal the wounds of earth;
till pain, decay and bondage done,
    when death itself has died,
creation's songs shall rise as one
    and God be glorified![37]

---

[37] A hymn specially written to celebrate creation care by Bishop Tim Dudley-Smith. Text © Timothy Dudley-Smith in Europe (including UK and Ireland) and in all territories not controlled by Hope Publishing Company.

Revelation 21:1 – 22:5
15. Certainties of the new covenant

A paralysing hopelessness is what marks the destitute, the guilt-ridden and those suffering from terminal illness. Fear and insecurity have also gripped many well-to-do people, especially in the wake of 11 September 2001 and the corporate scandals on Wall Street and elsewhere. In rich suburbs where hunger, disease and deprivation are not experienced, a pervasive sense of emptiness, boredom and triviality is apparent. It is the subject of an increasing number of films and novels. The popularity of postmodern writers testifies to the contemporary disillusionment with 'big ideas'; political resignation and fatigue have killed off the utopian spirit that came to the fore in the Paris of 1968 or the Prague of 1989; and increasing personal freedoms have, paradoxically, restricted the scope of our collective *imagination*. If the summit has now been scaled, and the view found to be less than intoxicating, what is there left to live for?

The social scientist Francis Fukuyama comments that

> In our grandparents' time many reasonable people could foresee a radiant socialist future in which private property and capitalism had been abolished ... Today, by contrast, we have trouble imagining a world that is radically better than our own, or a future that is not essentially democratic and capitalist. Within that framework, of course, many things could be improved ... homeless ... minorities ... job ... We can also imagine future worlds that are significantly worse than what we know now ... But we cannot picture to ourselves a world that is essentially different from the present one, and at the same time better.[1]

---

[1] Francis Fukuyama, *The End of History and the Last Man* (Avon, 1993), p. 46.

1. A tale of two cities

The book of Revelation is 'A Tale of Two Cities'; namely, the symbolic, antithetical cities called Babylon and the New Jerusalem. Babylon represents and sums up all those God-defying cities of the Old Testament from the Babel of Genesis 11 onwards: Sodom, Egypt, Babylon, Edom. It stands over and against the people of God as an oppressive, arrogant empire. In John's day the spirit of Babylon is incarnated in Rome, the self-acclaimed Eternal City, whose military conquests had brought the whole Mediterranean world under Roman rule. Roman propaganda depicted Roman rule as bringing the Pax Romana, or peace and prosperity, to all the nations of the world. Even today scholars write of the 'grandeur that was Rome' and are impressed by the glories of Roman civilization.

However, John sees Rome and the Roman Empire differently. He knows that Rome, like all colonial powers, sucks all the resources of its far-flung provinces into itself. A few provincial élites, whose loyalty has been bought by Rome, enjoy the luxuries of global free trade that the empire has made possible. But the vast majority of their populations are either sold as slaves or eke out an existence on the soil.

In chapter 17 John portrays Roman civilization as a gaudily dressed, expensive whore. She has 'Babylon' inscribed on her forehead and is seated on a beast covered with blasphemous names. She is drunk with the blood of martyrs, and seduces the nations of the earth with her clever sorceries and cunning charms. In the next chapter John calls the Christians living in the churches of the Roman province of Asia to 'come out' of Babylon; that is, Rome. Clearly it cannot mean to separate themselves physically (for Rome's power was everywhere), but to separate themselves from the idolatrous practices of Roman civilization: to refuse to worship the emperor as divine, to refuse to participate in Rome's exploitative commercial and trading practices, and to refuse to conform to the consumerism and other pagan values of Roman society.

It is not adequate to say John rejected Roman rule solely because of the imperial cult. Nor is it adequate to say early Christians avoided participation in the army for the same single reason. In both cases, imperial religion provided a means of expressing loyalty to an economic and political system that violated Christian standards of love and justice. Something more than cultic abominations tainted commercial networks of the Empire: Revelation makes repeated allusions to the greed and selfish opulence of Rome and her merchants (18:3, 7, 11–16, 19). Despite terrible plagues that came upon the earth in John's vision, people 'did not repent of their murders or their sorceries or their fornications or their *thefts*' (9:21).[2]

In chapter 18 John sees God's judgment of the whore and the beast on which she sits. In prophetic style, he gives a catalogue of all Rome's exploitative commercial relations that ends with the words

for your merchants were the tycoons of the earth,
and all nations were deceived by your sorcery.
And in you was found the blood of prophets and of saints,
and of all who have been slaughtered on earth.

(18:23–24)

Little wonder, then, that the book of Revelation has been called 'the most powerful piece of political resistance literature from the period of the early Empire'.[3] This is subversive counter-propaganda. John wants his readers to see Rome, not from the viewpoint of their contemporaries, but from God's perspective. God's perspective is the heavenly perspective, and, paradoxically, the heavenly perspective is the perspective 'from below'. John looks at Roman power and civilization, not from the perspective of its beneficiaries, but from the perspective of its victims. He himself is a victim of Roman power, being exiled on the island of Patmos. However, he not only accuses Rome of victimizing Christians, but of economic exploitation of the peripheral provinces, and of social and political oppression.

If the Christian readers of John's visions wanted to dissociate themselves from Rome ('Babylon') and its corrupting influence on their own cities, they needed an alternative city, one whose true beauty would expose the tawdriness of Rome's alleged civilization. If they were to come out of Babylon (18:4) they would need to move in another direction, to give their allegiance to another city. If they were to resist the deceitful charms of Babylon, they would need a more powerful counter-attraction. Since Babylon is the great city that has the entire world in its iron grip (17:18), even ruling over the earthly Jerusalem (which was destroyed by Roman armies in AD 70), this alternative could belong only to the eschatological future. It is God's alternative city: the New Jerusalem that comes down to earth from heaven.

---

[2] J. Nelson Kraybill, *Imperial Cult and Commerce in John's Apocalypse* (Sheffield Academic Press, 1996), p. 200.

[3] Richard Bauckham, *The Theology of the Book of Revelation* (CUP, 1993), p. 38.

The description John gives of the New Jerusalem is a weaving together of many strands of Old Testament prophecy. The principal Old Testament passages which resonate here are Isaiah 24 – 27 and 60; Ezekiel 37 – 48; and Zechariah 14:16–21. There are echoes also of the intertestamental book 1 Enoch. John's portrayal of the eschatological city not only reflects much of the Hellenistic aspirations of the ideal city, but as a New Testament prophet he draws on his Jewish treasure store of imagery to express symbolically and theologically the radical hope of the coming of God's kingdom.

2. The new order: God's creation transformed

Then I saw a new heaven and a new earth (21:1). What is 'new' about this new creation? The creation is now filled with the immediate presence of God. Hitherto, the book of Revelation confines the presence of God, as the 'One who sits on the throne', to heaven, where his throne is (cf. ch. 4). He is not absent from the world, but is present, paradoxically, in hiddenness and contradiction. He is present as the suffering and slaughtered Lamb. He is present to his worshippers who comprise the persecuted church and in their faithful witness as they follow the Lamb to death.

> But while the Beast rules the world and humanity in general refuses to give God glory, his evident presence, his glory which is inseparable from his reign, appears only in heaven. And when his glory is manifested in heaven, its effect on earth is the destructive judgment of evil (15:7–8). Only when all evil has been destroyed and his kingdom comes, will God's throne be on earth.[4]

I am the Alpha and the Omega, the beginning and the end (21:6). This is only the second time in the book that the 'One who sits on the throne' speaks directly to John, and on both occasions (cf. 1:8) it is to affirm that he is both the ground and the goal of the cosmic story.[5] What John meets at the end is not an event, but a Person. God is not simply another item in the city; he is the eschatological reality that embraces all things. No longer present in hiddenness and contradiction, the throne of God moves from heaven to the earth. The city as a whole shines with the radiance of jasper (21:11), which

---

[4] Ibid., p. 140.
[5] David Aune notes that the divine title 'the Beginning and the End [and the Middle] of all things' is drawn from Hellenistic religious and philosophical tradition and has a cosmological rather than a temporal significance, and gives many citations to illustrate this. See D. E. Aune, *Revelation 17–22*, Word Biblical Commentary (Thomas Nelson, 1998), pp. 1126–1127.

in John's earlier vision of the throne of God symbolizes the divine glory. God's own life is now the eternal life of the city (22:1, 2).

Christian thinkers and visionaries have always known that our ability to speak of ultimate things is severely limited. This is where language fails us. It is easier, perhaps less misleading, to say what the ultimate future of God will *not* be than to state what it will be. And so John weaves into his portrait of the new creation some significant *negative* assertions. In the New Jerusalem there will be

i. No more sea (21:1). The sea represents, both in the Old Testament and in Revelation, the chaotic power of anticreation, the primeval abyss which constantly threatens to engulf the earth and humanity. Always restless, it is a symbol of all those forces that attempt to undo God's moral order. It is from the depths of the sea that the Beast emerges to blaspheme God's name, to persecute his people, and to tyrannize the earth (13:1–10); and it is the sea that is the seat of the great whore, Babylon (17:1). The vanishing of the sea in John's vision is a sign that God's victory is now complete, his sovereignty absolute.

ii. No more tears, death, mourning and pain (21:4). This is the consequence of the disappearance of the sea. All the world's misery (*the former things* of v. 4b) will be forgotten like the pangs of childbirth. In a touching metaphor borrowed from Isaiah 25:8 God is depicted as a mother gently lifting her child on to her lap and wiping her tears with her own hands. Is there any comparable picture of God in the world's religious literature? As one writer observes, 'all that now robs life from being fulfilled, joyful, vibrant *life* will be absent from the transcendent reality to which he is leading history'.[6]

iii. No more uncleanness and corruption (21:8, 27). If the new Jerusalem is a holy city, embodying the awesome purity of God himself, then all that is incompatible with his will can find no place within its walls. It follows that all who continue to cling to deeds of *abomination* and *falsehood* (v. 27) exclude themselves from God's presence. Unrepentant sinners have no place in the New Jerusalem.

Several commentators point out that the catalogue of vices John lists in verse 8 is neither traditional nor arbitrary. Rather, it carries nuances associated with the specific political and religious situation that Revelation addresses; namely, one of pressure on Christians to participate in the idolatrous practices of Roman society. The *cowardly*, those first on the list, would be those who lack the courage to resist involvement in the emperor cult; the *liars*, at the end of the

[6] M. Eugene Boring, *Revelation* (John Knox, 1989), p. 217.

list, would be those who surrender to Roman propaganda and fail to declare their Christian faith. Further on, in 22:15, John returns to the theme of *lies*: excluded is 'everyone who loves and practises falsehood'. Clearly, this must refer not to the occasional untruth but to a whole way of life, organized around the lies of the Beast, radically opposed to the truth of God and persistently rejecting God's invitation to a restored humanity. Judgment has to do, primarily, with the recovery of the truth. The eschatological Day of the Lord is that day when we shall rejoice that 'Truth has come and Falsehood has been overthrown' (Qur'an 17:81).

All the other vices mentioned (faithlessness, pollution, murder, fornication, sorcery, idolatry) can similarly be linked to the life-world of John's Christian audience.[7] He never suggests that people who cooperated with idolatrous pagan institutions are beyond redemption: the good news of salvation is open to 'everyone who is thirsty ... anyone who wishes to take the water of life as a gift' (22:17). John, as a faithful pastor of his estranged flock, exhorts his hearers to faithful witness in the teeth of the overwhelming pressures of pagan society. They are to stand firm, for their new quality of life, however much out of step with their present social environment, is the life that characterizes the world to come.

iv. No more temple (21:22). For Jew and Gentile alike, the idea of a city without a temple would have been unthinkable. Cities in medieval Europe competed with each other to build the most beautiful cathedrals. Modern cities like Kuala Lumpur boast of having the world's largest mosque, and Hong Kong the world's tallest image of the Buddha. One of the first acts of almost every immigrant community is to establish its own distinctive place of worship in its new residence. Temples both symbolize the local presence of the deities and also map the public space of the worshipping community. Indeed, the priest-prophet Ezekiel in his vision of the restored Jerusalem, following the return of Israel from captivity in Babylon, gives the temple a central position dominating the entire city, and has instructions for marking out who may enter and who may not (Ezek. 44:5).

John sees no temple in the New Jerusalem. For the city as a whole is holy: its walls radiate the glory of God himself. We observe that the city is shaped as a perfect cube (21:15–16), reminiscent of the

---

[7] 'The word here translated "polluted" is from the same root as that used for the obscenities of Babylon (17:4, 5). "Murderers" are the monster's agents in the killing of the martyrs (13:15), who have filled the cup that made Babylon drunk (17:6). Fornicators, sorcerers, idolaters are variations on the one theme of idolatrous worship (2:14, 20, 21; 9:21; 14:8)' (G. B. Caird, *A Commentary on the Revelation of St. John the Divine* [A. & C. Black, 1966]), p. 267.

Holy of Holies in Solomon's temple (1 Kgs. 6:20; 2 Chr. 3:8–9). If what makes the creation new is, as we have seen, the direct, transforming presence of God pervading every aspect of it, then all that is now embraced by God is suffused with a glory of which the ancient temple in Jerusalem was only a transient shadow.

v. No more sun nor moon nor lamps (21:23), yet also no more night (22:5). In his funeral dirge on Babylon (ch. 18) John has declared that all the lights will go out in that city as the violence she has inflicted on others recoils on her own head (18:21–23). If in the New Jerusalem the lights also go out, it is not to plunge the city into eternal gloom, but to let the city be bathed in a splendour far more magnificent. The glorious presence of God filling the life of the city, no longer confined to a special sanctuary, makes all present sources of illumination invisible. Night-time, associated almost universally with fear, ignorance, the occult and the demonic, will be no more.

vi. No more curse (22:3). The immediate context of this verse (the nations worshipping in the New Jerusalem) suggests that it is better taken as referring to the Old Testament sacred ban of destruction, Yahweh's handing over of evil nations to slaughter (cf. Is. 34:1–2).[8] God's final word on the nations is not their destruction but their conversion.

Positively, the New Jerusalem, God's Alternative City, represents (1) the realization of true human community, (2) the consummation of human work and culture, (3) the reclamation of wealth and aesthetics, and (4) the transcendence of religion.

3. God's new order: the realization of true human community

John pictures the eschatological city *as a bride adorned for her husband* (21:2b). She is the Bride of the Lamb (21:9; cf. 19:7) who shares the throne of God and is with God the source of her light and beauty (21:22–23). The struggling groups of Christians in the cities of Asia Minor are given a glimpse of what they already are in the eyes of God and what they are to become at the end of time: a beloved, purified and radiant community in which all the barriers that separate human beings from God and each other have been destroyed. John hears a voice from the throne in heaven (21:3), echoing Ezekiel 37:27, 'My dwelling-place shall be with them; and I will be their God, and they shall be my people', but the final word is significantly changed to the plural *peoples*[9] and the 'them' (Israel in

---

[8] See Richard Bauckham, *The Climax of Prophecy: Studies in the Book of Revelation* (T. & T. Clark, 1993), pp. 316–317.

[9] The best Greek manuscripts carry the plural.

Ezekiel's prophecy) is now *mortals* (i.e. all humanity). The statement 'I will be their God and they shall be my people' is a covenant formula which occurs frequently throughout the Old Testament (Lev. 26:11–12; Jer. 7:23; 31:1, 33; Ezek. 37:26–27; 43:7; Ps. 95:7; Zech. 8:8). The covenant people have fulfilled their calling to be a light to the nations. All nations will now share in the privileges and promises of the covenant.

Thus the biblical drama, which began with a couple in an earthly garden, finds its climax in a multinational city in a renewed and transformed earth. A city is the realization of human community, the concrete living out of that interdependence which is an essential aspect of our human nature. We all long to love and be loved, to experience genuine human fellowship. Such fellowship is made possible by the fact that the Creator himself has chosen to link his eternal future to fellowship with us human beings: the covenant formula of 21:3 is the climax of all our longings for unbroken communion with God, symbolized in the wilderness tabernacle and old Jerusalem temple, but anticipated truly in the incarnation of the Logos of God, the Lamb himself. Now all peoples are embraced by the gracious indwelling presence of God. Beneath all the imagery of gates, foundations and walls is the fundamental truth that God's final dwelling place is not the isolated bliss of a cosmic void, but with, in and for humanity.

We note that all the dimensions of the New Jerusalem are multiples of the 'twelve' that connotes the People of God. The twelve gates in the walls of the city have inscribed on them the names of the twelve tribes of Israel, and the twelve foundations of the wall carry the names of the twelve apostles of the Lamb (21:12–14); the walls measure 12,000 stadia (21:16 NRSV margin) in all directions, 144 cubits by 'human measurement' (21:17). Translations that turn these figures into modern units of measurement obscure their symbolic significance. The New Jerusalem stands in continuity with the Old Testament people of God and is founded on the apostolic testimony. 'I tell you, many will come from east and west and will eat with Abraham and Isaac and Jacob in the kingdom of heaven' (Matt. 8:11).

> The community of God's people, at times seemingly limited to twelve Jewish tribes or to a small band of disciples, someday will cover the world. By reporting that the New Jerusalem is a thousand times twelve stadia, John calls attention to its extravagant scope and enormous capacity. Far from being a small place only for a chosen few, the redeemed city can accommodate all peoples of the world, with room to spare. If Rome was impressive

for its size and splendour, the region of God will be infinitely greater.[10]

This is not, then, a tiny religious enclave of the 'faithful few' who have turned their backs on the world and have retired within the walls of their safe haven. John is writing to Christians who must have been tempted to develop a narrow vision of God's eschatological future. They were a marginal, often embattled, minority; and the temptation all minorities face is to look inwards and dream of the day when their fortunes will be reversed and the majority will grovel at their feet. This is a vast, inclusive city. And John brings out its inclusiveness in several ways.

First, even the kings of the earth, who hitherto in the book of Revelation stand for those client-kings of Rome who are seduced by the wiles of the Whore and oppose God's rule, now find their place as redeemed citizens of the holy city (21:24). John thus holds out the hope of the repentance and transformation of those who are now enemies of Christ. Secondly, the city gates are open twenty-four hours a day (21:25). Ezekiel's restored Jerusalem also had twelve gates, but these served as exits for the Israelite tribes to go out to their allotted land (Ezek. 48:30–35). The temple in Jesus' day had a wall that separated men from women and Jews from Gentiles (cf. Eph. 2:14–16; Acts 21:27–29). John's holy city has no temple and its twelve gates are always open for one-way traffic, from outside to inside (21:24–27). Thirdly, John has also modified Ezekiel's vision of trees on the banks of the river (issuing from the altar in the restored temple) whose leaves are 'for healing' (Ezek. 47:12). John sees the river of the water of life *flowing from the throne of God and of the Lamb* (22:1) and the tree of life bearing leaves which are specifically *for the healing of the nations* (22:2). The verse immediately following (the lifting of the ban of destruction) reinforces the thought: the nations who enter the city and walk by its light have been healed of their sins by the leaves of the tree of life and are no longer subject to God's judgment.

4. God's new order: the consummation of human work and culture

Cities are not only people; they are also the places where we enjoy the best of human architecture, technology, art and music. From one point of view the Bride-city is God's achievement and gift; from another it is the consummation of human work in faithfulness to

[10] Kraybill, *Imperial Cult*, p. 211.

God's will (e.g. the bride's trousseau in 19:8 is made up of 'the righteous deeds of the saints'). Thus the New Jerusalem brings to fruition the original creation mandate (Gen. 2:15). It is a garden-city, humanity living in a renewed relationship with the earth. Just as God's gift of mortal life is mediated to us by this creation of which we are a part, so eternal life will be mediated by the new creation (22:1–2; 22:14, 17, 19).

It is not only the 'righteous deeds of the saints' that find their way into the life of the eschatological city, but also the *glory and the honour of the nations* (21:26). The gates of the city stand open to receive all the cultural wealth of the earth, the products of human labour. The heritage of the nations will be redeemed; that is, stripped of all idolatrous accretions and redirected to the worship of God and the Lamb. Thus John's vision, like Paul's letters, hold out the hope not of the 'junking' of history but of its redemption. God promises not to make 'all new things' but, rather, *all things new* (21:5). Salvation includes the final gathering up into the all-embracing worship of God and the Lamb all that is truly human in all places and at all times, those human acts that reflect the beauty, love, justice and truth of God.

This is what makes our human strivings to build more decent cities and a more just and beautiful world ultimately worthwhile. It is not that our efforts bring about the kingdom of God. That is to turn the gospel on its head! We have observed that the New Jerusalem does not arise Babel-like from the earth, but is a *coming down out of heaven from God* (21:10). From first to last it is a gift, God's gracious doing. But in the New Jerusalem fashioned by the triune God are to be found all our human 'doings' that have been (often unknown to us) aligned with his purposes for humanity and his world. If 'even the cup of cold water given to the least of these my brethren' will be remembered on the last day, how much more the tube-wells drilled to provide safe drinking water for a village community in Nepal or research into a vaccine for HIV sufferers in Kenya? Is it too fanciful to assert that, say, the music of Beethoven and Bach, the Zen paintings of China, Jazz and African drums, Moghul architecture, Arabic calligraphy and the dances of the Polynesian islands will all find their place in the life of the eternal city?

There is a moving painting of the resurrection of Jesus by the Latin American artist Adolfo Pérez Esquivel that expounds its meaning with simplicity and power. The empty tomb stands in the foreground to a dismal contemporary scene of war, slavery, brutality, pollution and destruction. The risen Christ stands in front of the tomb. Around him are gathered urchins from the streets of Latin

American cities, who have disappeared while in police custody, and native peoples massacred by conquistadors and multinational logging companies. Also standing there is Oscar Romero, the Salvadorean Roman Catholic archbishop who was murdered in 1980 by right-wing death squads while celebrating the Mass; the environmentalist Chico Mendez, also murdered; two American nuns, raped and murdered by the Chilean army; and other victims of torture and oppression.

In the light of the resurrection, we are able to affirm every act of love and justice, every word of truth spoken in the face of lies, and every work of beauty in a world of ugliness. It is only in the light of the resurrection that we can dare to affirm that history, our history, has ultimate significance. What happened in Jesus was the means by which the Creator God will bring his creation out of its bondage to evil and death and raise it to share in his own divine life. And, as Dietrich Bonhoeffer famously observed from his cell in Tegel prison, 'The difference between the Christian hope of resurrection and a mythological hope is that the Christian hope sends a man back to his life on earth in a wholly new way.'[11]

5. God's new order: the reclamation of wealth and aesthetics

It is only in comparison with the beauty of the Bride-city that the glamour of Babylon can be perceived to be the cellulite charms of a superannuated whore. When the whole city is said to have *the glory of God and a radiance like a very rare jewel, like jasper, clear as crystal* (21:11), we recall from 4:3 that the glory of God himself is 'like jasper and carnelian', and that the sea of glass before his throne in heaven is translucent, like crystal, to reflect his glory. Here the whole city, with its translucent gold streets and jewel-encrusted foundation wall (21:19–21), shines with the reflected glory of God himself.

The unimaginable splendour of the city – John is grasping at words to articulate the wonder of what is revealed to him – is also depicted in the list of precious stones that form the foundation wall. Commentators note that this is nearly identical with the list of the twelve gems which adorned the high priest's breastplate (Exod. 28:17ff.; 39:10ff.), and Caird explains the divergences as due to John making his own translation from the Hebrew (a single Hebrew stone could be equated with more than one Greek name).[12] Also, various Jewish traditions claimed that the stones in the breastplate

[11] Dietrich Bonhoeffer, *Letters and Papers from Prison* (ET SCM, 1953), letter of 27 June 1944.
[12] Caird, *Revelation*, p. 274.

and the gold used in the temple came from paradise (Eden). An identical list of jewels is worn by the king of Tyre (Ezek. 28:13). According to the prophecy in Ezekiel, the king of Tyre once wore these jewels until in 'the abundance of your trade you were filled with violence, and you sinned'. Then God 'cast you as a profane thing from the mountain of God' (Ezek. 28:16). In John's New Jerusalem, the jewels of the king of Tyre are restored to the mountain of God. Is this the Day when the 'expropriators will be expropriated' (Marx), and the wealth of God's world be shared equitably in a renewed humanity?

We have noted that the city is so brilliant it needs neither sun nor moon to illuminate it; and so impressively beautiful that in magnitude, symmetry, solidity and splendour it defies human power to envisage. Eugene Boring sums up well:

> 'Bride' also speaks of beauty, and the city is pictured as the eternal affirmation of all that is beautiful. The beauty of this world (gold, precious stones, pearls, dazzling light) becomes the vehicle of expressing the beauty of the eternal city ... Eternity is no odorless, colorless, tasteless void; it is (in contrast to the dead, silent streets of earthly Babylon, 18:22) a living city of light and colour.[13]

Thus, the present creation has an aesthetic, as well as a moral and religious, goal.

6. God's new order: the transcendence of religion

The city is without a temple, because *its temple is the Lord God the Almighty and the Lamb* (21:22). We have noted that all that is alien to God's character will not find a place within it. Its source of illumination is *the glory of God and the Lamb* (21:23). John echoes Isaiah 60:19 but, once again, significantly alters the tradition. Where Isaiah, speaking of the future glory of Zion, declared, 'The sun shall no more be your light by day, / nor for brightness shall the moon give light to you by night; / but the LORD will be your everlasting light, / and your God will be your glory,' John's vision has *the Lamb* sharing the glory and life-giving throne of God (22:1, 3). This is just one of the numerous instances in Revelation (and indeed throughout the New Testament) where the crucified and risen Jesus is, in a matter-of-fact kind of way, given the most exalted place imaginable. The Lamb is intimately associated with God, sharing

[13] Boring, *Revelation*, p. 222.

the prerogatives of God, yet without the suggestion that he is another deity.[14]

Thus John's vision of the redemption of the world's peoples and cultures is thoroughly Christocentric. The worship of the nations is directed towards God and the Lamb. We have also observed that the apostolic witness to Jesus Christ is what is foundational for the multicultural city (21:14). John's vision challenges all those theological tendencies, prevalent in some approaches to ecumenical dialogue, to marginalize the person and work of Jesus Christ in favour of a more 'universal' conception of God, who is said to be equally at work in all the 'religious traditions of humankind'.

In the New Jerusalem we witness the marriage of the particular and the universal. There are no 'religious traditions of humankind' standing by themselves in the eternal city, simply because the Lamb of God has gathered – presumably through his cross–resurrection–ascension and the outflowing mission of his Spirit through his followers in the world (Rev. 22:17) – all that is true and good and valuable in all such religious traditions. The latter have been transformed and refocused on the worship of the Lamb. Of course, the church needs humility in her witness among the nations, for until that final consummation of all things 'we see in a mirror, dimly' (1 Cor. 13:12) and our judgments of what is true and good and valuable are always fallible and provisional. It is God and the Lamb who will have the last word, not the church. But we can say with confidence that whoever and whatever is 'saved' to share in the life of the eschatological kingdom is saved not through the 'religious traditions of humankind' (including that which we call 'Christianity') but through the work within history of 'the Lord God Almighty and the Lamb'.

In the earthly temple, once a year only, the high priest, wearing the sacred name of God on his forehead and carrying the blood of a sacrificial lamb, entered God's immediate presence in the Holy of Holies. In the New Jerusalem, which is God's eternal Holy of Holies, all will enjoy the immediate presence of God without interruption. They will bear his name on their foreheads (22:4b), and God will delight to call them his *sons* (21:7b).[15] These metaphors

---

[14] Note, for instance, the way the self-designation *the Alpha and the Omega, the beginning and the end* uttered by God in 21:6 is applied to himself by the coming Christ in 22:13. Also, in 21:6 it is God who invites people to drink of the water of life, while in 7:17 it is the Lamb who will guide his people to the springs of the water of life.

[15] The inclusive language of the NRSV, generally laudable, fails in this context. 'Sons' carries echoes of the promise to establish David's royal line (2 Sam. 7:14), and unlike the term 'children' points to the freedom of adult personhood (John 8:31–36; Rom. 8:15–17; Gal. 4:1–7).

273

suggest the security of being perfectly known and freely loved by God. Furthermore, the glory of God in the New Jerusalem is not just a beacon that attracts the nations to the city; it is the light by which they live (21:24). Not only Israel, but also all the nations, will be instructed in the will of Yahweh and live according to it.

Unlike Ezekiel's temple, where the priests teach the people the difference between the holy and the profane (Ezek. 44:10, 15, 23) in the New Jerusalem of John's vision, all people are priests and all things are holy. John's vision thus enshrines the hope of Zechariah 14:20–21:

> On that day there shall be inscribed on the bells of the horses, 'Holy to the LORD'. And the cooking-pots in the house of the LORD shall be as holy as the bowls in front of the altar; and every cooking-pot in Jerusalem and Judah shall be sacred to the LORD of hosts, so that all who sacrifice may come and use them to boil the flesh of the sacrifice.

This is the ultimate sacrilege: the breaking down of the walls that separate the sacred and the profane, built up over centuries in all human cultures. Here the whole city is filled with God's presence, every nook and cranny of human life penetrated by God's life. The ordinary and mundane are the vehicles of the divine.

Moreover the kingdom of God and the Lamb differs radically from that of the Beast (13:1ff.). To worship and serve God is consistent with sharing in God's rule (22:3b, 5b); indeed, it is the other face of the coin. God's rule over his covenant peoples is for them a participation in his rule. This image, as Richard Bauckham notes perceptively, expresses the final reconciliation of God's rule and human self-determination: 'Because God's will is the moral truth of our being as his creatures, we shall find our fulfilment only when, through our free obedience, his will becomes also the spontaneous desire of our hearts.'[16] This is the paradox of our humanness: to serve God is to enjoy perfect freedom.

And *they will see his face* (22:4). This is the face no-one in mortal life can see and survive (Exod. 33:20–23), but to see God's face is the ultimate aspiration of all the theistic faiths. The face expresses who a person is: to see the Lord's face is to know him in his personal being. Do we remember those times when we have not looked at our watches and switched off our mobile phones, because of the sheer delight of being with people we love, or of having been enraptured

---

[16] Bauckham, *Theology*, pp. 142–143.

by the beauty of a landscape or a piece of music? The worship of heaven will be the eternal fulfilment of all those times.

In the words of St Augustine, 'There we shall rest and we shall see, we shall see and we shall love, we shall love and we shall praise. Behold what shall be in the end and shall have no end.'[17]

We shall 'rest': the busy and fretting ego, usually self-serving but often worried, often frustrated and often suffering, will be no more. We shall 'see': the restless search for certainty will be over and all eternity will be needed to appreciate what we see. We shall 'love': all the distances, disappointments, separations and enmities will be replaced by the never-ending union. And therefore we shall 'praise'.[18]

7. Conclusion

The sociologist Zygmunt Bauman has described the 'postmodern' condition in terms of the twin metaphors of the *vagabond* and the *tourist*.[19] Both express a lifestyle of non-attachment. The vagabond does not have any goals, plans or projects. He does not know how long he will stay where he is now. He sets his destination even as he goes. What keeps him on the move is disillusionment with the last place in which he stayed and the hope that maybe the next place or the place after that will give him the temporary satisfaction he is seeking.

Like the vagabond, the tourist too knows that he will not stay for long in a particular locale. But unlike the vagabond the tourist has paid for his detachment. For the tourist, therefore, 'freedom from involvement' means being able to ignore native problems, feelings or concerns. Like the vagabond the tourist is moving through other people's territory and has no commitment to that territory or to its people. Indeed, the freedom he has paid for is the freedom to be unmoved by what happens around him. He can always take the next plane home. The world is to be experienced aesthetically, purely as pleasure. The only meaning his world has is an aesthetic meaning. Physical closeness with spiritual distance – these sum up both the vagabond's and the tourist's lives. Neither feels any moral obligation to the spaces he or she inhabits.

Christians, unlike vagabonds and tourists, are committed to the places in which they live. For this world, in spite of all its evil and

[17] St Augustine, *City of God*, Book 22, ch. 30.
[18] David L. Edwards, *After Death? Past Belief and Real Possibilities* (Cassel, 1999), p. 163.
[19] Zygmunt Bauman, *Postmodern Ethics* (Basil Blackwell, 1993), pp. 242ff.

corruption, has a future. And God's future embraces and informs human actions in the present. Our hope is not that we shall be whisked off to another world when we die, but that this present world will be transformed, and into all that God intended it to be. Heaven, the ultimate reality of God's sovereign rule, will come to earth. And that vision is given to us, not to encourage idle speculation and curiosity about the future, but to motivate us *to live in the present in such a way that we give people around us a glimpse of God's future*. The church is that missionary community, drawn from all the nations, which lives God's future in the present.

Thus, in the words of Eugene Boring, 'the gift becomes an assignment'.[20] The promise that God *will wipe every tear from their eyes* (21:4) challenges those who believe the vision to point to it by their present actions, which bring healing to the sick, comfort to the dying, food to the hungry and justice for the oppressed. The vision of a garden-city, and of human beings restored to harmony with a renewed earth, motivates us to care for today's groaning earth and all its non-human creatures. The promise that the *glory and the honour of the nations* (21:26) will be brought into the New Jerusalem motivates us to seek the redemption of all human cultures, including the worlds of technology and the visual and performing arts; while the warning that *nothing unclean will enter it* (21:27) motivates us to proclaim a gospel of repentance to the nations and to fight evil in all its personal and collective manifestations. The promise that all nations *will be his peoples* (21:3) challenges the church to be faithful in her witness among the nations, seeking to practise costly reconciliation and to translate the gospel into every culture and language on earth. Likewise, the vision of the holy city filled with the immediate presence of God, with no more separation of the sacred and the profane, enables us to experience God in our day-to-day mundane tasks and to offer them to him in worship. It also impels us to align our work, our leisure and our relationships towards the eternal reality of God's coming reign. 'Blind unbelief may see only the outer world, growing old in its depravity and doomed to vanish before the presence of holiness; but faith can see the hand of God in the shadows, refashioning the whole. The agonies of earth are but the birth-pangs of a new creation.'[21]

[20] Boring, *Revelation*, p. 224.
[21] Caird, *Revelation*, p. 266.

Study guide

The aim of this study guide is to help you get to the heart of what Howard and Vinoth have written and challenge you to apply what you learn to your own life. The questions have been designed for use by individuals or by small groups of Christians meeting, perhaps for an hour or two each week, to study, discuss and pray together.

The guide provides material for each of the sections in the book. When used by a group with limited time, the leader should decide beforehand which questions are most appropriate for the group to discuss during the meeting and which should perhaps be left for group members to work through by themselves or in smaller groups during the week.

In order to be able to contribute fully and learn from the group meetings, each member of the group needs to read through the section or sections under discussion, together with the Bible passages to which they refer.

It's important not to let these studies become merely academic exercises. Guard against this by making time to think through and discuss how what you discover *works out in practice* for you. Make sure you begin and end each study by focusing on God in praise and prayer. Ask the Holy Spirit to speak to you through your discussion together.

PART 1. WORLD HORIZONS

Colossians 1:15–23
1. The glory of Christ (pp. 17–32)

1 In what way is the controversy that surrounds Jesus of Nazareth distinctive from that which surrounds other famous people (p. 18)?
2 What light does Colossians 1:15–17 shed on the question of who Jesus is (pp. 19–22)?
3 Why is it that 'only Christian faith ... can speak coherently of a universe' (p. 22)?
4 What do you make of the authors' suggestion about why universities around the world have deteriorated 'into tuition factories' (pp. 22–23)?

5 How do verses 18–20 of Colossians 1 fit in with the sequence of thought in verses 15–17 (pp. 23–25)?

6 What reality is 'presupposed in moving from verse 16 to verse 20' (p. 24)?

7 How would you answer someone who suggested that, in the light of verse 20, all human beings will ultimately be reconciled to God, whatever their present relationship to him may be (p. 25)?

8 Why was (and is) the message of the cross such a 'public relations disaster' (pp. 26–27)?

'*This crucified figure is the One through whom the universe came into being and also the One through whom the universe will be restored to its proper functioning*' (p. 26).

---

9 Do you have 'too puny a view of Jesus' (p. 27)? In what ways does this passage extend your vision of who he is?

'*Christian mission stands or falls with the absoluteness of Christ*' (p. 28).

---

10 How is your thinking about the scope of Christian mission influenced by this passage (pp. 28–30)? What practical implications does this have for you?

11 What is meant by describing mission as 'eschatological' (pp. 30–32)?

Genesis 1:26–31; 2:15–20
2. Life and dominion (pp. 33–52)

1 Why would the Genesis creation narrative have 'shocked' Israel's neighbours (pp. 34ff.)? What contrasts are there between Genesis and other accounts of creation?

2 According to Genesis, what is distinctive about human beings? How does this relate to how we think about ourselves in today's world (pp. 37–39)?

'*Human beings are to be treated as having an essential value that is neither given ... nor can it be taken away by human beings; it can only be recognized*' (p. 39).

---

3 What does a Christian perspective on human worth lead to in practice (pp. 39–44)?

4 What 'makes a society worth living in' (p. 41)? How does the society you live in measure up? Are things getting better or worse?

'Injustice is a violation of God's own being' (p. 42).

5 In what ways could ethics become 'the site of gospel proclamation' (p. 43) in your situation?
6 What does the teaching of Genesis on human worth imply for how we should treat other people (pp. 43–44)?
7 What guidance does this passage offer as we think about how to treat the rest of God's creation (pp. 44–48)? Which of these different aspects is most relevant to you?
8 To what extent are you affected by 'the idolatry of work' (p. 47)?

'We find our true identity not in our work of ruling the earth, but in our relationship with God' (p. 47).

9 How would you answer someone who blamed the cultural influence of the Bible for the current ecological crisis in our world (pp. 49–51)?
10 How might concern for the environment be a more significant part of your approach to mission?

Isaiah 44:24 – 45:25
3. The incomparable God (pp. 53–68)

1 What 'two fundamental biblical truths' are highlighted here (p. 54)?
2 Why is Jesus so 'worshipable' (p. 55)? How is this reflected in the worship you lead and/or experience?
3 Under what circumstances do claims about God's exclusive incomparability inspire 'a joy-filled liberation' (p. 55)?
4 What is 'fascinating and instructive' (p. 55) about the context of Isaiah 45:22?
5 What is so surprising about the prophecy about Cyrus in this passage (pp. 56–57)?
6 What does this passage have to say about God's relationship with his world (pp. 56–60)?
7 How would you answer someone who asserted that claims of Christian exclusiveness lead to 'incivility, intolerance and bigotry' (p. 61)?

> '... *a truly free society must include the freedom to share deeply held beliefs about the most important things' (p. 62).*

8 What is so surprising about this 'soaring faith which saw in international events the hand of Yahweh' (p. 63)?
9 What is 'elenctics' (p. 65)? Why is it important?
10 According to Gavin D'Costa, what is 'central to mission' (p. 66)? Do you agree? Why?

John 1:1–18
4. The Word made flesh (pp. 69–86)

1 In what ways is 'the Word' such an appropriate title for the Son of God (p. 70)?
2 What 'powerful missiological challenge' is presented by this passage (pp. 71ff.)?
3 What is so shocking about the claim that 'the Word became flesh and lived among us' (pp. 71–73)? Why is this bad for our pride? How does it ennoble our common humanity?
4 What similarities are there between incarnation and the Hindu concept of *avatara* (pp. 73–76)? In what ways are these ideas fundamentally different?
5 What 'problem of the evangelist' (p. 76) is highlighted here? How may it be tackled?
6 What is the 'crucial difference' (p. 78) between Christian conversion and religious proselytism?
7 What is so shocking about the way John describes the world's response to the incarnation of the Word (pp. 79–83)?

> '*Conversion has a beginning, but no end. It's a lifelong process of discovery and transformation' (p. 79).*

8 'The message of the cross is scandalous ...' (p. 81). Why? What impact does this have on mission?
9 What is the significance of John's use of 'the language of a courtroom' here (pp. 83–85)? Are you a witness too? What would you say is your testimony?

> '... *the closer we get to God, the more, not less, human we become' (p. 86).*

PART 2. THE INTERNATIONAL PURPOSES OF GOD

Genesis 12:1–4
5. Chosen to bless (pp. 89–106)

1 What emphases are suggested by the use of repetition in Genesis 12:1–4 (pp. 90ff.)?
2 What is the 'overwhelming emphasis' in the blessings promised to Abraham (p. 91)? How is this brought out in what follows?
3 How does the 'wider context' of Abraham's story contribute to our understanding of God's purposes (pp. 94–96)?

'The history of the internationalizing of the Christian community is full of sending, going and receiving' (p. 96).

4 What is described here as 'part and parcel of Christian identity' (p. 97)? How has your experience of Christian faith been shaped as a result of this?
5 What relationship is there between the promises to Abraham and recent events in the Middle East (pp. 97–100)?
6 What is it that makes the Christian message truly good news rather than mere propaganda (pp. 100–101)?
7 How does Abraham's story underline 'God's concern for the whole created order' (p. 103)?
8 What are the consequences of living 'for the promise' and 'against the promise' (p. 104)? Can you think of any examples?

Deuteronomy 10:12–20
6. A distinctive people (pp. 107–123)

1 What does the command 'fear Yahweh your God' actually mean (pp. 107–108)? Is this true of you?
2 How does this passage underline the universal sovereignty of Yahweh (pp. 109–110)? How is this reflected in what the New Testament tells us about Jesus?
3 How are we to reconcile what the Bible tells us about God's impartiality on the one hand with his particular love for Israel on the other (pp. 110–112)? In what ways does this issue continue to be relevant today?

'It is a part of our calling as the Christian Church to unmask these false gods that have taken over God's world' (p. 112).

---

4 Why is it essential for authentic Christian witness to include social and political action on behalf of the poor (pp. 112–114)? How is this being put into practice in your situation?

5 What is suggested as the 'ultimate challenge of the twenty-first century' (p. 114)? Why is this the case? What can you do to be part of the solution?

6 In what ways are religious world-views inextricably linked to social justice (p. 119)?

7 What practical sign of repentance is spelled out in this passage (pp. 119–120)?

8 What is wrong with nationalism (pp. 120–122)? Does it have any positive features?

9 What does the author mean when he suggests that mission is about 'being' rather than 'going' or 'doing' (p. 123)?

Jonah 1 – 4
7. A resentful servant (pp. 124–139)

1 What is 'striking' about how the book of Jonah has been interpreted down the years (p. 125)?

2 In what way is Jonah 'unlike any other prophet' (p. 127)?

3 How does what the author says deepen your appreciation of the story of Jonah (pp. 126ff.)?

4 What 'diminished views of God' (p. 131) are challenged by the book of Jonah? How does what is said bring this out?

5 What is 'unsettling' about the sailors and the Ninevites in Jonah's story (p. 131)? How is this reflected in more modern experiences of cross-cultural mission?

'He is not a God whom we can tame and box into our own neat theological kennel' (p. 131).

---

6 How does the focus on the city of Nineveh inform our thinking about cities today (pp. 135–136)?

7 What do you think Jesus meant when he talked about 'the sign of Jonah' (pp. 136–139)?

8 'Two questions from the final chapter of Jonah linger in the air . . .' (p. 139) What are these? What impact do these questions have on you?

Isaiah 49:1–26
8. A ready servant (pp. 140–153)

1 How do you react to accounts of the persecution of Christians – both in history and in the contemporary world?
2 What do we know about the background to Isaiah 49 (p. 141)?

'The church is not necessarily strongest when it is most powerful' (p. 141).

3 What is 'immediately striking' (p. 142) about the way the Servant describes himself here?
4 What effects of the Servant's ministry are described in this passage (pp. 143–144)?
5 What is the ultimate purpose of what has been going on in this chapter (pp. 145–146)?
6 What evidence is there that the Servant Songs 'profoundly influenced Jesus' own understanding of his person and mission' (p. 146)?
7 What 'extraordinary fact' emerges from considering the origins of this chapter (p. 147)?
8 How would you answer someone who criticized the Western missionary movement as 'a collaborator with, or even an instrument of, the juggernaut of Western imperial and economic expansion' (p. 147)?
9 What light does this chapter shed on the issue of Christian martyrdom (pp. 149–151)?
10 In what ways have the promises of this chapter been fulfilled beyond the expectations of those who first heard it (pp. 151–153)?

PART 3. THREE-IN-ONE MISSION

Luke 4:16–30
9. The freedom Jesus brings (pp. 157–171)

1 Who are 'the poor' in this passage (pp. 159ff.)? How does an understanding of ancient Mediterranean culture add to our appreciation of what Jesus means?
2 What significance is there in the inclusion of a quotation from Isaiah 58 in this passage (p. 161)?
3 What exactly does Jesus release people from (pp. 162ff.)?

4 What is the 'utterly unexpected direction' (p. 163) taken by Jesus in his sermon? What does it lead to? Why?

5 How does this passage demonstrate that the 'dichotomies of evangelical proclamation and social action are incoherent' (pp. 165–167)?

'Jesus seemed to have turned their world-view upside down, sabotaging the assumptions and values on which they had built their individual and collective lives. Such gospel preaching always generates opposition' (p. 165).

---

6 Why do forgiveness and reconciliation create 'new enemies' (pp. 167ff.)? What can peacemakers do in response?

7 Is the use of force by Christians ever justified (pp. 169ff.)?

8 What can Christian people do to 'reduce the temptations to violence' (pp. 169ff.)?

'Peacemaking is not a soft option for Christians' (p. 171).

Matthew 28:16–20
10. The mandate Jesus gives (pp. 172–190)

1 In what ways is this passage 'a key to understanding the whole' of Matthew's Gospel (pp. 173–176)?

2 How does Matthew underline the truth that the Great Commission 'was given to an ordinary group of devoted, failure-prone learners' (p. 174)?

3 In what ways is your understanding of this passage enlarged by what the author says here?

4 What makes some scholars doubt that Jesus commanded his followers to take the gospel to the Gentiles (pp. 177–178)? What do you think?

5 Why does this passage 'stick in the throats of many who have a more pluralist view of religions' (p. 179)?

6 What 'fear' ought we to feel and allow 'keenly to affect the way in which we go about our mission ...' (p. 179)?

7 What issue to do with baptism is raised by this passage (pp. 180–182)? What do you think about this question?

8 What does the phrase 'all nations' mean here (pp. 182–183)? Why is this a critical issue?

9 What do we know of the place of this passage in the history of world mission (pp. 184–186)?

10 What differences can you think of between the way Jesus tells us to fulfil our mission and the way we might 'think best' (pp. 186–190)?

11 How does Matthew bring out the authority of Jesus in his Gospel (p. 187)?

'Christian mission can never be understood apart from its authorization in the authority of Jesus ... ' (p. 187).

12 What parallels are there between the ministry of Jesus and the ministry of his disciples (pp. 187–189)? What effect does this have on how we see the task of mission?

13 'From first to last Matthew is the Gospel of ... ' (p. 189) What does the author emphasize here? What implications does this have for mission?

John 12:20–26; 13:34–35
11. The way Jesus commands (pp. 191–207)

1 How does the example of Jesus change the way we think about freedom (pp. 192–194)? In what ways does this run 'counter to all the religious teachings of humankind'?

2 What relationship is there between mission and suffering (pp. 194–197)? What distinctive feature of Christian suffering does the author highlight here?

3 How does 'this sort of thinking' challenge 'the methodologies of church growth that abound in evangelical circles today' (p. 196)?

4 How does the work of mission bring about transformation in the life of the church (pp. 197–201)? How is this illustrated in the story of Cornelius?

5 Why is witness 'a risky undertaking' (p. 198)? What experience have you had of this?

'For the Christian, dialogue is a fundamental aspect of bearing witness to the truth of Christ' (p. 198).

6 In relation to contemporary culture, how may we be 'guilty of idolatry' (p. 199)? What examples does the author cite? How can this be avoided?

7 What does the author identify as 'the biggest "blind spot" of evangelical Christians and the Western missionary movement in recent times' (p. 203)? Is this a problem for you? How can it be overcome?

8 In terms of mission, what is wrong with the aim of planting churches within people groups (p. 204)? What should we be seeking to do instead?

9 What are the 'two abiding missionary principles' left for us by Jesus (p. 206)? How are these reflected in your thinking about mission?

Acts 2:1–47
12. The Spirit of mission (pp. 208–224)

1 What strikes you most from this brief historical sketch of the early twentieth-century Pentecostal movement (pp. 208–209)?

'Mission begins with an explosion of joy!' (p. 209, quoting Lesslie Newbigin).

---

2 What actually happened on the day of Pentecost (pp. 209–211)? Does the author highlight anything you haven't noticed before?

3 How would you summarize Peter's understanding of the significance of what had happened on the day of Pentecost (pp. 211–213)?

4 Are Jesus' words in Acts 1:8 a command or a promise (p. 214)? What difference does this make?

5 How do you explain the tendency for revival movements to fizzle out in disunity (pp. 216–217)?

6 What is 'the very heart of the good news of the gospel' (p. 217)? Why is this so?

'He who cannot forgive others, breaks the bridge over which he himself must pass' (p. 218, quoting Corrie ten Boom).

---

7 Is there scope for more sharing of resources in the church today (pp. 218–220)? Why doesn't it happen more often?

8 What modern counterpart to the Pentecost phenomenon of crowds from many countries hearing the apostles speaking in their own languages does the author focus on (pp. 220–223)? Why is this so important?

9 What 'fundamental need for the church' (p. 223) is highlighted here? To what extent is this part of your experience?

Acts 19:8–41
13. A model of mission (pp. 225–240)

1 Why has the author chosen Paul's ministry in Ephesus as a good model of mission (pp. 225–226)?
2 Thinking about Paul's preaching, what point is worth 'dwelling on briefly' (p. 226)? What else do we learn from Luke's description of Paul's preaching ministry?
3 What can make apologetics 'unattractive' (p. 227)? How can we avoid this?
4 What 'three important matters' (p. 229) are raised by Luke's account of the miracles that accompanied Paul's preaching in Ephesus?
5 In what ways does this passage present the Christian faith 'as an alternative to the "popular religion" of the empire ...' (p. 232)?
6 'Cross-cultural missions rarely lend themselves to strategic planning ...' (p. 233). Why not? What elements are often 'ignored in mission studies and the writing of church history textbooks'?
7 How does Paul's experience in Ephesus illustrate God's use of 'the wise intervention of human authorities who do not acknowledge the name of Jesus' (p. 234)?
8 In what way does Luke's account serve 'as a political apologetic for his times' (p. 237)?
9 What is it about the church that makes her 'deeply subversive of the status quo' (p. 238)? What does this lead to? How subversive is your church?

PART 4. DOXOLOGY

Psalm 104
14. The consummation of creation's song (pp. 243–260)

1 How central is the care of creation to your thinking about mission (pp. 243–244)? Why is this such an important issue?
2 How does the writing of the poet Christopher Smart 'help us to praise God' (p. 245)? Can you think of any other examples?
3 What does Psalm 104 tell us about God's work of creation (pp. 246–248)?
4 What strikes you most about the statistics on pages 249–250?

5 Why is it important to insist that 'God cares for the whole creation and not just its human component ...' (p. 251)? What practical implications of this truth can you think of?

'The first obligation of every living thing is towards the Creator; worship and prayer come before work' (pp. 252–253).

6 Why are some Christians opposed to the environmental concerns raised in this chapter (pp. 253–255)? What do you make of the danger of our becoming 'social gospellers' (p. 255)?
7 What do Psalms 103 and 105 add to the picture set out in this chapter (pp. 256–257)? What question is prompted by these three psalms taken together?
8 What do you make of the policy adopted by St Molua's Church (pp. 258–259)? What would such a policy look like in your situation?

Revelation 21:1 – 22:5
15. Certainties of the new covenant (pp. 261–276)

1 What distinguishes the apostle John's view of Rome and the Roman Empire from that of his contemporaries (pp. 262–264)? What alternative does he offer?
2 What is 'new' about the new creation described in these chapters (pp. 264–267)?
3 What significance is there in the various things which are said not to be in heaven (pp. 265–267)?
4 What is so appropriate about the fact that the biblical drama begins in a garden and ends in a city (p. 268)?

'A city is the realization of human community, the concrete living out of that interdependence which is an essential aspect of our human nature' (p. 268).

5 What is it that 'makes our human strivings to build more decent cities and a more just and beautiful world ultimately worthwhile' (p. 270)?
6 Where is the focus of heaven's worship (pp. 272–275)? How does this inform and stimulate mission?
7 What do the twin metaphors of vagabond and tourist express (pp. 275–277)? In what ways does a Christian view differ from these?